READERS REACT

"In this extraordinary, shockingly personal, historically mind-expanding true-life adventure, he establishes himself as a major player in the ranks of America's greatest storytellers. Enjoy the ride!"

— Phil Proctor, actor (stage, film, Firesign Theater),
author of *Where's My Fortune Cookie?*

"A remarkable true story, well researched and engagingly recounted."

— Paula Bernstein, author of *How To Be Golden*

"A fine writer whose sentences are toothsome and nourishing, turning in unexpected directions."

— Ben Yagoda, educator, author of *The B-Side*
and *Will Rogers - A Biography*

"Takes us on a breathless thrill ride, confronting generations of family drama that leave us amazed and stunned."

— Ed Cunningham, Philadelphia broadcaster

"Clearly and evocatively told."

— Timothy Ferris, author of *The Whole Shebang*
and *Coming of Age in the Milky Way*

"Quite a 'larger than life' story... Kudos for his investigation and determination to find the truth."

— Jim McCarty, drummer for The Yardbirds,
Renaissance and other groups

The Weather

The Alice Daily Echo

Phone 1421
For All Departments of
The Alice Daily Echo

VOLUME NUMBER LV   (Member of The Associated Press)   ALICE, TEXAS, FRIDAY, JULY 29, 1949   (NEA News Photo Service)   Number 206

Bill Mason Shot, Death Comes Thirty Minutes Later

Charge Against Sam Smithwick

W. H. (Bill) Mason, program director of Radio Station KBKI, was shot through the left breast about 10:30 this morning near the west side Felipe street and died thirty minutes later in the local hospital.

Shortly afterward Deputy Sheriff Sam Smithwick, law enforcement officer in Jim Wells and neighboring counties for the past 20 years, appeared at the county jail and surrendered himself into custody.

The Alice Daily Echo

The Alice Daily Echo

VOLUME NUMBER LV   56   (Member of The Associated Press)   ALICE, TEXAS, MONDAY, AUGUST 1, 1949   (NEA News Photo Service)   Number 208

Move For Special Prosecution In Mason Death Cited

Smithwick Brought Back To Jail Here

Election Suit Is Dismissed

Artificial Aid Fails To Revive Sam Parker

Alice Area Residents Crowd Belton As Witnesses In Smithwick Case

Smithwick Says Mason Grabbed Gun And He Shot

Hunt For Gunman Who Shot At Prosecutor Evetts Intensifies

The Alice Daily Echo

THE WEATHER
PHONE 1421
For All Departments
ALICE DAILY ECHO

VOLUME 56   ALICE, TEXAS, TUESDAY, JANUARY 24, 1950   Number 149

For State Hospital Program

Shivers Says Cigaret Tax Hike Acceptable

Sam Smithwick Gets Life, Notice Of Appeal Given

THE WEATHER
PHONE 1421
For All Departments
ALICE DAILY ECHO

VOLUME 56   ALICE, TEXAS, THURSDAY, JANUARY 26, 1950   Number 151

Ainsworth Named Chairman

Membership Drive Is

Truman 'Hopes For Results'

No Relief Looms In

Search For Assailant Of Evetts Is Pushed

Smithwick Found Dead In Pen Cell

Fliers Ask For Probe Of Randolph

Discrimination Against Reserve Group Charged

Suicide Verdict Given In Death Of Mason's Slayer

Sam Smithwick Burial Is Set For Thursday

The Alice Daily Echo

THE WEATHER
ALICE DAILY ECHO
Daily — Sundays
For All Departments
PHONE 1421

please stand up

keith mason

please stand up

Visit the website at: www.pleasestandupmason.com

ISBN (Print): 978-1-66782-775-9
ISBN (eBook): 978-1-66782-776-6

Cover: David Margolis / Damarcom

For Jean, who started it all
For Melanie, who kept it going
For Cate & Alec, who carry it forward

*In an old saying from some old country, you
have to "dig deep to bury your father."*

I

RAPTURE OF THE DEEP

It seems I didn't exist.

That's how my father looked at it, anyway.

Yet there I was, sitting on my mother's bed, my summer-sneakered legs dangling, while she organized some boxes on the far stretching end of the closet shelf over the plastic-bagged winter coats. We'd recently moved at the beginning of summer before my fourteenth birthday to this boxy, white-brick garden apartment building with no gardens, down the street from the library and the volunteer firefighting garage, a ten-minute walk across town from my grandparents' home where I was raised.

She produced a manila office envelope, standard nine by twelve.

"This has something about your father."

OK, that was sudden. Out of complete nowhere. A subject barely breached across the years.

A little excitement bubbled in me, mixed with moderation, *oh, really.* Aloud to her I acquiesced, "Okay."

I didn't know much. The simple story was that my mother Jean was swept up young, got married and quickly created a baby. By the time I arrived, my father had gone off the radar, to be forever unspoken about, unreferred to. I was used to it. You don't miss someone, or something, that never was.

Now my mother was letting me in, had decided I was ready to see the past. Mom always assured her willingness to answer questions

1

about my father, but neither of us ever brought it up. I'd never demanded answers, forced her to confront it, put her through whatever she'd have to feel, remember, relive, to relate the whole where-I-came-from.

She left the room.

Something carnivorous in me wanted to rip into the envelope, but it was my nature to display reserve; I didn't even tear open gift wrapping but instead was methodical, humble. I gently extracted the contents.

There were two copies of a single edition of an old Newsweek magazine from six years before, October 1961, still reasonably fresh, not yet yellowed at the edges. Behind them were some black-tinged sheets off an old office copier, pages from a previous edition of the magazine. A doctor my mom worked for had a waiting-room subscription, and he drew her attention to these items figuring they'd be meaningful to her.

In the intact magazine a paper clip marked a story across two pages, running about nine hundred words, between an article on the mysterious death of a Danish diplomat (with suspected Soviet, i.e., Russian, involvement) and a profile of the brainy Senator William Fulbright. Headlined "Salvage: Golden Fleece," with a vertical, page-deep ink illustration harking to the cover style of a genre of *Gutsy Men* magazines, the report revisited a longer, similar story found on the earlier photocopy, relating the underwater adventures of a heating engineer in his thirties who hauled up from the seabed that which some would value and others preferred to leave undisturbed.

Secured by the clip was a photograph, passport size. A man appeared grim in the lukewarm portrait light. It was hard to discern if he was in his early twenties, younger, older, a northern European sort, but might have been Balkan. The suit jacket was plain, the wavy hair brushed up off a square brow. Had a hint of a German POW camp guard, or one of Dillinger's boys, as though there should've been a matching profile shot with a rack of sheriff's numbers beneath it.

I squinted as if to increase interpretive perception along with optical contrast, yet I felt no hopeful, rushing urge to resemble the photo, to establish some connection to the face; there was no *oh, boy, finally.*

I remember my salutation as quiet, maybe a touch sardonic, as if to the pizza delivery guy showing up two hours late:

"So… it's you."

I got into a staring contest with the picture. The man directed his left eye at me, but the right seemed a bit off-center, so the overall effect was of a subject looking at the photographer's collar, and then back to the lens, drifting. A man who wouldn't be caught looking directly or intently at you.

What was expected, required in this moment? Was I supposed to feel attached to this person *pro forma*, to the source of my brown waves and wide ears and small mouth? The guy who talked my mother into who knows what, pixie-dusted her, told her she was the one, this would work, but it didn't.

A man who, when given the opportunity to commit, confess, embrace, step up, "Sure, he's my boy," chose not to and disappeared.

Was this a face my mother saw upon my own? Did I present this man and memory to her against her will every day? Or was it only in particular moments of angle and light that her missing husband came back to her, reminded her, a faint glimmer, a washed-out figure on a humid horizon of her life?

An office envelope from a box in a closet held the only physical artifacts about my father I'd ever seen. The only available facts to record or impressions I might imprint, any evidence of personality or appearance, slid out of an envelope. No memorabilia, no *memento mori* existed; all the ritually catalogued family photos and albums and home movies were devoid of any image of a man whose presence in my mother's life was totally cleaned out one night years before.

Plenty of people learn about an ancestor when they riff through an unfamiliar drawer in an attic to discover some crumpled wartime letters, or grandma shares her grainy treasures on a rainy day, "Oh, look, kids, this is your Great Grandpa Antonio when he was a goat farmer in Palermo."

On this summer day a father was revealed to his progeny in an old Newsweek. A quoted man under a paper clip. A confident, striving explorer. A seeker of underwater mysteries. An aquaman.

The ruckus reported in the earlier edition of the magazine was about the last enemy submarine sunk in the Battle of the Atlantic.

In early May 1945, Admiral Karl Döenitz was aboard *Aviso Grille*, Adolph Hitler's little-used armored yacht of four-hundred-plus feet (designed for sailing up the Thames to receive Britain's surrender, a voyage never taken). Both Hitler and his right-hand man Josef Goebbels had just unceremoniously and permanently turned in their dog tags, and the loyal but realistic naval chief was elevated to head of state in Berlin. Thus it fell to Döenitz to admit Germany's capitulation in World War II and make a few other public service announcements, including the coded message *Regenbogen* – Rainbow, to "cease-fire and scuttle boat" – to all remaining submarines.

Aboard U-853, cruising independently off the American coast, Helmut Fröemsdorf might not have received the instruction through his bearded, hawk-nosed radio operator, Erich Schaadt. Or perhaps the young *Kapitanleutnant*, twenty-four, his facial hair sprouting due to a lack of hot shaving water, simply ignored it; rumors back in port pegged him as a medal-seeking Nazi fanatic. The two-hundred- and fifty-foot-long U-853, essentially a tube weighing as much as nine hundred Toyota Camrys, hadn't achieved much. (The previous year, under another commander, it had been outrun by the *Queen Mary*, at the time a crowded American troop ship. The U-boat had more luck with its deck guns shooting down attacking Allied planes than with torpedoes.) Under Fröemsdorf all they hit was an old American patrol boat in April off the coast of Maine, killing more than fifty seamen.

The European war was supposed to be over when the young

commander sent a torpedo that tore off the stern of the 5,500-ton *Black Point*, killing twelve and sending thirty-four others, along with 7,600 tons of coal, into the evening sea not far from Rhode Island.

As it sank by the stern, a sailor whose foot entangled in a lifeboat line found himself hanging upside down. A mate named Whitehouse freed him with a knife, and then cut the lifeboat loose as well, so that the last fourteen men could get off the ship.

It took only fifteen minutes for the *Black Point* to flood. The old hulk in peacetime would've long been decommissioned, but now it was the last U.S. merchant vessel sunk in the Atlantic war.

Thoroughly irritated, the Navy sent out a posse of ships and planes from New England stations and a blimp from the naval air station in Lakehurst, New Jersey (where Germany's pride, the *Hindenburg*, burned in 1937). The sixteen-hour chase after U-853 stretched through the night. (In contrast, off Newfoundland in those same pre-dawn hours, the destroyer escort *Farquhar* bumped into another German sub and knocked it out with a torpedo in five minutes.)

Four hundred and sixty-six bombs and charges hit the water around U-853 and shook uncountable numbers of fish out of their complacency. The sub relinquished some lifejackets, bits of wood and cork, bubbles of air and oil, yet still it crawled along the bottom, presumably having shot the junk out a torpedo tube in the old submariner's trick to give the appearance of its destruction.

In mid-morning the destroyer escort *Atherton* and frigate *Moberly* finally laid two effective hits on the target cowering in a hundred-thirty feet of water.

A hole about five feet wide buckled through a structural seam out in front of the conning tower. Fröemsdorf felt a hollow *whoomph* from a second blast toward the starboard side of the engine room, breaching both the outer light hull that absorbed leaks and battle damage and gave the craft a sleek design, and the pressurized inner hull that supported life both biological and mechanical. Some of the submariners would die almost immediately as their lungs and intestinal organs were traumatized by explosive shock. For others, all they had left was to wait for the water to rip from one compartment to the next and try to block out the noise of men.

That afternoon a Navy diver went down to the wreck to confirm its identity and report on the location of the damage. A nineteen-year-old sailor's body was brought up, a good-looking kid named Hoffman, who later was returned to the sea with an American salute, a bugle solo and a prayer.

U-853, nicknamed "Moby Dick" by Allied pursuers for its escapes while wounded, self-identified by its crew (for the same reason) as "Tightrope Walker," would spark postwar rumors of having been Hitler's private escape submarine, or hauling an immense treasure of silver and gold, or a big batch of mercury. Sport divers began visiting the wreck in the 1950s, acquiring minor souvenir objects, plates, cutlery, the soft-soled shoes crewmen wore for maintaining silence, some plastic tags from the engine room with the boat's number used for marking spare parts. Nothing expensive.

It wasn't until 1960 that two salvage divers removed bones from U-853 in search of some achievement or profit in the remains which had long had all flesh picked at by tiny creatures.

Getting down to the target was an effort for them. Sharks were a problem, and one diver said he shot a thirteen-foot mako. On one trip, a deck hatch dropped its weight on a guy's foot and pinned him.

The skeleton they brought up was partially draped in bits of sweater and leather jacket. Still somehow attached to the skull was a breathing device used for escape from a stricken sub, an apparatus based on the Momsen Lung used by the Americans, much less effective than the oxygen-rich tanks employed by the two explorers as they plucked the remains from the forward torpedo room.

The divers found the corpses strung out in pairs; the breathing mask technique dictated that sailors share what little substance it provided, but to affirm that all crewmen applied said procedure in moments of *blechkoller*, "tin can frenzy," would be speculative.

The explorer whose exploits were condensed in some articles in Newsweek didn't think he was adding any insult to the sailor's injury by acquiring the skeleton. He planned further dives and photography before removing more corpses, because "Those bodies have been there for fifteen years, they can wait a few more days." Each dive would be only forty minutes, and some of the available air supply would be saved for the twelve or fifteen minutes of decompression required to return from the depths.

The bones were transported to a Newport funeral home. Perhaps they'd be returned to a family in Germany or crafted into an exhibit under glass or added to a box encased in a granite obelisk overlooking a seaside town square and sporting a plaque that encouraged visitors' reflection on souls lost to a callous, fluid world.

The remains were probably not those of Fröemsdorf, who likely would have been at the command station, but one of the fifty-four others. Hardly any of the crew wore dogtags.

The summer before the first magazine article came out, I'd been bragging about how my mother took out my tonsils.

Jean had stabilized her medical career in Philadelphia by trading hospital shift work for a nursing position with a reputable ear-nose-and-throat specialist named Sataloff. He was an "ENT to the stars" who took care of roadshow Broadway singers with throats raw from belting it to the balcony, and balmed crooner Bobby Rydell's hoarseness just before an appearance on "American Bandstand" when the teen-dance show originated from a TV station in West Philly.

Quite fortuitous, my mother working for an expert when my adolescent tonsils became inflamed. No doubt she got a break on the bill.

They draped me in white on a table as the surgical team leaned over like fronds to the pond, filling my ceiling view, then turning away in their busyness and the lights would flood back. I couldn't see my mother's entire face, just the bridge of the nose and the eyes peering out between the hair cap and the mask. She was smiling in there, imparting confidence. When you're nine years old and having surgery for the first time, or anytime for that matter, you can't beat having your mom right in there, nobody's going to muck it up when mama bird has a tray of knives.

That afternoon I requested my unlimited ice cream in the post-tonsillectomy tradition (a bribery of children's cooperation that traced back to the Abyssinians). The celebration was limited, my throat so raw I could manage only a few swallows of the spikey, gummy strawberry crystals.

The hospital allowed my mother to stay in the room all night, professional courtesy. She fitfully dozed in a lumpy, pre-ergonomic padded chair, and when the terrible tearing soreness woke me, she'd rouse in the dark and bring me ice chips.

It was a fun story, poignant, one of my oldest, unique because nobody's mother ever did surgery on them. Despite having no pictures of myself in a hospital gown, it was a true thing, documented, on file, remembered.

Such picture stories in my mind went back another few years but with less clear recollection. The cranial library, the mind's eye-movie spooling back, would barely approach my fourth year and then crackle gray. Any earlier stuff was replaced by newer, ostensibly more essential material. My brain repurposed many of its original memory units, just like how the TV networks cheaply taped new programs over so much of their Golden Age because the old shows would never be missed or hold utility.

That's how it is with growth, tossing out the seemingly inconsequential to make room for the presumably critical, a scheme of the brain's real estate development that denies every human so much wonderful recall.

I was fairly certain I'd had an early childhood, as biological growth demanded I be small at one age and larger at another, presumably later, time. The only way to revisit those years, *sans* memory, was through boxes of pictures, where the living room chair's floral colors glowed, and the giant pink and brown fuzzy cloth horse, taller than me, smiled. Even then, with all these clues, I probably wouldn't really remember the scene but simply accept the photographic fact of it, "Oh, so the wallpaper in the front room had stripes?"

That life was two-dimensional, flat, archived by a family of keepers and hoarders and chroniclers of decades of some affirmed lineage. Photographs wrapped up in envelopes and taped into albums, everybody looking at the future: the unmarried aunt who always came on our vacations, sometimes an uncle, the great-grandparents who forever dressed as if it were 1910 and would die the year before I came along. There was a grandmother's brother who was estranged from the others after arguments about family gravesites and lived six blocks away, whom I'd see only at Christmas. Discretely attired people kicking surf at the Jersey shore. A childhood with the stick-thin family and hefty in-laws and those birthday cakes from McMillan's Bakery with plastic cowboys on top one year, baseball players the next.

All well worth protecting from fire or water or negligence by committing everything to a digital vault, using the technology of Now to hang onto Then. My future generations would appreciate it. I'd get to it one day.

If I still carried anything forward from the pre-memory, it existed only within intuition and dreams. A cache no therapist could unlatch, elements of childhood I could not remember, but nevertheless inhabited me. Experiences long since taped over. You knew of that age only what was saved for you. Sometimes the past was hidden until someone decided you were ready to see it.

I emerged from the past of Edwin and Elizabeth, Jean's parents, both born in 1896 not long after the boats brought their hopeful predecessors from Glasgow and Edinburgh up the Delaware River to Philadelphia, the country's busiest reception room for newcomers before Ellis Island was pressed into service. Their families were Kennedys and Scotts, names not requiring adjustment of spelling or pronunciation to fit into the Next World. They might have been on the same ship, in the same line to get checked for disease and anarchic intention.

They clustered with other Scottish immigrants across the river in Camden, a town to become known not for the eight hundred African slaves offloaded there in the mid-1700s, but more for Campbell and his Jersey-tomato soup, Victor with his RCA record player and that cockamamie tilted-head dog listening to "his Master's voice," and Walt Whitman's poetic waxings. Later, Camden witnessed Jersey Joe Walcott practicing a champion's right cross, and L. Ron Hubbard's early attempts to establish alien truths.

The old Scots (including the Scotts) gangplanked into the future pursuing the legacy of their forebears: Daniel Boone and Sam Houston, the economist Adam Smith and the guy with the pickaxe who started the California Gold Rush. Scots were innovators of penicillin, the inflated bicycle tire (for short distances) and the steam engine (for longer). Morse's code was for those who spoke in dots and dashes, Bell's telephone for those who didn't. Duke Ellington was said to believe jazz and Scottish music were the only two kinds of music with natural swing, but most opinions shared Lee Trevino's that "golf is a game invented by the same people who think music comes out of a bagpipe."

Elizabeth, known to all as Bess, dark-curled, of medium height, temperament, medium everything, inherited the image and aura of her mother, Jessie Hamilton Kennedy, whose high-collared, excruciatingly girdled portrait from the Robert Smith studio in Cowcaddens, Glasgow, would grace family parlors for a century. Bess was studious-looking and pursued secretarial training; her younger sister Ethel's features were less defined and a bit spongier, and she'd spend her life at a desk at a fuel delivery company.

On a Christmas weekend, their father Hugh cautioned their behavior and safety (this was a short time after the "Spanish flu" pandemic had swept through Philadelphia, killing many thousands who shared unnecessary proximity at Great War celebrations). The young women splurged for twenty-five cent seats in the B.F. Keith Theater in Philadelphia to enjoy headliner Henry "Squidgulum" Lewis, an "effervescent mirth provoker," with the Little Peacock, Muriel Window, plus Four Classy Girls performing aerial acrobatics, a pianist known for "agonizing the ivories" and the Mirano Brothers, the Flying Torpedoes.

While Elizabeth and the stringbean Edwin had grown up several streets apart in Camden, it wasn't until after the war that they met. He'd gone into the service late, his unit assigned in Germany to guard some Russians contained in camps rather than returned home to probable persecution or death at the hands of other Russians. Edwin enjoyed the variety shows the prisoners gratefully staged for their guards. He brought home a Luger, a German officer's sidearm. His doughboy hat still lives in a box of stuff.

Bess and Edwin were part of a young America that happens after war, headed back to family and Saturday nights and with any luck a job, and after a few years, stretching out into what would become known as suburbs. Edwin's parents, Joe and Eva, had moved him and his brother Walter to a town outside of Camden that developed around 1905 along one of the train lines headed to the Jersey Shore. It was natural, maybe expected, that Ed and his new bride took up in a house a few blocks from his folks.

This quiet, sturdy community produced three Medal of Honor recipients, more per capita than any town in the United States. It lay between a pair of two-lane pikes called the White Horse and Black Horse that took people from Camden (along with Philadelphia and its neighbors across the Delaware by ferry) slicing east past the tomato farms and blueberry estates to the beaches of quiet religious-retreat towns and, for some, the iniquities of Atlantic City, with rumrunners in the back bay and New York gangsters nosing around.

By the mid-1960s the town maxed out at twelve thousand people in a flat square mile and a half. Fifty years later the population would fall to barely eighty-eight hundred, after the baby boomers moved away and people pushed further out into tracts carved from farms and woods.

Jean was Bess's second child, born in the fourth month of the Great Depression. With her older brother Robert she was raised in the shingled bungalow perched on a slight rise on a T-intersection, a full story above street level, with two sets of concrete steps etched into a steeply pitched lawn that required muscling the rotating-blade mower on summer evenings.

Slim like her parents, a lot of Scottish teeth, a bit of point to her nose and wispy dark hair, Jean pursued nursing studies over in the big city after high school. She moved to a friend's home in a suburb on the other side of Philly, where they worked in the two operating rooms at a small hospital. Her brother, back from merchant sea duty after the second big war, left Bess and Edwin's embrace to marry and move away with a woman he knew from Jean's high school class.

If you worked the late-night shift downtown at Hahnemann Hospital in the postwar years, it wasn't for the gunshots, drunken crackups, bar fights and insistent newborns. It was for the extra money. Jean could save now that she'd moved back in with her folks and, at twenty-one, enlisted in Hahnemann's big-city surgical array. She'd want her own apartment someday, and the late shift pay helped, though horrifying to Bess its urban *noir* circumstances and effects may have been.

The elective operations scheduled each evening often sloshed into the emergencies, and frequently it was after midnight that they stopped the bleeding while most of the city slept.

The white-garbed crew sought respite after hours in Broad Street taverns that also catered to the overnight Inquirer crowd from the printing plant up the block. At the Press Bar, a place like any other where murmurs and outburst laughter punctuated glass tinkling and jukebox swaying, Jean met Burton.

The fellow had some stockiness that suited his handling freight with the Sword Line. A shade under six feet, close to two hundred pounds, he was from California, waved brown hair over surfer-blue eyes. Not yet twenty-five and doing three-week trips in the maritime union, Burton wandered into Philadelphia in the late summer of 1951.

It pretty much zoomed along between the two, even as Bess and Edwin, having married in their mid-twenties, disapproved of the transient they saw popping through their door every few weeks. Jean and Burt determined to secure their happiness, and on an October night in a Lutheran minister's house a few blocks away from where Jean had grown up as a Presbyterian, they exchanged vows.

Jean took two days before telling her parents. It crushed Bess and Edwin.

The honeymoon phase was slim. The new Mr. and Mrs. quickly created a potential person, not in the plan but there you go. Jean picked up a small used car and made the drive between her folks' house and the industrial port of Marcus Hook, an hour's drive south of Philadelphia, each time Burt came in or shipped out. He seemed to lose interest, though, and began taking jobs out of the port in Baltimore, a lot further away.

The pregnant nurse driving to work across the Benjamin Franklin Bridge, then standing for hours under the intensive lamps of the O.R., struggled with her thoughts as any woman would: what good girls do or don't do, caring for tiny babies, adoption, is shame called for? She had no question, though, about keeping the baby. Jean was forever grateful her folks never once said, "We told you so."

She was alone when the kid kicked his way into a warm Camden hospital room in the hot July of '52. Blue Cross denied coverage because the young couple hadn't been on insurance for the qualifying year, so she had to pay retail.

Burt was gone. His philosophy apparently did not embrace *ichi-go ichi-e*: one time, one meeting, a phrase common to Zen calligraphy, an admonition (originated by a nineteenth-century Japanese tea master, later

murdered) to embrace any gathering lest it never be repeated, to have gratitude for every second of a life. The introduction at the Press Bar, the seduc-
tion, the sloppy results, the commitments quickly dashed, those months, all
seemed one long moment Burton chose not to make the most of.

Maybe he hummed some Fifties version of "Billie Jean" as he
slammed up the gangplank; after all, the guy was always off on ships,
keywords: adventure, escape, elusion, footlooseiness. Was the nurse his
first big mistake in life, or a window to a full-blown *modus*?

Immature, inexperienced or corroded, insanely stressed or simply
selfish, fearful of family, dismissive of expectations, scruple-short, maybe
a career con, this guy really messed up Jean's life and stuck her with a kid,
a kid he wouldn't claim.

Maybe the guy's duffel bag was packing too much already.

For a youngster, it was like living on the bridge of a battleship.
The big world was right outside all those windows, elevated up from the
avenue.

Most of the houses on Pine Street were simple single-story bunga-
lows with storage attics and half-buried cellars. Edwin had enclosed the
original open porch with siding, creating the window-lined front room I
used as a neighborhood-sweeping command post. Lining the curbs were
sycamores of pale green with bark that peeled off in crackly sheaves bigger
than my arm.

The grocery across the street was a quarry of five-cent Creamsicles
and caramels filled with white stuff and Tastykakes, a regional snack
specialty that laughed at Little Debbie.

On Sunday afternoons the unmarried, quiet Aunt Ethel walked over
a few blocks from her apartment. Having been raised by Jessie in an *e.
coli*-adverse kitchen culture at the turn of the century when ice was delivered in blocks by horsecart, the sisters knew how to boil vegetables into

surrendering their flavor, and just hammer the chops, and the ground beef became dark aquarium gravel. Alternately, the infrequent and expensive baked crab imperial was spectacular, buttery-bubbling in individual glass crustacean molds, and I gobbled my grandmother's sweet stewed rhubarb while resisting her prunes.

Milk in glass bottles still arrived by truck in the morning (until a time came when a market's TV jingle asked, "why pay more for milk at your door, when you can get it fresh at the store!"). For a youngster, the delivery guy in white pants was one of those faces of the larger world you'd glance through the front-door glass, an emissary of civilization.

Twice a year the kitchen would be off-limits and stinking of cigar smoke with the windows open regardless of the season. My lanky grandfather, nicknamed Scotty by his friends and co-workers in the art department for N.W. Ayer, a big advertising firm next door to the Saturday Evening Post over in the city, hosted old poker players from the neighborhood. I was permitted to enter the kitchen on card night only once, squeezing by the men from sclerotic industries who grunted "heyhowyadoonkid" as I scrounged for a bottle of Hires root beer. (Grandma had her crowd, too, a ladies' church group that rotated parlors for monthly gatherings, and I'd make my appearances, all adorable for Bess's friends, and cut a deal for some pound cake.)

The kitchen of white wood and white appliances was cramped with chairs and a folding table capped by a heavy, fitted hardwood top Scotty had handcrafted, six sides polished keen with carved snack receptacles, ashtrays, cup holders and a drum-stretched vinyl playing field the shade of a dark lime you'd see on ponds, reflecting every lively or sallow clink of tossed chips from the maple poker-bank box he also created.

The gaming table emerged from a table-saw workshop, overrun with dust and every screw size imaginable, sitting at the back of the shadowy, granite-block basement. Anything could emerge from Scotty's atelier – knickknack shelves, wedding-gift cabinetry, bureaus, wrought iron candelabra, Pinewood Derby racers for my Cub Scout rallies. Mounted on a stand in a dark corner was a tall, robot-thin lathe with a frosted-lens light atop it, and from the other end of the cellar it resembled a massive alien eyeball that spooked me from an early age. At the bottom of the stairs where Bess stored onions and potatoes on shelves, wall brackets grasped my mother's childhood American Flyer sled with its Rosebuddian eagle motif and riding boards much-shellacked by Scotty, now bubbled with age and crisp-topped like crème brulee.

Grandpop Edwin's usual daily roost was in a corner of the glassy front room, a maple rack by his chair stuffed with stacks of National Geographic, Popular Science and American Legion and coasters for Schlitz beer (poured bottles, never cans) fresh from the brewery district around Front and Poplar in north Philly.

The Scottys watched weekend sports on a black-and-white television, and for the evening variety shows and sitcoms Bess and sometimes Jean would take the sofa along the wall. They'd come through the Depression and a world war linked to the universe by radio, same as everybody, but now the family's electronic hearth was on a rolling stand of brassy, wobbly aluminum. (The family's first television, in a side den later to become my Western-wallpapered bedroom, was a fifteen-incher encased in a dark wood console the size of a tipped-over cigarette machine.)

Through these electro-boxes came what passed in that era for imme-diacy, supplementing but hardly supplanting the three daily newspapers from Philly and Camden. We'd gather for Ed Sullivan's Sunday night talent parade and glitzy New Year's Eve pageants of ball gowns and crooning saxophones in posh Manhattan hotels.

There were special occasions for which I was glued to the magic machine, as when Kennedy became the TV President, showing off the high-altitude photos of Russian missiles trampling Cuban cane fields, Americans don't put up with this crap, Moscow better turn those ships around, and it comes-this-close to Goodbye Miami.

It was exciting for me to connect with a big shaky world instead of just the relatively unanimated one on Pine Street. There was the wide-eyed boom of the first astronaut lift-offs, the death of Winston Churchill that so affected my grandmother and the weekend of JFK's assassination with its special reality featurette, the live shooting of suspect Lee Harvey Oswald in a Dallas police basement. A few months later on Sullivan, The Beatles said *yeah*, more than once.

In early times, while my mom and grandpop were working, Bess and I would watch the daily game shows with ticking clocks and dunks in water tanks. *Queen for a Day* was particularly engaging, in which three women much like Bess, Depression survivors, choked out tales of deprivation, suffering attractively, competing for a new appliance.

Evenings saw a variety of quiz show that extended a white-gloved hand to the great swath of interior Americans, bidding them to dabble, however briefly and distantly, in the sophisticated world of Broadway's sky-sweeping floodlights and glitzy nightlife. These guessing games had celebrities who looked like they'd stopped off on the way to a Manhattan party: bejeweled newspaper columnists and wise-cracking radio humorists, singers in 50's musicals, approaching-elderly movie stars.

On *What's My Line*, the celebs tried to unmask a person's job, likely to be amusingly on the edge of middle America – the midget beekeeper, the lady who'd been painting garages for sixty years, the man who caught salmon from a helicopter.

On another night came *I've Got A Secret*, invented by a TV adman, Allan Sherman (who a few years later as a Jewish folksinger parodist would go top-ten with "Hello, Muddah, Hello Faddah" about a miserable summer camp). The guests would whisper their secret – he had the world's largest toaster collection or she had fourteen cousins all named Gladys or, as in Pete Best's case, he was The Beatles' first drummer – to the host Gary Moore, he of the Marine crewcut and cigarette perennially in his right hand.

(And the smokes weren't unusual. A cigarette haze lingered over many of these programs sponsored by Pall Mall, Kools and Chesterfield, with messages assuring viewers back before tobacco ads were chased off the airwaves that "more doctors smoke Camels.")

On the third and last of the available channels of the early broadcast era was bow-tied Bud Collier (picture Matthew Modine in the film role) with a trio of contestants claiming to be one person who had done something of interest. As the camera gave a panning examination of their faces, they'd assert their identity ("My name is Rudolf Shamongi" … "*My* name is Rudolph Shamongi… "*My* name…"). The actual person could not lie about themselves, while the two duplicates could mislead the judges. Depending on who fooled who, they'd win a sparse few hundred dollars and likely receive a complementary carton of cigarettes or a nice gift package of headache remedies.

Names not-yet-household, like Kim Novak and Ossie Davis, appeared to promote movies and careers. Many spouses and children of the famed filled in the lineups, such as nine-year-old Anderson Cooper, son of the fashionable Gloria Vanderbilt, pretending to be Wally Norton, the world's youngest professional bear trainer. Year after year the show spilled out a clown car of contestants – a man who tunneled beneath the Berlin Wall, a guy who was half a horse in *Hello, Dolly!,* Everest climber Edmund Hillary, Miss Rodeo America, a Native American who posed for the nickel, three women with ribcages lit by fluoroscopes, Motown's Berry Gordy, Jr., a dinosaur footprint salesman and Oriana Pallachi, author of *The Useless Sex.*

The diver couldn't seem to keep from tangling in a knotty net of opinions.

Burton's company, SubMarine Research Associates, was planning recovery of more of the thirty-six distinguishable skeletons from U-853 and returning them to West Germany. The government in Bonn wouldn't invest anything, so the business raised about four thousand dollars from magazines seeking publishing rights to the tale. The outfit was still nine grand in the hole and scraping.

In Newport, the city council and a group of clergy led by The Rev. John Rossner, curate of Trinity Episcopal church, were disenchanted with what they considered a desecration. Stories that the salvagers, who'd been down dozens of times, had also sawed off a portion of the periscope and grabbed some life rafts caused consternation in some quarters.

Rhode Island warned that the U-boat wreckage was in what it claimed as its "tidal," albeit international, waters and would permit no violation. Burt argued that rulings by the Coast Guard and U.S. State Department permitted him to move forward, and with help from a Swiss and German salvage crew and as-yet-untested Swiss diving equipment they would float the entire vessel. "Maybe we can raise her and put her on display," he trumpeted. "If nothing else, she'll be a memorial to the stupidity of war."

Fed up, West Germany declared U-853 to be its property and any further attempt to remove its contents, much less raise the vessel, would be "akin to piracy." The naval attaché at the German Embassy in Washington, D.C., Edward Wegener, said his government agreed with the traditional American position to "let the ships and seamen rest on the bottom."

One counter-argument was that the sub belonged to Hitler's Third Reich, not the Republic of West Germany. If the government of the 1960s pressed a claim to the site or its contents, then West Germany would also be saying the Third Reich did not fall. Couldn't have that.

Voices in Bonn insisted the diver's plan was "a commercial venture aimed at exploiting the dead, and no civilized society approves of this."

Retired admirals sounded off in interviews, among them Henry Eccles, who said, "I have hundreds of old friends who are resting in submarines at the bottom of the Pacific Ocean, and I would defy anyone to start bringing up their bodies." A former president of the Naval War College, Stuart Ingersoll, couldn't reconcile how clever, energetic young American divers could consider conducting "such nonsense" when "a nation with which we are now in peace and harmony pleads with them to leave the submarine rest in peace."

The guy they were all yelling at insisted, "We told the German government about our plans and received their sanction. Now I'm beginning to feel they're putting the squeeze on us," that there was a tacit agreement about an eighty-twenty split on any treasure they pulled up. Burt seemed pretty serious, having turned to professional diving full time. "We're going right ahead! Whatever thunder they want to throw, let them throw it!"

New England newspapers blazed garish headlines about German corpses, stoking lurid embers of wartime emotions less than two decades distant that had yet to fully cool among a coastal population that had seen the smoke of burning ships across the horizon.

The salvager asserted his dignity, relatively. "In 1950 a Navy guy brought up a body and then they threw it overboard and the head came off. This is the type of thing we're trying to prevent."

Atop this mound of yell and counter-yell, Burt's plan once they raised the wreck was to sell tickets. That would fund scholarships for families of the dead on the *Black Point*, followed in priority by the kin of the U-853 crew, and after that, American children of those lost at sea in the war and finally, whatever smattering of "deserving orphans of war dead from any country" might be on the waiting list.

The claims ping-ponged among diving enthusiasts and offended observers: that because the boat was in an easily accessible hundred-plus feet of water, the dead could not really be considered "buried," that the Germans had reneged on a deal to provide funeral expenses for the first recovered sailor, that U.S. Senator Claiborne Pell should petition the United Nations to block the sacrilege.

Stories about, and opinions generated by, these underwater dramas and above-ground wranglings would go on and on in professorial U-boat histories and prickly naval enthusiasts' newsletters. Sixty years after the sinking, an online forum on German military history was still attracting posts about U-853, spanning from let-bygones-be-bygones to hang 'em. In language of varying degrees of lucidity were posts from Michigan and Sweden ("That is just disgusting, I wonder how those divers would feel if someone dug up the graves of their relatives and stole their skulls?"),

Madrid and Peoria ("MY God!!!!!! They should be taken out and BULL WHIPED Holy Christ that is disgusting!").

A Scandinavian perspective on treasure-hunting, in awkward English speckled with [*sics*], was posted in 2002: "All sunken german ships in Norwegian waters was/still is norwegian property. It was owned by the Norwegian state, and sold to private salvaging firms. They where raised, some repaired, some ended up as scrap. Many of those had human remains(Tirpitz for instance), few got as far as a cematary afterwards. No warship is a wargrave until declared as such. Still its sad when it happen."

A West German photo-news magazine called New Illustrated located seamen assumed to have perished on U-853 (and Fröemsdorf's mother as well). Among them was Theodore Womer, part of the crew since it first launched, who took issue with a death certificate indicating his demise. Helmut Sommer, one of the sub's early skippers who took more than two dozen wounds in a strafing attack, also hadn't made the last patrol as he was stuck with some of his family in a Russian-occupied part of Germany.

More than fifty did indeed perish, the young men who do the dying. Friedrich Volk, almost twenty-one, wrote to his mother he was afraid of Fröemsdorf's inexperience. A radioman, Karl Wurster, had cut short his shore leave to ward off guilt that his mates might die for Führer and country without him. Engineering Officer Christian Wilde, who celebrated his 26th birthday just before he was killed, told a friend there was something aboard the U-853 that he could not discuss.

A woman in West Germany found a letter written by an eighteen-year-old named Helmut, the youngest aboard U-853. "Dear Christl," it began, "I received your letter of the 25th of January with great happiness. Now at least I know that you have survived so far... When I come back from this trip, everything will work out. Maybe we can celebrate our reunion at home again... When you receive this letter, I will already be in Norway. If you don't receive any news from me in five months, please turn to the base (of the sub fleet)... There you will learn whether U-boat 853 is still on a trip."

Of course, it wasn't. The Navy punched holes in her and seawater did the rest.

As for the young man whose retrieval in '61 kicked off the fireworks, three very casually dressed men lifted his inexpensive coffin from an unmarked station wagon. A graveside fusillade and a bugled *Taps* was attended by a German consul general, a commander in the German navy and the chief of staff of the Newport Naval Base. A person unknown and unseen came around annually to clean up the plot.

Jean gave her boy a name meant to be taken straight, that you couldn't reduce to Timmy or Dick or Louie or Ham. My name from the old Scottish meant *from the battlefield*, or in a quieter interpretation, simply *wood*.

In my first years I was alone, no kids my age on the block, no play dates. Mother started sending me in a station wagon to somebody's house a few towns over, a casual pre-school, where I could socialize, energize and acquire the nickname Bouncing Ball.

Adolescence saw plenty of solo afternoons creating Napoleonic battlefields on the bedroom floor with boxes of little plastic green soldiers and knights upon horses. *South Pacific* and the dueling pianists Ferrante and Teicher echoed from my mother's room. I read the Hardy Boys series and, later, the entire World Book Encyclopedia, a practice that would make me seem a genius in high school geography and history and eventually a perfect candidate for *Jeopardy!*

Outside, a generation of original town residents moved or passed on. As the neighborhood nurse, Jean would be called for whatever comforts or counsel she might provide to elderly neighbors in their last night. People passed as she sat with them in rooms of dim yellow lamplight behind drawn curtains.

Our Presbyterian home eventually became encircled by Catholic families moving in. The Parochials from St. Rose of Lima seemed to have far more holidays than the Publics enjoyed; their school-off days differed from mine, which was patently unfair, all those entitled saints. In summer afternoons I could look three backyards over and see the Catholic kids in a pool, the families picnicking together in the evening.

The only Jewish kid I knew had a dad named Milt who owned the Sweet Shoppe, the candy milkshake emporium across from the train station. Then when commuters started driving the freeways and McDonald's opened in the next town, people bypassed old places and Milt lost his Shoppe.

If there were any African-American kids in the world, they lived on corners in a deteriorating Camden, visible only through bus windows on grandma's drag-me-along shopping trips to the Market Street department stores in Philly. There were rumors of one or two Black families in our town, way over on the edge of the park by the municipal swimming pool everyone called the Polio Pit, but nobody actually saw them. First time I met a Black youngster it was after seventh grade, a randomly assigned tent mate at a Christian summer camp in north Jersey. Perfectly fine chap.

Jean and Edwin's incomes provided Little League fees and ortho-pedic shoes and vacations in the green-finned pre-seatbelt Dodge to the Jersey Shore and Niagara Falls, Florida and Nova Scotia. In the picturesque, rolling-hill Poconos between the hamlets of Mehoopany and Tunkhannok, we guest-roomed on a family farm, where I helped milk the cows and almost drowned in a slippery-rocked creek.

In the late baking summer of '65 mother and son took a train north for a few days' sightseeing in the wizardrous Capital of the Civilized World and its stupendous World's Fair. To start things off, our cabbie from Penn Station had to machete a path to the Hilton Hotel on Sixth Avenue through rings of police and mashed-potato corners of amassed throngs. The Beatles, having played two nights before (through teeny hundred-watt speakers that were massive for their time but ant-like at Shea Stadium), were just leaving the Warwick across the street. With the taxi locked in like an arctic frigate betwixt icebergs, we got out at the corner and waited for a short limo parade to pass. In the rear window of the final car I saw the bowlish haircuts of

George Harrison and Paul McCartney.

All of which to say, I had the security, the toys, the space to run around, views of the world. In thin-millimeter home movies collected in boxes, Jean's outstretched arms were covered in birds at Parrot Jungle and white-gloved Boy Scouts smartly marched in July parades.

In plaid flannel shirts long before their rediscovery by craft brewers, in a white American suburb instead of Appalachia or Uzbekistan or the Skeleton Coast, sitting a scant six miles from Cherry Hill, the first enclosed, air-conditioned mall east of the Mississippi, I was unburdened by deprivation. I'd never been tugged aboard a sloshing raft or carted along an unfathomable highway from and/or to hell.

Heck, I was born in one of the best places on earth. Maybe not as happy as Sweden, but a lot more daylight.

Television confirmed my experience to be the American Way. I had a likeable family that fit in with neighbors who knew each other's cars and patio floral habits and bowling scores and clinked iced tea in George Babbitt's backyard. Although there was that one thing I was dimly aware of, the differentiating thing that no one spoke of at the dinner table. In the early days an older couple next door made unsolicited judgy noises, but for the most part the neighborhood was polite. A local conducting a sidewalk tour for a visiting relative might point out, "We like it here, although the guy in that gray house never cuts the grass; that's Mr. Sinkler's, he's the beer lover around here; and that one has an older couple and their daughter, she has a kid now but we don't know what happened."

In the Odyssey, Telemachus said something about how no one truly knows his own begetting. There are facts and there are mysteries. There is what you were told and what you discovered for yourself.

Around the age of six, some kid asks "Where's your dad?" and in older years, "Where's your dad, how come you never, what happened to....?"

Children asking pointed questions in the way they do, before they clue into the demarcation between curiosity and intrusion, usually via a *shush* from their mother.

I don't recall anyone ever calling me a bastard, an acutely rude sobriquet. My mother never allowed me to regard myself as *enfant maudit*, an accursed child of suspect lineage, like the kids born of French girls and Nazis.

There was no moment of big sit-down, nor unintended revelation overheard, no smoky Betty Davis neighbor spitting venom over the fence, "You know *why* you turned into such a brat? Because you don't got no father, that's why!"

So I'd draw on the explanation my mother gave me: "Some people don't have a mom and dad, only one of them. It's just what you have."

A father-free life seemed not quite average but satisfactorily normal, what with grandpop Edwin there to throw the ball around the yard and fire up my later interest in growing tomatoes. I'd make him alternate Father's Day cards in my early school grades and there was no turmoil.

In the early 1950s around three million children under eighteen in the U.S. had no father, through death or some other form of complete cutoff or harsh abandonment. Kids whose fathers disappeared in a mortar pit in the Ardennes or froze in the Chosin Reservoir, who dropped over with a snow shovel or walked away in North Philly, who got T-boned at that bad traffic circle in front of the diner in Brooklawn or went down on the *Edmund Fitzgerald*. Paternal orphans. As information about my old man was less than sparse, there you go, I qualified for membership in a sociological group, how about that. Not that it got me a government check.

On a late spring morning, my father wasn't draped over the chain-link dugout fence talking with me between Little League innings. So here I am, nine years old, crossing the diamond from the third base dugout to first, volunteering to provide my teammates the strategic partner that was the Base Coach, a role I was serious about, implying veteran skills and decisive management. I waited for the other team to wrap their mid-inning toss-around, glancing up at the fastball the second baseman wailed over the stretching first baseman's glove, ziplining a centimeter past the webbing and on its split-second approach to the immovable object between my eyes.

I awoke on the grass across the field behind my team bench where I'd been carried, my nurse mother and an umpire and quiet teammates hovering. I'd been disconnected that long. Once on my feet I had a strawberry snow cone, no doubt some kid joked about applying it to my head, and Jean took me home.

Some weeks later, my head became a TV set. Without warning, accompanied by no other affects or pain, my field of view would roll. It was similar to the instability televisions had in those days, when the picture lost its sobriety and the bottom of the image would slide up, or side-to-side, the edge of the scene emerging and repeating from a thick static line, *flip-flip-flip*, requiring a fiddling with the hold dials on the side of the cabinet to calm it.

Everything I was seeing, all that my eyes registered and brain interpreted, would slip at a deliberate pace to the left, followed by the exact same image filling in from the right like a slide show. In such an episode, the rest of your life stops happening and the prime reaction is to grab something. Bad luck if I was riding my bike in traffic.

The episodes overcame me every few days or weeks. If I held still, closed my eyes, the phenomenon would wash away. After the first half-dozen seizures I adapted, resolved to treat the attacks as science in action, to study and chase, a brain tornado. I kept my eyes open to observe how long the sliding image would run, slowing to a crawl, until settling back into place. Twelve seconds of psychedelia.

In a lamplit, darkly furnished office at a Philadelphia hospital, an old-school neurologist tested my reflexes. I had to undress in a curtained cubicle and pad quickly to an examining table so that my mother couldn't see my privates. But the doctor had me do straight line-walking and other exercises in the middle of the room, so all I could manage was an ineffective tuck-in. I avoided eye contact with my mother. I didn't know if she'd watched me naked the entire time or had, for my modesty, studied the certificates on the wall.

Then came tests in the sleep lab, encephalogramatic wires acupuncturally pin-pushed into my skull, a pill-induced nap rudely awakened after thirty minutes by a technician dropping a stapler into a trash can.

For what was diagnosed as *petit mal* epilepsy, tiny bad, a daily Dilantin was prescribed. It all went on for four or five years until the episodes spread thinner and then stopped occurring, the brain stabilized and not so argumentive. My sense of balance outdoors after twilight would forever be affected.

So I had to take pills and parade naked in front of my mother after an optical-interpretive system went *flip-flip* haywire because I wasn't with my dad behind the dugout talking about my excellent last play at third and instead ran over to the first base coach's box and looked up at a spinning white meteor.

Eventually, the man in the wetsuit, easily taken for a garrulous sandwich maker at a deli, never confused with the chiseled Lloyd Bridges of the *Sea Hunt* show that was currently popular, would achieve a pinnacle of fame (or notoriety, depending on one's point of view) in an appearance before an inquiring panel.

He had to be prepared for anything. They might focus on *l'affaire Fröemsdorf* that first brought him to their attention, or another scheme of his that was percolating. They might ask how, if the one-time heating engineer was by his own accounting broke, he and his junior partner, an X-ray technician, had acquired *Summer Palace*, a forty-foot motor cruiser built by the wealthy Astor family in 1929. Had this purchase created his insolvency, or ensured perpetuation of existing debt?

The diver sensed that his banter had limits, responses to be carefully weighed, exuding enough credibility to buffer any cynicism lest the inquisitors become cautious of, even doubting, the explorer's abilities or explanations. He'd boasted that "Only five out of a hundred divers are capable" of reaching the depths where the temperatures drop to forty degrees and the pressure on the body is four times greater than at the surface.

Perhaps they would concur with a published account that described a "solid citizen of Connecticut," or they might arrive at a different estimation. No wife or family or business associate would be on hand to provide character references; he would testify alone.

There had been times when the diver may have exaggerated the narrative or insisted on his honor, integrity and reliability despite scant evidence of either.

But in the face of the questions to come, he knew only the facts about U-853 would suffice.

There was a time I figured I might make a good Frenchman.

A music aptitude test when I was five suggested aptitude for keyboards, rather than bowed-string or breath-based instruments. Handily, against the living room wall in Bess's home was a spinet piano in dark burnished maple. A piano offered affordable culture for thousands of American homes early in the century; Jean learned on it, and Bess played hymns. But for me, nah, pianists were common as bubblegum.

The accordion, now that was delightfully eccentric, with those stripe-shirted Parisians under streetlamps, wandering Roma, or maybe Lawrence Welk if lederhosen was your game. (Nobody beyond Lake Pontchartrain knew much of zydeco yet). Accordionists were respected, at the time anyway. It was an emotional instrument, creating a wall of sound, the melody, bass and orchestral fill all at once. (Rumor once had it that the Phantom of the Opera was originally an accordionist, not an organ player, but Gaston Leroux's publisher forced a change to make the character sexier.)

What inherent talent I carried was mined and polished over years of weekly tutelage at a local music school with Walter Pedozek, the very model of the distinguished, tall, bald-in-front, serious Polish violinist and pianist. Elementary school teachers enlisted me onstage as a special guest star after the rest of the class had done whatever choral nonsense the annual variety assembly called for, and on my red and white Italian-made instrument, plastic clip-in letters spelling my name down the grill, I'd play some ultra-speedy European score from the *Book of Velocity* and impress the heck out of everybody.

Alas, the rattling moment of *rockus interruptus* came in July of '65 when I saw *Help* at the fifty-cent matinee, three afternoons in a row, at the Century Theater on the White Horse Pike. Life as exemplified by The Beatles was far more hilarious than waltzes and polkas. (The only accordionists I saw in pop music were the guy in Gary Lewis and the Playboys, which was just silly, or the one in The Cords, a sort of pre-Devo sextet of Franciscan monks in Wisconsin. Al Yankovic was but a wee lad back then.) I blew off the scholarship Mr. Pedozek insisted he'd get me at the Curtis Institute, Philadelphia's version of Julliard or Berkeley, where the instructor was on the faculty. After eighth grade I relegated the monogrammed squeezebox to its case, although I kept up with lessons on the piano, and anyway, guitars looked really interesting. No more Paris for me.

By sixteen I was fascinated, consumed, by the four thick strings of a Vox Apollo IV sunburst hollow-body half-cutaway thin-necked bass guitar that was practically vintage when I acquired it in a closeout sale for about a hundred-forty bucks that I split with my mom. The electric bass (developed by Leo Fender in 1952) suited my stubby single-note fingers, its low aural register and propulsive character instilling that intrinsic magnetism that instruments have when they find their players. Four plunkable strings to pull gutbucket jazz from the open viol body with a particular stroke high on the neck, with a fuzz switch to Hendrixise the psychedelic tunes. (I disliked the Fender basses many players deployed, the Precision, the Jazz, their strings and the neck too fat, the tone all bottom and no zip.)

I listened to everything, playing between my ears the bass part of all of radio and every record in the house, following the headlights of Paul McCartney and then Brian Cole of the harmony group The Association, then on to Peter Cetera from Chicago and Chris Squire of Yes and John Entwhistle from The Who and a dozen others, and off to the side absorbing the cool from a few Ron Carters and trying to figure out Mingus.

The aforementioned Association, a tight show band from California in three-piece suits and four-part voices, performed my first rock concert, in the same theater where I saw *Help*, and they sang "Windy," "Along Comes Mary" (a pot song!) and "Looking Glass" and by the second tune my knee began jerking spasmodically with an excitement as if juiced by electric current, and it was so loud and mindblowing and perfect.

Oregon left South Africa on its maiden voyage at the end of November '41. The freighter's lights were blacked out and the crew had been scanning their binoculars for German submarines the entire trip across the Atlantic. Late on a Sunday as it approached Cape Cod, the wireless clicked out Pearl Harbor, and the captain knew the American Navy would be scrambling like beads of water in a hot pan.

A day out of Boston, in the clouded blanket after midnight, *Oregon*, a C-1B transport with steam turbines and a top speed of fourteen knots, made the acquaintance of an equally darkened battle group bound for the Panama Canal.

Once she'd unknowingly slipped between four destroyers, *Oregon* was found by the battleship *New Mexico*, which cleaved into the freighter's starboard side. The damage was serious, but it took on very little water.

After sunrise, satisfied with her stability, *Oregon's* captain dismissed a destroyer left behind by *New Mexico* to maintain watch, and resumed course alone.

Onward past Nantucket she progressed at full speed, until the wind changed and the water battered its way into the hull and the mass of it went down in a few hours, taking along seventeen of the forty-two petrified crew.

Two million dollars sank with it, with some estimates pegging it at three or five. The cache wasn't oil or raw rubber. The treasure was 14,076 bales of high-grade African merino wool.

Theoretically, if you could get the latches open and give the thing a good shake the tightly-packed bales would bob to the surface. Encased in thick lanolin like diamonds in wax, they'd presumably never lose their value.

Then, if you really wanted to sweat, there was the possibility of six thousand tons of manganese ore.

But the numerous recovery operators, recreational divers and fishermen out there after the war hadn't ever spotted the ship. Searches turned up empty perhaps because the last bearings taken by *Oregon* were affected by its list as it foundered, its position under what stars were visible through the smoke noted incorrectly by some nerve-wracked ensign before he took to the lifeboat. A magazine reported one diver saying he'd reached the ship in 1958 out in the cantankerous currents off Nantucket and found a dangerous mess. Nobody with any sense would tackle this one.

The salvager who'd been pulling history out of a sunken U-boat wanted *Oregon*. Bereft of funds, with barely "thirty two cents and a second-hand razor blade" to his name, Burton was said to be willing to forgo the profits just to accomplish it and relinquished salvage rights to the insurance company in return for its financing the hunt. Another day, the diver said he was getting the biggest share of the split and no friggin' arguments. Couldn't seem to get the story straight with him.

The safari embarked aboard the *Captain Bill III,* a well-equipped seventy-six-foot dragger designed for hauling fishing nets, underwritten by a Massachusetts attorney named Bottomly (possibly the same one who'd soon get wrapped up in the Boston Strangler case). To peer into the deep, they adopted a bird's-eye view: a Beechcraft pilot from an aerial mapping service flew patterns with a magnetometer, a very effective metal detector, to locate underwater anomalies. Previous searchers hadn't thought of that.

It took less than an hour to find *Oregon*. It was a few miles from the Air Defense Command radar station called Texas Charlie Tower, as well as the gravesite of *Andrea Doria*, the passenger liner that had reacted badly in 1956 when it, too, was rammed.

They made the usual calculations upon reaching the site. A diver has to figure out the current and develop a fair idea of what the sea is like, its personality at the time. That means watching the rope lines or other drifting objects laid out to run alongside the boat, to see where the water's going because it sure isn't just sitting there.

The most perilous part of the dive is just getting out of the boat, or back in. A diver can pack seventy or eighty pounds of gear, and squashing something or breaking a limb is as easy as it looks. A wrong move or sudden motion to the boat can crunch things.

The trip down to a wreck is like traversing a rockface. It's mountaineering in water, hand-over-hand the entire way, no swimming or leg kicking. There's the possibility of irritated sea life turning a human into target practice or lunch. (Shooting an annoying mako from topside was one thing, but it was something else to be on the buffet for great whites up to sixteen feet long that were known to come up from Cape Hatteras.) Or nitrogen narcosis that impairs judgement and sensory perception. Or barotrauma, an increased pressure on the middle ear that comes from descending too fast without using proper techniques of swallowing and blowing to force air into channels in the skull.

The current is not a friend. A current of two-point-five or three knots, about three miles an hour, can tear off gear or rip a diver away from the line. If it's stronger in deep water, much more than expected when the dive judgement was made topside, a diver can lose grip of the line and not have what it takes to get back. There's little to do then but drift with the current, maybe drop some gear (goodbye to a bunch of money, not that it mattered in this sort of moment) and hope to float up naturally and slowly enough to avoid the ever-unpopular bends, the agony of decompression and unruly nitrogen bubbles in the tissues that go pain-crazy in a too-fast ascent. With any luck, the diver can find the boat's trail line moving in the same direction. If a diver can't get to that, now perhaps hundreds of feet from the boat, unless he was on an expensive radio when he broke loose, he's likely gone.

The first dive to *Oregon* could have been Burt's last. The ocean was rolling hard at depth, pinching off face masks and hands from anchor cables.

By the time the *Captain Bill* returned for a third descent, the seas were less agitated. This time the crew attached a massive concrete block to the cable, so wherever it hit bottom, it was going to stay.

As the lead diver followed the line down, a massive school of tuna smothered him.

Visibility was as expected, ten feet at the most with lights. Ambient sunlight can filter through, but this wasn't dappled blue Caribbean turtle-snorkeling. Somewhere after twenty-five feet the sun goes away and there's nothing to be seen up or down. You got the lamps you can carry, maybe 1000-watters if you're serious, attached to a thirty-five-hundred watt onboard generator. Although lights do little past a few feet, annoyingly bouncing back off the swirling silt, you still need something to see your dive mate's language of more than two dozen hand signals to communicate operations, directions, air supply, danger, distress and leave-me-save-yourself. "That's feeling alone," the descent into dark, said one who'd known it.

Well past a hundred feet the concrete block sat on a hard, flat corpse of a ship.

This was a moment of exhilaration for any diver on a target. To be first to a wreck is stunning, like Major Powell moseying up to the Grand Canyon. A small moon step. Most targets in New England waters had been tackled by the early '60s, so getting first to one of the long-missing ships was an achievement.

There was no sign of a disturbance since the day in '41 when *Oregon* nestled down in a fairly flat posture. As the visitor to the rammed ship looked about, there was no sign that Nick Zinkowski made it to *Oregon* before; the experienced Ukrainian diver and one-time Navy submariner, age thirty-one, had been trying for six months to locate the wreck. (Zinkowski also dove to U-853 and wanted to raise it.)

Zinkowski's company was Submarine Specialists, Inc., based on the old T Wharf in Newport Harbor. The company held $125,000 in equipment alone, and some of it was the newest technology. It took several of the crew to get him in and out of his diving suit, with its eighteen-pound shoes. The outfit cost twelve hundred dollars (eight times as much now) and he'd be lucky to get six months' use out of it.

That kind of diet usually eluded guys like Burt Mason, who likely used old regulators and fairly unsophisticated gear. "Back when Burt was diving, what he had was nowhere near today's technology," an old-timer said. "He was the guy who would be grasping at straws just to get the work." Borrowing, bartering, scraping by. They were called scrappers.

Equipped this day with scuba gear, Burt made his way into a cargo hold. There wasn't usually much fear, strictly business, and a minimal concern with the equipment once a stable stance was achieved. But he wasn't in a hard hat suit with buoyancy compensation and a topside air supply pumped through a tube that made him a "dog on a leash." He was at the mercy of larger forces and whatever he could grab onto.

There were wrapped bales down there, no telling how many, any accounting would wait for the next, more organized dive. He couldn't linger, at those depths it's thirty minutes to work, thirty to decompress on a slow rise.

As recounted in that second copy of Newsweek in my mother's

bedroom envelope, what mattered now was to tear off some samples to bring back to the air and light, to show off in a newspaper, convince somebody. Tests would ascertain if the wool on *Oregon* had withstood the time and the water.

Bess and Edwin's hospitality extended until just before I hit fourteen. Grandma Bess would forever be my most-admired woman, generous of heart, supportive and sympathetic, but I conflicted with her old-school husband. Passing years brought along a measure of "not my real father" anger and refusals to submit. Scotty was well within his rights to expect a defined set of feelings and experiences after retiring from the advertising company, watching his children grow and leave the house to him and the wife. But the current scenario wasn't relaxing.

In the aftermath of a particularly bad screamer about me with her folks, Jean stopped after work the next day and rented the small apartment across town. We would relinquish some privacy from each other to gain an autonomy from everybody else.

With mom now working for a facial reconstruction surgeon in Jersey and no herding grandparents or snitch siblings, the freedom of the apartment worked against me as a refuge from the obligations of high school, sometimes for an hour or a morning, but there were full days in a row when I skipped the irrelevance of algebra and biology's worm deconstruction and the expected social conformism.

The mixed academic and social results at school (far from when I graduated at the top of my sixth-grade class), the class-cutter's detention, the weight I'd put on since I was twelve, the physical and verbal pushing from the more-shit-than-brains members of the Future Dead Gas Station Attendants Club who targeted my overweight nerdism, all compounded the anguish of the worst four years of my not-very-long life. Frontier maneuvers with the Boy Scouts every month on my way to the Eagle medal carved off a few pounds, but they always seemed to crawl back.

Jean's many Tuesday nights out to enjoy a few hours for herself was totally earned, great, mom, go see a movie or have dinner with some nursing friend or be a grownup, whatever that means and let's let that drop. It gave me the night open, too, meaning a bakery bag for *The Jerry Lewis Show* and *N.Y.P.D.* and *Dick Cavett*.

Through television's window on the world, there were shots fired, King, another Kennedy, brief invasions of the dinner hour by tear gas and burning tires in Parisian streets, gray tanks securing boulevards in Prague, the police riot drawing student blood in Grant Park. Small steps and giant leaps, a great time to be alive but you'd better run through the jungle. Woodstock happened, but all I saw of it were the lines of traffic headed north into the New York hills as my bus ran south from a Scout wilderness camp.

My last year in high school I attached to a group of the smartest students as a poker player and wit with an unmatched mastery of the sarcastic arts, and that clique integrated further with another, of dateless, facially unconfident weekend misfits. I auditioned for rock and show bands seeking a bassist, but the players were always much older and offered gigs on the bar circuit or touring Army camps a clean-cut sixteen-year-old couldn't accept. Thus, my early career was in wedding bands booked by a catering business, a gig consisting mainly of "Fly Me to the Moon" and plugging the *oompah*-tuba parts for polkas.

Handy with words, unfazed when Mad Magazine rejected my script for a *Hawaii Five-O* parody, I was appointed by the faculty as editor of the six-issue high school paper. I took up as the go-to funny character actor for annual stage productions. Audience laughter and teachers' back-pats for pointed editorials on student apathy offered a glimmer of a future, a Something out there.

At graduation – during which the principal failed to call my name in the chair-by-chair list, leaving me seated as a missing tooth in the row until I stood up unannounced – they conferred upon me the Dr. F. Herbert Owens

Award (provided by an alumnus who liked having his name mentioned every June) for "achieving the greatest progress during his senior experience." Didn't get a plaque, only a newly published five-dollar bill.

Two months after graduation, my birthdate was matched to a number pulled from a bingo cage. A slip from one set of numbers was paired with a date from the calendar, birthday after birthday, the method during the Vietnam conflict to select draftees for a future of M-16s and My Lai and mosquitoes the size of Hershey bars, rooting out the Vietcong crossing the rice paddies by spotting their black pajamas, ducking air strikes on "strategic hamlets" and hoping that the woman with the two half-naked toddlers you just shot up because she wouldn't stop rooting in her reed laundry basket for what might have been a grenade actually had a grenade, because if not you'd feel a lot worse than you usually did out in that beautiful overgrown stinkhole.

I talked big to some friends about escaping, should the bingo balls turn against me, to Toronto or Montreal, the *el norte* of East Coast escapees from an immoral, inexplicable war, as if I had any money from a cheeseburger job or parental support or skills for managing a starving stupid future when I was eighteen in a strange cosmo town. But my number came up in the three-hundreds, made me untouchable, so I stayed in my mother's apartment while other boys fell into 'Nam where fifty-eight thousand of them were killed. (Almost fifty-K of them were white, a statistic at odds with the tenor of the times that assumed the brunt of it all was borne by Black city kids drafted with no college excuse or medical deferment. African-Americans did bear quite a load, as they were eleven percent of the total forces in 'Nam but made up a quarter of those sent into the jungles to fight. Seventy percent of the dead were not draftees but army volunteers who signed up to Battle Communism and the threat to Our Way of Life, as if Our Way of Life had any reason being in Southeast Asia.)

Not to mention another three hundred thousand who returned with holes in them or who left behind parts of their bodies and minds.

The lucky number meant no military for me. But my best friend's ticket was around forty, a good shot at a call-up to the bungle in the jungle, so Bob had to leave art college and enlist for three years on an Army promise for helicopter repair training in Germany, which, lucky for Bob, it honored.

Life with two parents would've meant another house, maybe siblings, other kids at a different school, Sundays maybe in the same stone Presbyterian church, or in some bland New England burg that always smelled like autumn or a Louisiana parish where they at least appreciated the accordion.

Jean answered my question when I was about ten, if she'd get married again, "No, I'm past all that. Once was enough," she firmly stipulated. No more wondering about that.

While there were no Hamletian visitations nor Vaderesque confrontations, no father to compete for Oedipalified attention, still, I had men to disgruntle about. It was a shadowy, molecular resentment of the guy who victimized my mother that I didn't fully comprehend at some grad-student level. Silent, powerless as a boy, I'd circled the wagons early, demanding she never be judged, tried to protect her by withholding regard from the men who crossed into Jean's life, like the twit who took me to a father-son Cub Scout dinner to impress her, and later the attentive healthcare colleague.

Yet a proper dad and the good example, the right talks, might've brought some confidence-building, wisdom for the dating life, the exploring life, the serious adult relationships to come, that all could have used a boost. Maybe a father who pursued physicality might've helped me stave off the useless, embarrassing poundage I acquired in junior high. On the other hand, perhaps my old man had thick-waisted genetics that brought on the teenage weight in the first place, in which case, thanks for nothing, Pop.

There was plenty of father in the construction of a child-face, a shape of the lip, the hair that wouldn't stay down and the ears pushed car-door wide even before the eyeglasses in fourth grade. (I did not inherit my father's natural buoyancy, though. I sank like a stone.)

My skeleton held so many X factors, gifted by predecessors. Years later when my first wife was pregnant there was anxious breath-holding – an entire genetic half of him, the Burton blood, might introduce who knows what burden upon my children or theirs. As it turned out, the kids were born and grew just fine in the big-picture sense, whatever DNA they carried.

Anyway, Ralph Waldo Emerson said men are what their mothers made them.

Burton was sitting amidst what he called a shambles.

A decade after *Oregon* and some national attention, one might say he'd been reduced, working aboard the *Barney*, one of the fleet of tugs, dive-support vessels and underwater mechanics craft of a maritime firm based in the Gulf of Mexico.

As Burt observed it, the *Barney*, a tug more than a hundred feet long and just twelve years old, was operating with a hole in the number two fuel tank, a caved-in bow and leaks in the stern. Not to mention, according to the engineer's complaint, no operating refrigerator, no working toilet, air conditioning or washing machine.

Most of the old crew was gone, including the other engineer with whom Burt shared duties. The captain disdained him, talked him down in front of the crew. He expected a few more days' pay due him, "beer money."

The early 1970s had become just as unprofitable for Burt as the early '60s, certainly more aggravating yet far less adventurous. And minus the magazine coverage.

The next job for the company in mid-January would send him a hundred-forty miles into the Gulf to haul back a disabled tug and barge, voyaging first past the Yucatan peninsula, then across to the Dry Tortugas (some specks of sand beyond Key West), north to Tampa and over to New Orleans. He wasn't thrilled, as the tug being retrieved was "in very bad condition, very bad, out of the country for a year," but the barge was estimated to be worth more than ten to twelve million dollars, well worth retrieving.

The trip was both erratic and nostalgic. There were "too few men, six on the on barge, six on the towing boat," and food stocks were scarce. The waves crested to five or six feet and some days more. They were barely making four to five knots, less than six miles an hour on a trip covering maybe two thousand miles. "This is just like the good old days," he said, "when I worked a boat and dove from it with a two-man crew, and some of the tricks are out of sight," referring to shortcuts and jerry-rigs that made the job possible at all.

Visiting schools of porpoises lent entertainment, yellowfin tuna and red snapper avoided their fishing lines, and they watched masked boobys diving for squid off Cuba and soaring, black and orange-patched frigate-birds migrating from Florida to Texas while rarely landing on the water.

Burt felt the crew was doing this job under protest of sorts. His inoculation papers were incomplete, but the outfit told him not to worry about it. Likewise, he had no papers for foreign travel and was, technically, illegally at sea. Wary that any heavy storm could disable and sink them, the captain declined orders to go faster.

Avoiding Cuban waters was also a priority, as incursion across those lines would leave them open to being picked up by a patrol and hauled in to face, for who knows how long, unpleasant accommodations in some beachside jail with the riff-raff of an economically distressed local society.

At the commuter university a thirty-minute ride from home on the #61 bus, I spent most of my time in an old brick two-story building where

40

the student newspaper office gave me a place to claim a desk as my personal locker. The earnest high school reporter who knew practically nothing about any real world (beyond my contempt for Richard Nixon and the "love it or leave it" hardhats who approved of the students getting shot at Kent State and Jackson State) now sat with senior editors questioning the quiet, sympathetic Irish revolutionary Bernadette Devlin.

In my community affairs column I could complain about being mugged twice; angry cursing in print, the epithets woven into journalism and thus ennobled, was heady. I dashed off record reviews and an unimpressed commentary on a barely attended free show in the cafeteria by a striving, rough-hewn pianist, Billy Joel.

On Friday nights, after dumping my pages into a typesetter's in-basket, I navigated a rumpled back staircase down into the black-walled, three-spotlight burrow of the campus folk club. A spinning galaxy swirled me in, personalities and patchouli vans, pranksters and songwriters (including the later-national blues guitarist Walter Trout).

The upstairs people offered me the editor's chairs at both the paper and the poetry review in my junior year, but staying in school just didn't feel functional. Nor did a transfer to a larger school in Philly with a TV major that could've propelled me to a career in Big Time Entertainment, which is what I always wanted but at the moment didn't have the clarity to pursue. So I dropped out after the sophomore season, besides which the university told me not to waste its time with my crap grades and don't come back. Jean tried to understand.

What appeared achievable was across the river. It was an era of weekly urban newspapers, call them alternative, underground, radical, like the L.A. Free Press and Village Voice, free or cheap, covering entertainment, politics, city life, youthful rebellion and the economy that catered to it. Philly had the Daily Planet and the Drummer, and after leaving college I took my stuff about local coffeehouses and movies to them and they actually bought it.

The Planet, ensconced in small third-floor walkup offices around the corner from one of the city's hippie villages on Samson Street, paid me sixty-five dollars a week to write, help the layout designer and drive around three counties distributing bundles of the paper to colleges, record stores and boutiques. (A few years later in a movie about that underground paper life, *Between the Lines*, my emerging-adult character was played by Jeff Goldblum and Bruno Kirby. Thanks, guys.)

In my twentieth summer my mom was away on a vacation with her brother's family, so I had the apartment to myself. The solo life, sleeping late. Liked it. Upon her return I announced my nest-departure and Jean waved goodbye in that parental amalgam of sadness and whoopee.

With Alan, a thin, goateed manager for a rock band who also worked at the Planet, I took a small flat in Germantown, a lower-middle seen-better-days Philly neighborhood of outer-urban rowhomes and overgrown twins. It was in an immense, faded four-story structure of porches and shredded-white columns. I invested in a sign-of-the-times waterbed and made the mistake of painting my windowless back room dark blue.

It was twenty minutes from my little retreat near the meandering wilderness park to a noisy downtown, the Planet, the bop language, the Liberty Bell's old pavers and horse-carriage clip-clop international gawkers, heyday restaurants of dimming quality, the barely licensed rockanroll warehouses giving way to arena shows.

Now-unruly rubber-banded electrical hair surrounded newly adopted wire-rim glasses. I took stabs at playing in bands with an underpowered amp. Away from my mother's cooking and that season ticket to Pastrytown, pounds steadily melted off my frame. Not all, but enough to count. Women started speaking back.

Living on the pay at the Planet and record stores and overnight warehouse jobs was a slim circumstance, but the art was free: boxes upon boxes of records, press lunches with city-hopping movie stars, concert seats to impress women and overcome teenage total-no-confidence.

The generations prior to the Fifties-into-the-Sixties found their understandings and inspirations and mantras mostly in books, while the tunes of their time were a backdrop to romance and war. Here in my times, sound became the literature and the poster. As international commerce threw popular music quickly between continents and cultures, and more iconoclastic cities and college towns initiated buzz-free FM, the poetry and literacy and politicizing of music solidified.

Music was wallpaper, you always had a record on. The descendant of rock-'n-roll, just plain Rock music, rooted in the blues with acoustic and ethnic cousins across the spectrum, was a liberator, a connector of tribes, a shared escape and entry to a freer world, its ideas and aspirations. In 1963 a British psychiatrist postulated how the "open hero worship" of the early Beatles was "an indication of how fully emancipated adolescents have become," the early screaming-teen furor "a sign that adolescence is now a proud experience rather than a shameful phase."

America had plenty of couches and barstools with fans who tracked sports and the stats, immersed in player minutiae and yelled at the TV play-by-play guys who just, won't, shut, the hell, up. I inhabited, instead, an alternate living history – musicians and bands, supergroups and studios, record deals and release dates, sideman trades and spousal swaps. (There was also the drag of moving four thousand records, one apartment to the next, year after year, trying not to bump into landlords with all those shelves of cinder blocks and lumber.)

I chased it, plunging into a deep backstage-pass pool. Lounged on a ritzy Manhattan couch with Jerry Garcia, tonsorially-challenged and black T-shirted, the Grateful Dead's galactic guitarist and smoke-sleepy dream-weaver sniffling cocaine mist from a repurposed Afrin bottle, analyzing post-Nixonian politics and what that new movie *Star Wars* was going to be about versus *Close Encounters*. Revved up the tape recorder for Jerry's mate Bob Weir, post-show at one in the morning back at the hotel, the singer exhausted and still chatting it up, while I'm grimacing through a raging molar infection because you have to get the story and the dentist can wait.

There was dim-florescent theater-basement jocularity with prematurely balding, hey-let's-go-bowling Phil Collins in his pale Henley shirt and overlong trad-plaid scarf, and photo-posing the gangly-limbed, reserved thinker Peter Gabriel in a badly lit stairwell. Slithering around TV talk show makeup cubicles, overpopulated nightclub hallways and Playhouses in the Park, trying to be academically penetrating with smiley Pat Metheny, relevant with perennially annoyed Frank Zappa, confidence-boosting for fizzy new bands like Boston and Steely Dan. Chatting up guitar intricacies with Leo Kottke and David Crosby, analyzing concert sound mixes with the Eagles on their first tour, welcoming a new generation of British Invaders. Hanging onto my seat in the third row when the newcomer Springsteen's band took over a little folk music joint, crunched onto a stage the size of an Impala convertible, to break his debut record.

Introducing the acts at the Kool Jazz Festival at the big outdoor summer theater and on the European stage of the Academy of Music (a tailored audience shushed for me, now that was a thing). Getting whupped at chess more than once by Mal Waldron, who'd been Billie Holiday's pianist.

Dissembling the evolution of hip humor with George Carlin, laughs about race with Dick Gregory, sketch construction with the Monty Python guys, off-off-Broadway musicalia with Belushi, Gilda and Chevy in the days before Saturday Night.

The papal audiences for me were with Steve Allen, my studied idol, the comedian, author, composer, actor, the original *Tonight Show* host without whom there'd be no Letterman or Fallon, the hilarious commander of language, smart, quick, the man who had more ideas in an hour than most anyone else in a week, a writer of books, songs and sociological study, biopic portrayer of Benny Goodman and improviser of piano jazz in a Chelsea saloon while Jack Kerouac snapped poetry. I wanted Steve to adopt me.

One night the voiceover actor and spoken-word auteur Ken Nordine was in town to tape Mike Douglas' national talk show. Nordine was the epitome of the thin-tied, white-shirted, buzzcut, jazzy Chicago ad man. Later, in a series of restaurants we imbibed assertive joy-absorption indicators and the stories that follow. At night's end, driving my visitor along lumpy asphalt backstreets to his hotel, the baby-napping rhythm put Nordine in a swampy mood and a song emerged, Ken remembering a father in a low tenor, like an old Irish thing you hear from a guy at the end of the bar. Somewhere out in that night I lost my wallet.

(Forty-five years later I spoke to Nordine just before the grand old man of Word Jazz died at ninety-eight, and asked about the late-night ballad he'd sung for his father in a car long before. Ken couldn't remember it, but he was still a sweetheart.)

While it was just doing the job, it would be disingenuous to suggest there wasn't a "can I believe this?" sparkle in taking Marcel Marceau to a fine Chinese restaurant and feeling positively knighted when, backstage at the Academy between scenes, the greatest of French pantomime artistes gave me a friendly wave while he changed his jockstrap. Or drinking too many Seven-and-Sevens with filmmaker John Waters and his Baltimore drag starlet Divine. Or ghouling about bloody-faced on a decrepit movie set in an uptown warehouse, helping diminutive actor Herve Villachaize (later to be the *Fantasy Island* plane-spotter) hungrily seize an ingénue in the low-rent lesser-classic *Doctor Malatesta's Carnival of Blood*.

On pre-digital, typewritered, correcting-fluid newsprint (long before any primate with a computer could ruminate and opinionate) I alternated flashes of brilliance and insight with middling plonk and outright swill. In the fourth largest musical pond in the country, I branded myself "Philadelphia's most respected unknown writer."

Yet the minor celebrity did not accrue to me for actually doing the thing, playing the music or acting the role. It came only for observing and remarking on the creating and thinking and performing by others, many of whom weren't much older, like Collins who had just two years on me.

No appropriate rock band to actually play in ever turned up; the life of a table-serving, garret-shivering, hope-dangling auditioning actor wasn't for me, either. Guess I could've pushed myself into what wasn't yet a business in the '70s, when I thought short movies about musicians might be big on TV, but, well, I didn't.

To be the critic *ta-dah* was to be at peace with not having enough ambition to do it all, that what I did do was enough, a way to emerge from a mayo-on-white town to some kind of somebodyism.

Ambition was mercurial. Even though I became a reviewer at one of the city's big papers, the Bulletin, I stopped writing when it became tedious. I couldn't imagine a career reviewing prog-rock music forever (like a contemporary who could and moved to Rolling Stone for forty years).

But I still enjoyed spinning records and telling people "check this out." My high school geography teacher who worked nights as the announcer at Philadelphia Flyers hockey games, Gene Hart, encouraged me to get into radio, of which I'd long been enamored, listening at night when I was small to AM in the bedroom darkness to voices from who knows where. (As an eight-year-old I was impressed that a local station had its own orchestra and managed to bring in so many stars like Frank Sinatra and Dinah Shore to perform just one tune, because I had yet to understand that they were playing records.)

So I moved to a brainy-rock FM show and sonorously voiced Friday-midnight jazz and snoozy-quilt Sunday mornings, while writing comedy sketches and reporting traffic jams. It went on until I got tired of driving in at midnight in every weather or awaiting buses at five in the morning. Years later there would be forays into voice-over work, from the studious and sleepy *("The eco-system of the Jersey Pines is a diverse environment full of mammals, birds and its share of amphibians, too, with sixty-five distinct varieties of trees...")* to the downright brutal *("With unheard-of prices that almost defy gravity, Miller Toyota's Fantasy Days have been extended for another full week!")*.

If this Path was not of actual doing, but rather the explaining and relating what other people strove for and accomplished, still, it was identity. It was storytelling. It segued to a career at the raised-eyebrow edge of the city culture in an artsy theater called The Painted Bride, producing and promoting hundreds of shows with musicians, actors, dancers and all manner of eccentrics, including Saturday night jazz concerts on the local N.P.R. station. Then it became public relations, megaphoning for nonprofits pursuing public embrace: Drexel University, the new orchestra hall, jobs for the disabled.

In my fifties, I landed at an addiction rehab network, writing for a real human need where the words I enlisted, the feelings engendered, prodded people to get off drugs and alcohol, and every so often my practical, empathetic encouragements brought somebody in, saved someone from dying. That was worth getting out of bed for.

A reasonable Path for a regular uneven guy. A guy with as much chance as the next for a collision avoided or a tumor acquired. The same as every person, millions of go lefts and go rights, look another way, take that leap, find a golden ticket, choose that fork, round that bend, enter Publisher's Clearinghouse Now. Sometimes you hit the baseball or maybe it hits you.

When I turned thirty life's grand pageantry deposited me in the midnight hallway of an after-hours avant-garde radio program I created with three other oddballs, an amalgam of multi-form music, technical experiments, comical theatrics, interviews with whoever showed up at four in the morning. There I met a co-performer's girlfriend's sister, and then it was off to the dance and the vows and two children and after thirteen years a wrenching divorce, not my idea, depositing me in a sullen, bankrupt hole. Through it all I clung to my mission statement, doing all I could to teach and hold a daughter and son who coped, and not always well, but as I never had to, with angry parents in separate houses. To refuse to replicate my father required no thought: it was implicit, organic, to be integral to my kids and enjoy each delightful minute of their lives and to bear the weight of the terrors from which I could not save them.

Don't you want to know something? It would pop up on second dates,

47

my casual yet insistent disinterest in discovering anything about my father, met by the woman's bemused curiosity, sometimes mixed with incredulous exasperation.

"I know it's supposed to be a point of fascination," I'd agree with people, "but I honestly don't care." Be it an offhand insult or well-contemplated adjudication, why should I legitimize the putz with my curiosity?

Therapists would mumble "Now, *there's* something to look at" when I outlined my dad-free insouciance, and they probed for sublimation and denial. It was not that I felt sing-song unwounded by it all; I was simply *okay* with it, had always just felt *okay* with having come to terms in childhood. My waving off the whole subject was easier than examining it and finding buried hurt. Why sink a pipe into something if it's bound to bubble out? Or burst.

This wasn't an emptiness *per se*, as that would imply a vessel to fill. More of a blandness, the unvarnished gray feeling one gets from a gym locker. This was an inborn aversion, as if to gorgonzola, never subject to evolving taste.

Indifference didn't even appear on Plutchik's Wheel. A few of the psycho-graph's dark blue petals matched some of my feelings, but it assigned no designated color to the central emotion I carried about my father.

"Sure, I'll talk to the jerk," I long said, "if he calls up one day with a massive inheritance to assuage the guilt." Who wouldn't want to know about a rich relative, even a crappy one? Getting a letter from a lawyer or deathbed telegram or knock at the door with the deed to some gray-skied estate as the only living male relation of Sir Gwynneth Kennedy-Peatmoss of Goatbridge?

Decades later that *closure* thing would become popular with many, but I wasn't ever going to search actively for the missing and presumed.

As to other twigs of my genetic branch, I had moments of imagination: ringing a doorbell on the ancestral street of Hugh the Edinburgh postman and shocking some woman who didn't know she had an American twice-removed half-whatever I was, a "hey, whaddayaknow!" embrace with some newfound cousin across the Atlantic, or among grandpop Edwin's brother's progeny supposedly in Florida.

But any of Burton's clan wouldn't automatically qualify for love because of the supposed blood tether. They'd be more of an entertainment, to regard with the sentimental sense of kinship I felt with other humanoids in the Great Primate habitat at the National Zoo.

There was a mild reflection, however, about Burton's wiring, a distant man's betterness or worseness, if and how it conferred down the line genetically. The potential latent diseases or molecular abstractions that might skip a generation to my own kids. The behaviors and temperaments of a man long gone yet quietly bivouacked in me like a terror cell awaiting the igniting password, the call of *Regenbogen*.

I was grateful for my blank space. Better off than the guys who'd endured a Great Santini or a belt-swinger. There had never been a bad shout-up for me at the front door, no Tom Waits going out for cigarettes when he didn't smoke and never coming back. No glimpsed figure with fingers curled around the link fence at the schoolyard. No arrestingly familiar stranger sitting with my distraught mother on the sofa when I came home one night.

Never in my life did my father appear to me in a dream.

Melanie was a businesswoman, an authentic Middle Eastern dancer with international credits and an actor with parts in *Moonstruck* and *Jersey Girl*, a bunch of off-Broadway and Philly stages, on TV in *Hack* with David Morse and a very expensive AT&T commercial. I'd been fortunate enough to meet her via an online site a few years after my first marriage collapsed. On an early date, along with the "don't you want to know about him, what are you, nuts?" quiz, we exchanged game show anecdotes.

She'd been on *Wheel of Fortune* in her thirties during a West Coast trip with her mother. Her Fortune was a series of lost turns and bankruptcies that sent her away with barely a sad Pat Sajak handshake. They offered her some conciliatory goodies including the boxed home game, a case of Ricola cough drops and a shoeshine kit, but when she learned it was all taxable as income she told them to park it where even the California sunshine had no influence. That misadventure perpetually annoyed her, thus any glimpse of the show was a disaster flashback. Combined with my own scant talent for dictionary puzzles, as a later couple we had no impetus to watch *Wheel*.

Meanwhile, she loved *Jeopardy!* but I couldn't bring myself to enjoy it. One rainy spring day in the late '80s, having wrangled my media connections to access an audition for the show, I took Amtrak down to a Washington hotel ballroom. Cluemaster Alex Trebek made an encouraging appearance for two hundred hopeful smarties. Guessing badly on opera, the periodic table and glorious moments in dentistry, I didn't get past the written-quiz first round. Alas, to get on *Jeopardy!* one could not punt on unfamiliar subjects as one is apt to do while "playing along at home" (an activity unique to *homo sapiens* among all the mammals). Despairing of my not-know-it-all-ness, schlumping back out to the wet D.C. streets through the towering hotel atrium, I glanced to see Trebek, alone, rising in the glass elevator, a minor Greek god heading up for a check-in with Zeus to confirm that this schmo in the lobby was not worthy of the pantheon. The failure soured me on the show for years.

In our later married cable life we rarely tuned in the Game Show Network, not too engaging with its 80's-90's disco hybrids of high hair, giant lapels, giant playing cards, charades or surveys saying.

Then in the early twenty-teens, a channel called Buzr took some Comcast space and mixed in really old programs, stuffed-away archives refreshed by a video distributor called Fremantle. This was a pale resort for rainy nights, sick-day companionship, in the two-dimensional black and white of the medium's infancy, its toddling years and adolescence. With these shows I could sit again on a Pine Street sofa with mom and grandmom.

I could be ten. The technology of Now allowed me to experience what before was only in Then.

For a few months in spring and summer we watched the new channel from our resplendent red and gold amoebic-patterned couch with its individual powered leg-lifters. Playing Statler and Waldorf in the balcony, we flung peppery remarks about the contestants, the hosts, the judges, sets, animals, commercials (including the original Hertz flying man) and the entertainers who visited game shows in the '50s as they now did *Dancing with the Stars*, to keep themselves above the waterline of public belovedness.

After six months, though, the vintage Buzr shows rerunneth over, shorn of novelty, and by my sixty-forth July birthday, our vintage game show viewing dropped by ninety percent.

In the mid-80s Edwin died of emphysema, the first of the family to go away from me, and this ruined me for days and weeks. I couldn't bear to leave the chapel after the memorial service, didn't want my grandfather to be alone in the room after everyone departed for their cars. Same thing happened at the gravesite, the showrunner in the dark suit shooing me away so the shovel guys could come in.

Edwin never saw the two great-grandchildren from Jean's boy, but Bess had a year to spend with my first baby, a girl who now holds her name.

Aunt Ethel passed with Alzheimer's, then Bess followed, from cancer.

We buried the elders in a Camden cemetery beside Hugh and Jessie, Bess and Ethel's parents who'd shipped up the Delaware from Edinburgh. I'd visited the immigrants' gravesite as a boy with the folks many times after church, trips that included a stop across the road for a floral spray at a shop that was dank green and jungled from an overload of ferns. When you turned into the cemetery off the street at the side entrance closest to the

Kennedy/Scott plot, the first thing you'd see was a large, upright gravestone engraved with my own last name. Nobody I knew was parked down there, but it was a quaint foreboding of eventuality.

Edwin's gravestone conveyed his Army service, a simple foot soldier in a complicated world. My predecessors were a few minutes' walk from Walt Whitman's tomb, a gated stone-block structure and the star attraction of Harleigh Park, commanding a view of the splash pond at the golf range next door.

In Manhattan, Shelley was hoping to run into a yachtsman with a jaunty cap, or maybe a Gloucester fisherman. That would solve her problem.

Four years after graduating high school in the mid-'50s in a doo-wop Queens neighborhood, she'd tripped into a job as a TV production assistant thanks to a new customer in her dad's dry cleaning shop. The guy worked alongside Bob Stewart, a prolific conceptualizer of television game shows and the creative brain for the more well-known producers Mark Goodson and Bill Todman. Stewart's original idea for a quiz show was called "Cross Examination" and later "Three of a Kind."

They'd sought more help because the Tuesday night show had taken off. The pressure of a one-chance-to-get-it-right weekly live broadcast was replaced by the recently adopted videotape process, and the insanity of multiple shows each week required dozens of participants jammed into a short schedule.

They hired actors when they needed a physical type like a jockey or a female basketball player, but Shelley and the other P.A.'s were directed to find people who were "more regular than regular." These were folks with no special plans for the next day and who could, within an hour or so, learn to be somebody else. Then some celebrity judges would figure out who was real and who was not.

The team of assistants beat the city's bushes for people who fit the profile *du jour*. Last week it had been diamond experts and egg-harvesting champions, and her deskmate Rita bagged a couple of faux bison hunters standing in the Manhattan tour bus queue on 47th Street.

While the other two assistants normally hiked through the Theater District, by cab stands and the banks, waylaying apple pie natives and heavily accented foreign tourists, Shelley pursued her own tactic. Approaching customers entering or leaving restaurants, she could go upscale or down-home, depending on the cultural look that was required for a part. The pretty brunette, short and energetic in a breezy front-stoop fashion, found a talent for talking people into doing something they'd never imagined.

Back in the summer someone at the office spotted a magazine article about an adventurous fellow, and by the time the subject had been located (and readily agreed to be on the program), an even fresher story angle had surfaced. Setting off on Monday morning to locate two men of the proper physique and agreeable to impersonation, within an hour of leaving the office Shelley signed up a thickset Air Force sergeant and the owner of a vacation ranch in New Jersey. The next day they were coached on the subtleties of truth-stretching that could earn them as much as a thousand dollars to divvy up and a great story to tell the folks back home. They sat through a practice run with a team of actors filling in for the judges, trying to spot fixable problems. In the afternoon the orchestra (also on tape) was playing them in for a broadcast scheduled for October 30, 1961.

Bud Collier kicked off his popular program with a trio of men claiming to be the U.N. ambassador from the new nation of Sierra Leone. One imposter was chief of residents at Bellevue Hospital, the other a Jamaican native and administrator for New York state housing. Next came a woman who was a professional rabbit breeder and cottontail-contest judge, but the poseurs – a concert pianist and a retired librarian – convinced three of the four celebrity panelists to guess their identities incorrectly.

After a commercial insinuated smoking Salem cigarettes was akin to an oxygenated stroll by a stream in the Rockies, it came time for the third set of individuals who each claimed to be honest about their identity.

The camera swooped forward and up to the darkened, backlit figures on a raised platform suggesting a hangman's scaffold, the string orchestra arpeggio rising into tingling excitement. As spotlights engaged, famed announcer Johnny Olson asked their names. They each gave it, in turn. All the same.

As the camera panned again across the trio, Collier read some text about the subject's claim to fame. Studying the who's-what were the panelists: television comic Tom Poston; Margot Moser, a fill-in that week, who'd replaced Julie Andrews in *My Fair Lady* for nine months; Johnny Carson, a game-show host himself, young and smart-alecky in his years before *Tonight*, harboring an illusion about the taste of his leopard-print vest; and in the cleanup spot, the most well-known at the time, Kitty Carlisle, an elegant, smart actress who had faced off with the Marx Brothers in *A Night at the Opera,* married playwright Moss Hart and was a lifelong diehard arts advocate, the epitome of the sophisticated New Yorker.

They all had questions prepared.

The World Wide Web, a new thing in my modern lifetime that had also seen the introduction of minivans, odor-free kitty litter and unisex milkshakes, began infusing people's lives with information and data points. Everyone with a scanner and a collection of old stuff was copying their history and throwing it into the Web. The Then was becoming the Now.

While intellectually curious, I undertook no serious genetic trace or genealogical study. No, it was simply spare-hour sifting through tall internet grass, idle queries about U-boats and diving, searches compelled by some vague impetus, poked along by the "look what you can find these days" expansiveness of the Web. Let's face it, when you acquire binoculars, you're bound to peer through them and view things hitherto unseen.

I was in my late fifties when I began with the tinkering, the probing, the sly creaking open of a rusty door and prying up an uneven floorboard of my life. Melanie nosed around a few times as well, because if I wasn't interested in my old man she'd be happy to do it for me.

Burton was mentioned out there a few times, what with 1960s New England newspapers reporting on U-853, and there was a sizable piece by a wartime buff and Midwestern TV newsman, Adam Lynch, in a U.S. Naval Institute magazine.

One of those sessions fell on a night in early autumn when I was sixty-four, in the basement office below the casement window with a view of the tops of the backyard spruces, sitting at the Ikea gloss-maple table-desk framed by bookcases piled with copy paper, outmoded software disks, accumulated travel books and maps, binders for a public relations course I designed for Temple University and Melanie's old theater scripts.

I typed a variation of some typical keywords in a Yahoo query box. Most of the results populating the first page were things I'd found before, with Burt's sub-hunting in the Bridgeport Sunday Herald and the Chicago Tribune and arrays of file photos: U-boats, exploding depth charges and smoking ships, blackened faces of German sailors picked out of the water, American swabbies with energetic girlfriends cavorting on leave.

The results were all on paper, well, images of paper on PDFs and JPGs; what else from the old days would there be besides newspapers and magazines and the contents of filing cabinets?

At the bottom of the scrolling list, something new.

In a header text were some of the searched-for terms. But the accompanying thumbnail picture was of an older white woman in glasses with hair bunned back, like one of my grandmother's church buddies in the parlor. An incongruent pairing of words and image.

Scanning the screen I woke up a bit to the moment, as happens to a person just before walking onstage or leaning out to skydive or signing on the bottom line for three years in the Army. By clicking the mouse, I'd be stepping into somewhere, no turn-back. The fraught leap, *salto mortale*.

It was a moment ripped from every cheesy don't-go-in-the-cellar thriller: alone in darkness, casting a flashlight beam side to side, knowing it would catch the target, a smirking face or a splattered knife. To know all this, understand what it was and how the result of my next moment would be a dissolution of innocence, took but a micro-second.

With a properly placed click on Mrs. Whitehair the next page flashed up, with a video screen and an arrow-right play button, titles announcing an old TV show, the date, the names of the celebrity participants. Apparently the video company Fremantle had released its inventory of decades of game shows to those cable TV channels devoted to the form, and this, like everything Video these days, cross-pollinated into YouTube.

My thinking plunged forward, racing as the brain will, why would this have popped up unless it's some coding mistake, but this is going to be what it looks like, it couldn't be but no sense in saying that, it has to be something, it's here, it's arrived, this thing. I tensed as if awaiting a deep injection in the soft bicep.

I clicked the gray arrow on the screen. The old two-inch videotape rolled. The counter showed almost thirty minutes to play.

The presentation was familiar, a page from a chapter of childhood. A diplomat from Sierra Leone and his doppelgangers. The host holding up a small package and reading commercial copy off a teleprompter. Then the Bunny Lady with the hair and the pretenders to her rabbity crown.

The digital file ticked along. Twenty minutes in, the final contestants were in shadow on the raised stage, outlined against the whiteboard back-drop. A simple black-and-white entertainment to most viewers then and now, a grand guignol for an audience of one.

In these hazy few seconds, one silhouette among three intimated a familiarity. But with no reference or memory it was impossible to say for sure. I waited for the orchestra, and the faces.

What is your name, please?

Spotlights engaged. As Bud Collier narrated a story about a sunken submarine and plans to salvage the wreck of a freighter, the camera panned the figures, chest-up. The first man was solidly-built, clean-shaven, a pretty stiff headlamp-lit animal, like a humorless math teacher who would hesitate to give his name at a faculty mixer. The second was bearded with a mustache, black-rimmed glasses and an ill-fitting jacket, easygoing, smiling at the celebrities in hopes of getting some autographs. A balding, nasally guy in seat number three just completed your forms at the D.M.V., relaxed but examining, eyes in motion, as if well-practiced at waiting to speak at the right moment.

The audience applauded, cued by an overhead sign as the trio descended to their seats behind a long desk with electric numerical displays facing the camera.

Margot Moser was first to question. After Guest Number One stumbled trying to describe a mechanical underwater process, Number Two characterized his business as a company of "one and friends." Number Three mumbled about the historical purposes of exploring a wartime submarine and a bright ding was heard, ostensibly a pre-set timer but actually being applied by a producer's hand throughout the show to keep things moving.

Johnny Carson in the leopard-print vest quipped about his intention not to vote for Two because the guy looked too much like a German sub commander. Then he had questions for One and Three about some technicalities of diving and salvage. Kitty Carlisle began with Two on some quick diving math, then briskly moved to the others. She was fascinated with the topic. Tom Poston got in a few lines, asking Two about agreeing with Three's testimony on cargo still being valuable after twenty years at the bottom of the sea. Two barely got in a nod when the timer chimed for the end of the interrogation.

I just didn't know. Honestly couldn't say who to finger, who to be amazed by, saddened or elated by. Which of the three to adopt. Gear still in neutral.

The celebrities bantered as they marked twelve-inch ballot cards, befuddled as to which of the three men before them could be trusted. They took their time recording the votes, awaiting a spark of revelation, before

Poston waved his hands and what-the-hecked.

Collier polled the panel. Poston selected Number Three based on imagining the guy's voice through a diver's headset. Moser voted for Two but still doubted if a man with a beard could fit into a helmet. Carson went for Three based on suspicious answers from One. The last vote went to One, Carlisle declaring this was the only contestant who looked healthy enough to be a deep-sea diver.

Some of me knew who it was, the rest less so or not at all. Even at this point, it was still a toss-up among three grainy guys. That's how far away Burton had been from me, even with the photos I'd seen in old newspaper reproductions.

At his podium, Collier made his catchphrase call for the sole truth-teller to confess.

"Will the real underwater salvage expert please stand up."

As often happened, there was a blip of suspense, one man shuffling in his chair, another beginning to rise and then declining. Finally, a commitment. Number Two stood, to applause. The panelists turned to each other, wide-mouthed, "how about that!"

As on another day, when I sat on a bed with a photograph under a paperclip, I could react only in a modest way.

"So… it's you."

Alone at the table in the little cubbyhole of a moderate existence, in a lifetime of imposed indifference and defensive avoidance, all was relinquished, not completely willfully. The missing was found, the unknown now embodied, to be stared at and absorbed in a six-by-four inch live-action souvenir from an album in history's closet.

As the clip played through seven and a half minutes, I absorbed the moments of introduction, astonishment and quiet exclamation. Watching a face, a body, movements, all of a sculpture, a lost antiquity brought back to the surface, reclaimed from darkness. Then as I ran the segment a second time with a more dispassionate examination of Number Two, I stabbed the pause button, on and off, to catch a frozen frame without distortion. A clean shot to study, thus to finally admit I was being studious.

It wasn't really an intense biopsy, as if through a magnifier to catalog strands of hair. Neither was it a languid, removed viewing like you'd take with a documentary about wildebeest migration. It was a togetherness with a person I could not articulate and to some degree didn't want to be a part of.

Now that he'd arrived, it was like a very long handshake, a connection thrust upon me as if someone had burst into my remote underground safe-room with intent to sell insurance. A grip that wouldn't let go, thus limiting what could be spoken between us, confined to pleasantries because serious talk must wait for the grip to break.

I found a slice of notepaper to arrange against the monitor, covering half a face, parts of the paused portrait. Finding familiar features of jawbone, the corners of the mouth, the eye sockets. I studied Burton with one part of the intellect while another was experiencing it, just as I'd observed the ocular *flip-flip-flip* during those teenage *petit mal* flashes.

The quiet "shit!" of it all, watching the frozen face for an interminable moment, reflecting how my own features more echoed my father's than those of my mother, which I'd long realized since I started shaving.

Then I prodded the play indicator back to the end of the white-haired ladies' segment and let the piece run through again, King Rupert of Ruritania studying the commoner enlisted as a body double. Seeing aspects of myself reflected in the other man's expression, in this move or that. The way my father clumped down the steps to the seats, some stroking of the chin, the confident, smiley relating to the famous people in the TV studio he was trying to impress.

I didn't know what I should be feeling, if, as had always been the case, there was no emotion to feel, at least emotion I'd admit or claim. Or if I could detect my conscious avoidance, hiding behind the damn academic attitude, the forensics.

It was stupefying. What were the odds of such a thing poking out of the mile-high haystack of the Web? Finding this clip among all the mechanisms, caverns of microfiche, the possible pop-ups or no-shows on any given page of detritus in accordance with the twinkling mysteries of Googlerythms? It was if I'd taken a random flight to a distant city selected by a dart tossed at a wall map and flipped a coin to choose a restaurant and walked in to notice across the room some guy I'd never met and yet could've been my brother.

I called Melanie downstairs and shared it all and she nearly had a urological accident. Yet she refrained from immediate shouting, respected my need for control, my declared non-sharing with the kids, or anyone. My silence.

One might think at this point I'd have Burton move in with me, copy the file to my phone for regular replay, screen-shot him to the refrigerator bulletin board. But after the accidental meeting on a fall evening, it would be the December holidays before I went back to the bookmarked YouTube page, awaiting the courage, or the calm, the necessary screwing-up of nerves to handle it, as one needs to muster to rise from the waiting room chair for a root canal. I sure didn't want to do it when I was tired, emotional, wary. I had to pick my moment to confront Burton again. When I did, the feelings were no clearer, no remarkable crystalization.

In the New Year I didn't jump to many viewings. There were months between sittings; I held a caution of peeling back layers, examining pores. When I did look, it was to apply the paper against the monitor to cover the image and isolate the facial identifiers, to study the smile lines and shucksiness of the voice.

Yet the increasing familiarity didn't manifest any evolving closeness to the man cavorting down at the end of the telescope.

Was the diver watching me back? Would he ponder who might see him? Burton's family, whatever that was, would be on alert the night of the broadcast in 1961. Maybe some pals at a bar, but anybody else? What likely mattered most to Burt about being on TV would be to impress a backer for grabbing the wool from *Oregon*.

Maybe Shelley the studio sprite whispered in Burton's ear just before the countdown that a nurse in New Jersey would see him on camera. What was the risk in this medium, in a pre-*Most Wanted America* television era, for a game show contestant to be discovered by a bounced-check creditor, a small-town Inspector Javert, or a fist-shaking parent of a debased daughter?

There was an equation in play: for Burton, the spotlight + notoriety + cash, while for someone else in a living room the shock + scream + WTF. Back in '61 nobody imagined they would witness this in another time and place beyond that single October night. There was no minutes-later viral anything.

Burton calculated the percentages, ignored or willed himself past any potential threat and climbed up to the darkened scaffold with two men pretending to be him.

The payoff for flummoxing the panel would be seven hundred and fifty bucks to split with the army sergeant and the dude ranch operator Shelley had coached on how to pass for a deep-sea diver.

At the end, One, Two and Three went backstage to sign a form to get their checks mailed out and receive a complementary carton of Salems. On the set, Kitty Carlisle was having the last word before the commercial. "I know why Number Two didn't look healthy. He was suffering from rapture of the deep."

It had been twenty years since Jean moved into the senior-citizen high-rise next to the Black Horse Shopping Center and the township police station that lent the residents a veneer of security and quick coronary-crisis response. Each night I called my mother to ascertain her daily medical benchmarks and open the valve on the news of the day, even if it wasn't the first time she went on about Louise's hip replacement or what Dick the drinker did in that parking space.

On a Saturday morning in January, I drove her to the library (she'd given up the car because of all the maniacs on the road), stopped at CVS for Ensure on sale, then returned to the apartment on the fifth floor with the skyscraper twinkles and blinking bridge lamps of the big city seven miles distant. (A view better than from apartments at the rear of the building, which eyed the WalMart parking lot and delivery doors to Five Below and Golden Happy Buffet.)

At the light oak drop-flap breakfast table by the window we reviewed the week's worth of penciled notes she habitually gathered to discuss banking, appointment scheduling and television shows of interest.

I knew my intention for the day. It required an opportune moment to cast out the line. The best moment, the one with proper breathing and confidence.

The topic needed a careful approach. Jean's short-term husband was more distant than old yellowed vacation slides, and on those rare occasions when we glanced upon the subject, she was always Scottishly stoic.

How far away was memory? I sure wouldn't ask her how much she remembered, bust in on things, force open a stuck drawer. Although that was exactly what this exercise would amount to.

I opened up the ten-inch tablet computer that let her take part in the world, where she'd read the daily newspaper I emailed her, and look up puzzle definitions, summer shirt sales, recipes and Google Earth views of golf courses she saw on TV. I located the file planted in my email so I could punch up the video right after prepping her with small talk, her warmup announcer.

I laid it out: my idle grazing for the father, the weightless curiosity, how I recently came across something new. I segued into a quick setup about the old game shows that Jean and I now watched on cable during my visits, the shows from when I was small, America's black and white Manhattan entertainments when dazzling and urbane celebrities stopped by Bess and Edwin's house on their way to a party.

I didn't say specifically what was to come, only that it would be impactful. She was curious, ready to accept whatever this was I brought to share. I clicked.

After the show's introductions of celebrity panelists, I fast-forwarded through the ambassadors and rabbit-contest judges to the final trio on the scaffold.

She didn't immediately see that which awaited her. Then came the first set of close-ups.

She'd I.D.'d right off. "Ah, yep, look at that. That's him. Son-of-a-gun." Mom said that kind of thing.

There was an echo of a sigh, her chin tilting upward, turning away from the table for a brief contemplation of the outside treetops, then back to the tablet. She showed no sign of upheaval, but naturally it was taking time to sink in.

The segment played through to the final moment, Kitty Carlisle's observation on Number Two's pallor. Then I rewound to a frame I'd mapped out and used first my palm, then an index card from the table, for the exercise of isolating the man's eyes, the smile, all that.

How it all struck her in the deep layers, like a collision on dark water, I couldn't say. No telling what her emotional memory bank held. She kept her visible response to the man on the screen, as did Carlisle, light and fascinated.

Jean hadn't seen the program when it first aired in '61. If a colleague at work mentioned Burton's fling with national exposure, she would've remembered something that substantial. But in those days when you missed the original program, or a summer rerun, it was gone.

Sometimes the past was hidden from you until someone decided you were ready to see it. Or was able to show to you at all.

Mom said later she'd left the pain of her youthful travails long behind. It was now her history, but no longer her trauma. Like a broken bone healed, the part of her damaged by Burt hadn't actually hurt for a long time, even if the crack line was always there.

Besides, the bandage on the Burt-induced injury was this wonderful boy with the wavy hair and wide ears who marched in a Scout uniform in 4th of July parades and wowed people with the accordion and had met lots of famous stars, and brought two delightful kids to play with their grandmother, and he called her every night.

She was pleased, not with Burt, but with the bundle he'd left with her.

The internet, the transporter, the stargate, slowly tugged me awake. What had been incidental trawling of the Web on a rainy day's whim every few months picked up speed and intent, more keywords and archives dusted off, one scrap and the next. Still, there would be no ancestry-site subscriptions nor swab samples. All that serious stuff lay across some river I chose not to transverse. The old remove.

Much of the search results became repetitive or uncorroborateable. Just as one can unearth dozens of people with your own name in a self-Googling, it was likewise with Burtons across the counties of the Republic, in local news extracts and death records from humble towns that required a prospector's pan-sifting.

There was enough to get a general outline of how Burt conducted himself after the TV show around the docks and divers of New England.

U-853's original commander, Helmut Sommer, kept a valuable trove of photographs and documents – portraits of crewman, interior pictures of the vessel's architecture – and loaned it all to Burton for research fifteen years after the war. According to the German officer's widow, Burt never returned any of it.

A week before the Kennedy assassination in '63, firemen investigated a false alarm on the waterfront in Portland, Maine, and found a half ton of dynamite aboard Burt's tugboat. Once the entire area was evacuated, he watched the Coast Guard tow the leaky vessel out and dump it all into the ocean, as he had no permit for the hot stuff and had danced around explosives regulations. He was duly fined for the transgression, while a

Portland supply company complained about an outstanding six thousand dollar tab that went unpaid by a guy some locals marked as the "Mad Bomber of the East Coast."

Burt often went after artifacts from American test subs purposely sunk during the war as targets for depth-charges or other munitions. It was four months after the dynamite debacle in Maine when one of the diver's sidekicks went down to pry brass fittings off one of those subs and drowned. Burt found him face down in the sand a few feet from the stern of the sub, possibly felled by oxygen toxicity, when extra unprocessed oxygen in the body disorients with tunnel vision and respiratory failure.

After multiple dives to the old steamer *Larchmont*, a vessel he'd been first to locate, Burt took another enthusiast out and brought back a small safe with some coins. The other guy was a fourteen-year-old named Earl. Lucky for them both that Earl came back.

In '66, while percolating ideas about another *Oregon* – this one a Cunard liner rammed in 1886 by a schooner off Fire Island – Burton was also touring department store gift galleries in New England, Cincinnati and Pittsburgh with his "Twenty Fathoms" collection of polished-up artifacts. Working with a "Spanish artist," he crafted drowned lamps, ashtrays, clocks, vases and other nautical bric-a-brac and just plain junk into supposedly desirable *objets* with certificates of authenticity. Some of them came from the Victorian salon of *Larchmont*; others, from U-853.

Amid this, another New England paper revisited Burton's career as the diver now anticipated his end, with his health problems mounting and the money gone, with no mention of profiting from antiques.

In a New England newspaper's graytone image of old compressed inkdots, Burton and a comrade from U-853 knelt on a dock, unwrapping a German life raft. The photo hearkened to a favorite framed moment of my own life: in a wetlands park in the Bronx, I'm half-crouching in a forest-blue fall coat, a watchful wingman to my four-year-old boy's Huckleberry moment exploring the slime-edge of a pond in an autumn afternoon's aching light.

Two images from their times, me and my father a half-century apart, men crouched by water's edge, one inspecting history, imagining his fortune, the other watching and protecting the man of the future as he threw sticks in the mud.

Additional shiny internet objects kept popping up like corpses in a city river's spring thaw. A woman's obituary from 2008 listed a father named Burton, a brother named Burton (already deceased at a plausible age) and a big family east of New Haven, close to the ocean. Maybe this dead brother of Caroline of Guildford was *the* Burton, the "solid citizen of Connecticut" as Newsweek described. Or just a coincidental Burton who may or may not have known how to swim.

A namesake in those parts worked at a brick company, married with two kids, kept getting speeding tickets in the '60s and lost a huge judgement after running over a stockbroker, but this defendant's reported age was suspect. In the following decade a teenager with the same name, somebody's son, survived a fatal car wreck. Not only were men with this name clustered in one specific suburban geographic tract, they kept getting into crashes.

Meanwhile, twenty-five miles west of New Haven in Trumbull, home to SubMarine Research Associates, Burton was fired from his own outfit by its investors (including a metallurgist and a sales manager for a Chicago publisher) because they couldn't locate the guy.

The internet camera panned the suspect Burtons across time zones, faces unlit, each declaring "*My* name is…" Behind them, gauzy curtains shrouded anyone attached by DNA, who still celebrated Thanksgiving with Burton or toasted his memory. Newsweek reported in '61 the diver had five children. That many? [or] Only that many? Maybe I had a half-sister who owned a catering concern in Bridgeport or filed insurance forms for a Cincinnati dentist. Or, dishearteningly, I imagined a half-brother killed in the jungle war I'd been lucky to avoid.

The weathervane twisted back to some long-buried reports from the Midwest. Around 1950, a guy just into his twenties in Ohio, name with proper middle initial, had far too many troubles: five years in prison (suspended) on a burglary charge, a wild acting-out the suspect claimed was rooted in emotional trauma after his own father William, a public relations man and community-morals rabblerouser, was killed in Texas by some cop who had a business interest in an adult joint.

A complaint filed by an ex-wife charged this Ohio Burton for failure to support a three-year-old.

This stuff was getting ridiculous. If I couldn't zero in on one Burton, *the* Burton, it was all just noise.

So, what happened was Jean married a guy she barely knew who got her pregnant right after the wedding. She saw little cash coming home from a merchantman's good pay, and her husband Burt was quick with a variety of excuses.

Then a financial company in Philly sent him some mail, and being defensively nosey as any spouse might, Jean opened it to discover her husband had manipulated the title to her car and used it as collateral for a loan she never heard of.

Another piece of mail would seal the deal. At the bottom of a duffel bag her husband left behind while he was on a shipping job, she uncovered a note from some woman in Ohio imploring Burton to make good on child support for their son.

Amid this collapse of marital stability and hope, with a baby due in a few months, Jean went with her dad Edwin to the loan company, paid off the debt and got the car back in Jean's name. Then Scotty looked around for a safe place to keep the vehicle and stashed it in the underground parking lot of an apartment complex in the next town.

Jean and her dad notified the local police that the guy might be troublesome on his next stop home.

When Burton came off the ship in Marcus Hook a week later, Jean tossed the duffel to the pier, said her piece, and drove off with Edwin in the car she'd reclaimed, carrying a baby-to-be. Took with her the other wife's address in Ohio. And that of a sister of Burton's from up in New England who'd written an empathetic letter to Jean about getting mixed up with her shady sibling.

On Pine Street, only Edwin would pick up a ringing telephone. Burt called his next time in port, making the expected "you can't do this to me" noises.

Jean never spoke to Burton again.

A lawyer she engaged to handle the divorce reported back there might've been another wife *besides* the Ohio lady who'd sent that letter.

Number Three, what is your name, please?

Burton counter-filed his own papers against Jean, in Lucas County where Toledo is. There, Burt claimed "no children were born of our union." Jean was really pissed. When her lawyer threw that statement back at Burt, Jean could gain a divorce on her terms. There would be no child support for the non-existent kid and thus no excuse or legal grounds for Burt's future contact. He wanted to be undone, to be gone? Wish granted.

It was the letters, stamped and relayed, that connected Jean, and thus me, to a man with two possible pasts. Or two men with one past.

There was a Burton H., possibly named after his old man, who pursued a slippery career in the waters off New England that got him on TV, and whose family might've included a woman who sent a sorry-you-went-through-this-letter, postmarked in Connecticut, to her young sister-in-law in New Jersey.

More tabloidian was a Burton H. from Ohio who got a social security card at age fifteen and would use it to join the merchant marine. May have been guilty of burglary down South, and the son of a murdered William. An Ohio newspaper noted a custody suit by a woman whose name, many years later, my mom would vaguely recall as very familiar, from that letter in her husband's duffel seeking child support.

The letters in Jean's hands about the men from Trumbull and Akron didn't fully coalesce them into a single creature. It would be fascinating if it had worked, details in jigsawed alignment, one big, complicated, well-traveled, flamboyant, tawdry, oddly plausible biography. But with the foggy element, the first names of the two Burtons' fathers, a Burton, Sr. and a William seven hundred miles apart, there was no final clarity, disallowing my hand-whisking "that's that."

There was also the pile-on that one of these Burtons sold maritime antiques in Ohio department stores, and that the photo in the advertising was of the same guy from the Rhode Island pier with the German life raft. And who showed up on *To Tell the Truth.*

As to the born-in-California entry on one of Burton's union papers that Jean kept in a box in a closet with the old Newsweeks, this birthplace was claimed because a) it was true, or b) it was not, and such a lie could disconnect the applicant from a past in some other state. Big if.

In only one life, son of only one father, could the real Burton stand up. But he just wouldn't. Not while there were others that might be him.

Covington, Louisiana, is a few miles north of the causeway across Lake Pontchartrain in the sort of moist flatland a hurricane swats aside. It's where Burton was employed around '77 at Dixie Carriers, part of Kirby Industries, a Houston-based petroleum exploration and transportation outfit. There, his name appeared on a patent application for a "rotating work arm system for a submergible chamber," some jargon-laden underwater mechanical pincer thing.

A phonebook Web page of unreliable certainty insinuated this inventor was alive in Texas. Must be ninety by now. I looked at this record on the computer for a moment. I had no intention of tracking the lead further. All I was doing was batting around a detective story, taking notes, and just because a phone number popped up didn't mean I had to get all intense and actually call it. What to say after *hello*? That was a whole bucket of mess.

Even if the patent filings held something I'd seen on no other document or news account, not just a middle initial, but Burton's uncommon middle name: Hoster.

All three names were in Covington.

Paul McCartney included no line in the jaunty tune he wrote when he was fourteen, "When I'm Sixty-Four," as to "one day we'll discover what became of him... if he's dead or simply too thin."

I had my own lyrics about being sixty-four when, in a mesh of unwitting dot connectors linking Bob Stewart, Goodson and Todman and the Fremantle company and those three guys who invented YouTube, vintage episodes of *To Tell the Truth* popped on the first page of organic returns for a particular Yahoo keyword query, and a bearded man, age thirty-four, appeared, asking to be believed.

This surprise from a monochromatic TV show in a past world comes through the time tunnel in a form that probably never happened to anybody else, ever. How bloody nice that it was to *me* this was happening. Like John Hurt in *Alien*, discovering he'd been selected to Caesarian-birth a temperamental creature with teeth. What the hell.

A few days after the YouTube, I knew I had to write it up. It was too special and bizarre not to, there was a journalistic responsibility to not just sit on it. I figured to take three months of spare time to develop twelve or fifteen pages, a nice article Esquire probably wouldn't buy but somebody would publish. After six months and twenty pages I stopped pretending to know what the last page would look like and how far away it was. All the nights, the clutter, the characters named in those glimpses and reports, some of them dead, some not so much as yet, the findings, exclamation points, holy-shit days, big days and nothing days, the living of it and the writing about it entwined like a Möbius strip in an Escher etching.

I didn't keep watching the video, no need to keep confronting it. My memory of it was precise, the panel and the host and the wiseacre in the leopard vest and Number Two.

Along the way, Melanie got a new TV loaded with internet access and a million YouTube entertainments. That meant the forensic hologram of my past could fill the family room flatscreen with a few clicks of the remote. Number Two could be large as life. But I didn't watch the clip of *To Tell the Truth* on that big screen any more than I did on the small one at the basement computer. Last thing I needed was a giant smiling Burt on the wall.

And there was still a feeling, made not of fear, more of irrational caution, that if I saw my father again, the father could see me, might break the fourth wall, turn from Kitty Carlisle and speak to *me*, and I might discover that all along I'd been only a character in an episode of *The Twilight Zone*.

After a bunch of months, a point came to just be over with the writing and the fixing and the fixing and the fixing. Put an end to it, a finite number of pages, a nonfiction novella or unsellably-long magazine script. But putting an end to it required an ending, not an unresolved *Maybe, Could Be*.

The last page of the manuscript was wobbly, no rebar, some weight to close a story that had no closure. I had nothing new or zippy, search terms were returning the same stuff. It was as far as I could go without committing to a darker punch, and that meant paying genealogy service subscriptions that dock you monthly and you forget until you notice it on your bank statement if at all, and copier fees to dozens of county registrars in six states, a big huffing chase after who-knows-what. My brain was tired.

I went back to the video with an idea to wrap the tale with *how many people have seen that YouTube of a game show and did they know they were watching somebody's missing father?* YouTube expediently provides a number under the frame that counts how many views a video's logged, from the superstar's multi-million viral visits to the two dozen for some pet ducks ballroom dancing.

I opened the bookmarked Web page to its startup slide of three unde-fined figures in shadow. The counter below showed more than two thousand views of that ancient episode. That seemed like a lot of visits. Must have been game-show aficionados who watched every *To Tell The Truth*, good-old-days random novelty browsers, Johnny Carson fans.

That's a productive detail, I thought, *anything else?* I twisted my hand on the mouse to idly roll the cursor down the screen under the video window. Below the viewer statistic was an additional item that hadn't been there nineteen months earlier when I first came across the clip of my father smiling at Carson. Wasn't there a few months ago, either, when I tiptoed back to the video to confirm some details. This was recently added material.

Someone left a comment.

II

AN EIGHTY PERCENT MAN

The streets were uncomfortable in the rundown neighborhood of Alice south of the San Diego highway. Hard winter rain potholes crunched dust in July, too many pickup trucks with full beds taking shortcuts.

It was this kind of thing that Bill Mason covered on his radio show on KBKI-AM. About what people were doing in that corner of Texas, or what they weren't doing and should be. Traffic safety, meatpacking cleanliness, vacant lots, public works contracts, how the Mexicans were treated. Bill just talked and talked, because Alice needed plenty of attention.

Around sixteen thousand people, mostly Mexican extraction, lived in this hub of Jim Wells County, parked between Laredo and Corpus Christi. Oil was discovered around those parts in 1931 and herds of cattle moseyed among black Eiffel Tower pumps in a landscape of cracking clay soil, mesquite and toasted grassland. Flat, flat, flat fanning out forever.

Alice was a place where most people's bank accounts, if they had one, were as dry-crinkled as the crusty dirt out back. The county's high school graduation rates usually wandered below fifteen percent.

Main Street went on straight to both horizons, lined with inexpensive black sedans parked at Bright's Market, Karl's Shoes and the Rialto movie house, which would close in the 1980s but remain standing another thirty years adapted for other business or simply left a ghost.

On the last Friday in July of '49 Bill was out to see for himself the extent of asphalt degradation that somebody or other in the county commissioners' office should have taken care of. While he was out there, he'd also make some stops to pick up account copy and ad revenue for the station. At fifty-one, he was program director and that entailed doing everything a rural radio station required short of repairing the transmitter.

At around ten, Avelino Saenz, thirty-five, was at the Tex-Mex Depot, a small station for a local railroad line. Saenz, a father of four, was a lanky war vet attending night school classes. Saenz was talking to a part-time telegraph operator at the Depot, Luis Salas, who was also a part-time sheriff's deputy and thus might have some pull in nudging a city inspector to look at Avelino's friend's plumbing.

Mason stopped in to say hello to Salas, and then departed for the morning's pothole surveillance with Saenz, who came in handy as a translator with the mostly Mexican population. They cruised slowly back toward town and cut through a shabby neighborhood to the highway as Bill took a right off Beam Station Road onto San Felipe Street.

This red pickup truck comes at them from around the corner off what's now called Apple Street.

Across from a tavern called the West Side Patio, the truck straddles the center and comes almost parallel to the sedan. The driver motions out the window for Mason to stop his car, so he does. A guy gets out of the truck and lumbers over with some of his two hundred, sixty pounds rolling over his belt and yells, "Are you Bill Mason?" Mason says, "Yes, I am," and then leans back from the open window with his hands out over his face, toward the passenger Saenz.

The big guy shouts at Saenz to get out of the way and the passenger does a half-fall out his door. Avelino hears Bill say something like "Wait a minute," and the truck driver fires a gun at Bill.

Saenz runs across the street to the doorway of the bar. Mason gets out of the sedan, leaving a loafer behind, and crawls under the front end of the pickup, seeking a barrier to further attack, the wind and the sense knocked out of him. The shooter is standing there, cursing to himself, a .45 automatic in his right hand and his left hand messing with it. Mason drags himself out from under the other side, stumbles across the road, red-splotting the hard dirt, calling for help a few times, and he gets a long forty or fifty yards away to the loading dock at the Alice Pipe and Supply Company and passes out. The driver gets into the red truck yelling about Mason being an SOB and takes off.

A fellow at the pipe outfit comes out with a customer and shields the crawling man's body from the sun with a folding chair. The owner, Joe Gleason, calls the cops and then notifies Moyer's Mortuary. A car from Moyer's rolls up after awhile and hauls Bill to the hospital.

Thirty minutes later he expires on the table from a "profuse internal hemorrhage." No autopsy necessary.

Meanwhile, the guy with the gun drives across town, over the industrial railroad lines that split the Mexican section from the white one, to a police station on Adams and Main a block over from the Rialto. It's quiet there at eleven-thirty on a Friday morning. He goes in the side door and uses a key for another door, then another key and shuts himself into a jail cell. Easy for him. Sam Smithwick is a deputy sheriff.

Seems the day before on his fifteen-minute show, Mason had fingered Smithwick as the owner of Rancho Alegro. This was a one-story, dressed-up windowless dump with a windmill out back, four miles west of downtown and four blocks outside the city limits, turned into a dime-a-dance joint with a long mahogany bar to accommodate the young Latin men in splashy vests with money to spend and ranch workers with less. To entertain them were Mexican girls who lavishly displayed their talents for dancing and cheap erotic appeal. Mason thought there was prostitution and said so on the air, and the liquor violations were already famous. Not a classy place, but out there classy wasn't the point.

Mason complained, too, that the sheriff, Hubert Sain, permitted "the ingress of fifty girls to take from the men of Alice... money which should go to the families of these men." A snide remark about venereal disease was thrown in.

That was typical of Mason's direct approach. He'd been a real pain the past couple of months on KBKI in the role of voice of the people, the ones being stepped on by George Parr, the "Duke of Duval," boss of adjacent Duval County, commander (following his father, the state senator Archer Parr) of assorted shenanigans around this King Ranch territory where the empowered profited from oil and cattle, from cheap labor, shakedowns and kickbacks, enforced by *pistoleros* like Sam and the worst of them, the violent Luis Salas, the telegraph operator known as "Indio."

So Smithwick got all bent out of shape and shot Bill in the chest, then turned himself in because running rarely pans out. The deputy's gun and badge were locked in a desk that afternoon when the district attorney charged him with murder with malice aforethought. A planned killing.

Friday afternoon the papers in Alice and Galveston flashed out the first copy on the crime across the Associated Press wire, and the next morning major urban papers coast to coast ran it. AP reporter William Barnard filed story after story for days, and there were plenty of angles.

The New York Times ran the AP text on Saturday at the bottom of the first page, headed "Crusading Air Commentator Slain; Texas Deputy Sheriff Surrenders." In a font usually reserved for World Series wins or World War surrenders, the Chicago Daily Tribune blared "Deputy Kills Air Crusader."

In Bill's onetime hometown of Akron, Ohio, the Beacon Journal ran a pair of five-inch front-page photos – Bill in a business portrait and the slouching deputy wearing a ridiculous racket of a tie that barely reached his third shirt button.

Every Texas paper followed the story for weeks.

Bill had a mother all his life. He had a father for a few years. Then another one.

His mother, Clara Valenta Olmstead, one of a family of eleven, was born in 1876 in East Bethel, a small Minnesota town, and she would die at age eighty-three in another, Saint Peter. Her ancestors were among the first twelve immigrants to populate Hartford, Connecticut, before 1640. The family took its name from a moated house in Bumpstead-Helion in Cambridgeshire during the time of Edward II.

Clara met William Lovejoy Heywood, almost twenty years her senior, in Minneapolis and with him raised three children: Bill, who came along in 1897, followed by Katherine Ellen and Elden. They lived in a two-story box house that still stands on Colfax Avenue, a half mile from the Mississippi River.

As soon as the third kid was born, the stern Heywood took off. In those days it was not too problematic to walk out of State A and set up shop in State B and start meeting unknowing women, friends and business contacts without threat of revelation. William recreated himself as a civic leader in New Buffalo, Michigan, started up with a new girl in 1905 and produced two more daughters. In Heywood's eventual obituary, his three kids with Clara went unmentioned.

When the census taker knocked on her door in 1900, Clara told him she was a widow. Perhaps she said that to everyone after the divorce to cut back on the fallen-woman-with-kids embarrassment, and explain her move to a small place (a woman sure didn't get the house in a settlement back then). Clara supported the family as a seamstress.

Love did find her again, with some economic and cultural security, in Burton Bailey Mason, a Michigan native two years older. B.B. adopted the children and the couple produced a fourth, Marian Eileen, in 1911.

At North High School, firstborn Bill was the sports-card kid, baseball, basketball, football in striped jersey and leather pants, chin up, nose in the air, a full head of hair brushed up and back, almost a helmet in itself.

Right after the U.S. entered the Great War he enlisted in April of '17. He asserted himself into sergeant's stripes in the 135th Minnesota Infantry regiment. But then, the way he told it, he had himself busted back to a private as the only way to get into a replacement division headed for France.

He got out of the war in one piece and enrolled at the University of

Minnesota. At the same time his courtship of dark-haired, thin, wide-smiling Harriet Rose Hamilton, 22, led to marriage. (Herein one of many tidbits of circumstance among these stories from the *Strange Snick*® collection: my great-grandmother in New Jersey was from a family called Hamilton, and my grandfather in Minnesota married a girl from a family called Hamilton.)

To afford a rented house, they took in a boarder, a thirty-two-year-old woman with a young boy. Adding to the purse, in his spare time Bill pursued inauspicious part-time work at the daily Minneapolis Journal, assigned as cub reporters normally were to rewrites, obituaries and the late-night police beat. He could still spend afternoons practicing as a half-back for the Gophers.

Harriet, known as Hallie, interrupted that flow in March of '21 when she delivered a daughter, Harriet Iris.

Whatever charms the frosty upper Midwest proffered, Bill found a warmer West Coast dream more uplifting and he pursued it after graduation in 1922. The young family wound up in San Francisco. Later he told a folksy story, none too self-effacing and probably not Hallie's favorite, that he'd gone there for a veterans' convention and lost all his money in a craps game, so he had no reason or means to leave.

He parlayed his rookie newspaper chops into jobs at two Bay papers, soon moving to the larger Examiner. If they wanted a guy to dog the police radio and be first in on a sensational murder, Bill dove right in "without taking off his bowler hat," the "a hard-boiled, hard-drinking reporter."

There was no shortage of newspapermen in the Twenties, "an era possible only in the Prohibition decade with its fantastic upheaval of conditions," Bill wrote in some notes. There was no minimum wage or eight-hour day, just "hundreds of men" after the war "seeking a continuation of the excitement they had just experienced... confident, not afraid of anything or anybody, turned loose at one time to insist on jobs as reporters. Men (who) descended *en masse* upon unsuspecting editors and took over the country's reporting."

At home, Hallie, who Bill also called Rosie, was drifting into unhappiness. This wasn't the life, or he wasn't the man. The couple split up with a reasonable amity, Hallie adopting a self-preservation to mask her heartbreak. She and her daughter made their way back to the Hamilton family home in Minneapolis. That's where Hallie took up office skills and later was a private secretary to the guy who built Foshay Tower, a Minneapolis skyscraper that's now a hotel.

It's also where the younger Harriet Iris developed her operatic voice. In her twenties she energized church choirs and later filled Twin Cities music halls like the Flame Room, swinging alongside a young Liberace. The girl would see her dad (who when writing about her called her Hi, as in H.I.) from time to time on his visits there in the 1940s. She sat with him on a floral-print sofa, holding his arm, big smile, her dark tresses ruffling under a wide, ribboned hat, her errant dad with a cigar, in the sort of show-biz image you'd find captioned as "photographed exclusively for MovieMag Magazine as the beaming starlet and confident producer enjoyed an after-premiere VIP moment at the Mambo Club."

Hi went East one time to meet up with her father, who, according to one of her daughters, "treated her like a queen and got a sash of flowers for her to wear. She had a wonderful time, but when she woke up the following morning, Bill was gone and left the bills, and she had to wire for funds to get home. That's how he treated women."

At lunch in San Francisco one day he strolled into the catalogue store Montgomery Ward where Charlotte Irgens, twenty-four, rang up his purchase and consented to a lunch date. He wasted no time in bringing this little package with the soft, wide face and wavy brunette hair in front of Superior Court judge T.W. Harris in March of '24. It was her second marriage as well. Mrs. E. Whitman Chambers, wife of a California novelist and potboiler screenwriter, was matron of honor.

Charlotte's dad Louis Irgens, an orphan and physician from North Dakota, was well known in Hill City society. Thus, the ceremony rated mention in the premiere issue of the Cupid Journal of Oakland, a small upper-crust newsletter, that described Judge Harris as "guilty of tying the knot," and how "except for the immediate family, none of the vast number of friends got dressed in time for the ceremony."

Charlotte was swept up in Bill's ease of transit between jobs and states. They went off to Minnesota, where she'd also been born, and Bill took one more round at the Journal. He cast a wide net that lassoed twenty-six officials for graft in street paving contracts, and found an ex-convict working with two other swindlers to relieve widows of their property before the women ended up dead in accidents.

Exciting though the work was, Bill longed for the figurative and literal racket of the Barbary Coast, and Charlotte missed the sun. So came another cross-country ride in an explosively packed sedan, back to the Examiner where Bill waded into how things were "rotten in Oakland." Characterized as "an expert at taking up where the police left off," he piled up evidence on a city commissioner, the sheriff and several deputies in a case that sent two dozen people to jail.

Mason launched into a second family. Burton, named after Bill's stepfather, was born at Saint Francis Hospital in early '27, and sister Marilyn arrived late the same year. Charlotte gifted her children with the lineage of the Hosters: Burton's unusual middle name came from grandmother Nina Irgens, descended from folk who lived for decades in northeast and central Pennsylvania, the line going back through four generations to Christian Hoster in the 1700s and beyond.

The clan first ensconced in an apartment close to Telegraph Hill on Taylor Street (around the block from Mason Street, no relation); about fifty feet up from the building you'd roll over the top of a rise and Alcatraz was dead ahead. But the boisterous kiddies demanded more space, so Bill rented a small Mission home with a big porch on a dead-end street, Pleasant Valley Court in Alameda, for $47.50 a month. Just as when he set up housekeeping with his first wife, this family enhanced the budget by renting a spare room, this time to a gravel pit operator named Ernest.

They maintained as much fun as the Depression allowed. Bill brought in enough money to provide toys and distractions. On a holiday card Bill dressed as Santa Claus visiting the brood, and in the next year's message he overlaid the faces of all four on Christmas stockings pinned to the fireplace.

Every story that attracted Bill seemed to be a Great Chase. There was the one about Charles Schwartz, a chemist of some reputation around the East Bay, who was selling stock in his company in Walnut Creek. Its chief enterprise was a machine he built in which a roll of toilet paper inserted in one end would turn into silk coming out the other. Of course, investors finally came calling about his production numbers and their dividends. It was a shame that the factory burned down with Schwartz in it, his corpse charred beyond recognition and identifiable only by the objects in his pockets and a missing tooth.

Mason and other newshounds smelled more than the soot when insurance policies for $200,000 popped up, along with a report of a knapsack found under the body holding a Bible and a tin can such as that used by Depression hoboes for coffee handouts. Bill located Schwartz's dentist on a camping trip, hauled him to the coroner's place and ascertained that whoever was lying there, a charred log of gristle with dental problems, it wasn't Schwartz.

A reporter named Tinning took a cue from the dead man's Bible and wrote to every religious settlement and cult along the Pacific coast. That bounced back a tale of an itinerant preacher in a town downstate; he'd received a letter from someone in Walnut Creek and hit the road with his knapsack. Once the pastor's dentist was tracked down – dentists being the coroner's go-to – the victim's name came out. That left Schwartz a fugitive.

Every development in the mystery became a front-page update. Tips came in from across California and a few other states as well. Reporters sat by the telephone taps the cops had put on Schwartz's relatives. One writer applied his usual extravagant technique, spreading a rumor about a big black car near the scene of the crime, grabbing a byline to enjoy one day's fame without concern that his tip would ever pan out.

(Bill had seen this do-it-your-own-way methodology flourish when he first came to the Bay, where the overweight silent film comic Fatty Arbuckle, in Hollywood's first major scandal, was crucified by the truth-be-damned papers and movie studios over a starlet's messy death in a local hotel. Get a real story or make it up: this was the tenor of the times.)

One rumor had the chemist hiding in a town outside Oakland called Martinez, where a train ticket for the night of the factory explosion had gone unclaimed. So Bill grabbed a batch of complimentary passes to a local Saturday night prize fight there and shooed a dozen reporters to the arena to roust up information. But he held back in the hotel the news crew had taken over. That's where, at two on Sunday morning, he grabbed a call from a local police inspector who'd heard from a boarding house manager, just out of the fights, about a new tenant who kept to his room. Bill in his Ford Lizzie coupe and a caravan of screaming cop cars headed for the house. As they surrounded the place, two shots echoed from the second floor.

Breaking in the door, they found Schwartz on the floor, a written confession beside him claiming he'd killed the preacher in self-defense. The letter didn't really cover the part about the factory blaze, but it no longer mattered to anyone except the investors. (As to the pair of gunshots heard from the street, one could only surmise Schwartz's first suicidal attempt was badly aimed. Unless…)

Through the rest of the dark morning, Mason was on the phone dictating the details to the Examiner office, the whole "Stop the presses – Flash!" thing. The curtain-closer on the "Toilet Paper Murder" sold fifty thousand more copies of the Sunday paper than usual.

Bill stayed busy on the waterfront, in poolrooms and over at City Hall on Van Ness two blocks from the courthouse. There was always something amiss in town to write about, either the bums on the street or the ones in high places. As he said about the endgame of reporting, "It doesn't do any good, another batch of crooked officials always comes along."

He liked to talk in later years about helping with graft investigations undertaken by Earl Warren, the district attorney in the '20s for Alameda County (covering from Berkeley and Oakland down to Fremont and east out to Livermore). Bill ticked off Warren, eventually an occupant of the governor's office and later the big chair on the U.S. Supreme Court, by spilling off-the-record information. Warren barely acknowledged how the reporter's tactics, exchanging inside access and securing witnesses, benefited him in a maze of shifting criminal-justice alliances and circular hand-washing.

There was some basking glow from it all and Bill donned it, branded it, as the provocative and annoying protector of truth, responsible to the little guy and his money, well-thought of by the common folk. This contrasted with his reputation inside the Examiner building where he was attributed with a drinking problem and remembered for firing an employee by throwing him through a plate glass window.

If Bill drank more than he should as a responsible citizen, he was a product of his environment. The police raided Prohibition stills and boot-leggers, delivery trucks and boats from Canada landing at small inlets along the northern shores. The seized liquor was usually stored in City Hall, divided by 1) what was in the evidence room for trial of the small fry and 2) the decent bond liquor found in "cheating drug stores" that made its way to police events, election day handouts and gifts the chief of the vice squad would slip to the boys in the press room with a note from the mayor about their fine coverage of how the administration was handling things.

Then there was "division three," the storage room apparently anybody could get into, the "moonshine section… the products of the stills." It was "terrible stuff, filled with fusel oil (from fermentation), in some instances made from garbage, from decayed fruit, from rotting grain. But it never actually killed any of us outright… right there in the same building with us, ours for the asking, hundreds of gallons of moonshine." Hence the term *drank the moon.* The reporters of San Francisco and Oakland enjoyed the perk. A lot.

Bill's writing wasn't restricted to the Runyonesque Bay. In October 1930 he took notes for an article while flying at ten thousand feet over the

Wyoming Rockies as a crew from Boeing searched for an Army aviator carrying "important papers" who didn't show at Laramie after a blizzard. Twenty-five miles north of the airport, all hands watched the passing white landscape until the pilot spotted "a yellow blotch against the snow, a great hole in the seemingly level plans, a drift fence bent and broken" that marked the final landing, unintended and at high speed, of a flyer named Caldwell. Two days later the narrative was headed "Examiner Man on Plane that Locates Body."

When Bill managed time with the family, they enjoyed getting away to a quieter climate. Summer meant a cabin on a hill, the last stop on a gravel road near remote Grass Valley, northeast of Sacramento. There were probably not more than fifty people in the area. The nearest neighbor, a mile away, was a carpenter named Frank who built their cabin and was known for making his own pasta.

Up the mountain, the chopping and sawing of loggers filtered through the clean, cool air among immense fir trees and the smell of pine sap. Below the house was a steel culvert that channeled the rain runoff under the road. The kids acquired this as a fort from which to combat invaders, hide from parents and on one occasion face off with a rattlesnake's piercing red tongue.

A week before Halloween in '31, the family grabbed a three-day getaway. Bill drove the convertible up and back, kids on the back bench with the maid, Argentine Lizzal, twenty-three, between them. On the way home Monday Charlotte rested her head toward the passenger window, absorbing the poetry of rolling hills and a tree-lined two-lane county road with apple stands.

Just before noon a guy at a service station about seven miles south of Napa at what used to be called Kelly Station saw an auto zipping into a loping curve around what's now an industrial park.

A tire popped and the sizeable car filled with camping equipment swerved off the curve, crashed through a wooden fence and crumpled into a telephone pole.

Burt and Marilyn thudded into their parents' seats and then to the rear floor, but the maid went over the bench and broke her arm in the crush. Bill sustained cuts and bruises, blood streaming down his face from a laceration on his forehead, lucky the steering column didn't impale him when the front of the car folded into the pole. Charlotte snapped forehead-first onto the sturdy upper dash of the black sedan and into the window glass, fracturing her skull.

The gas jockey ran over, cars and people slowly gathered. Charlotte was on the ground. On the way to the hospital in Vallejo, she died at the age of thirty-two. Burton was not yet five.

It was a quiet winter in Alameda. Bill thought having a nine-to-five job might cheer up the kids and make things whole again, as long as it engendered some enthusiasm for getting out the door in the morning. He tried to leave behind the noise of the city's underground, the crooks and obits, by taking a job at Gretchell, a big advertising agency that specialized in Plymouth and DeSoto automobiles. One in five cars those days was a Plymouth.

The change didn't sooth the emptiness for any of them. The generations before Bill's often lost parents to sickness and death at what would be "way too early" by the later standards of the mid-twentieth century and beyond. In those days there were plenty of ailments, no shortage of accidents. For Burton and Marilyn, with something so essential to their identity and safety wrenched asunder out at Kelly Station, Bill tried to maintain that parental epoxy of the stoic and supportive.

The old-time notion held that familial stability was best achieved with two parents. (Thus, when William Heywood decided he had enough of Bill's mother and walked out, Clara found a new dad in B. B. Mason; Bill's stepfather passed in 1929). For his youngsters, for his loneliness, Bill got hitched a third time.

Vera had a schoolteacher's motif, dark straight hair parted on the right, thin lips and eyebrows, a stern manner under a sensible coat. She was capable of a smile, though, particularly when toying with her black cocker spaniel or enjoying her new higher life out on dates with Bill. Where others might dine in something plainer, Vera donned a pinstriped ensemble with a tied kerchief, a Katherine Hepburn hat with big Hollywood bow and a shiny brooch the size of a police badge. At restaurants and racetracks, with a casually raised cigarette, Vera shined alongside her hefty husband.

The reconstructed family bumped along from one home to the next, near Merritt Lake in Oakland, then Berkeley Hills, where Vera had relatives, overlooking the bay a few miles off. Then back to the city, up in Laguna Honda, under the giant cement cross on Mount Davidson. Before the trees grew up around it, the cross was outlined with Christmas lights. Each night as the holiday approached, a newspaper ran a daily strip of the Christmas story, and Burt and Marilyn would sit by the window while Vera read the story to them. It was one of the few gentle times they experienced with her.

Far more often, one of Marilyn or Burt's transgressions would be followed by her offer, "Do you want the whipping now or after dinner?" Burt's usual choice was for after, holding out for the remote possibility she would forget the mischief by then.

Whether Vera might not have been able to have children or simply didn't care to produce her own, for a life with Bill she'd taken on a pair of pipsqueaks. Little Burt didn't give her much of a chance, those "not my real mother" attitudes, who the heck did she think she was? Kids will calculate their own estimates about what they owe a replacement parent, and what their temperament delivers.

Burt was a nice-looking boy, but disliked elementary school, and he wasn't popular. Seems he was a thief. Small stuff, a sandwich from a boy's jacket, pennies from a girl's coat. He was almost always caught, or at least suspected and interrogated. Reflecting on it much later, he hadn't the foggiest notion why he did it, either for adventure or profit or some sort of payback to an unfair world.

When a boy at school upset him, little Burt got on top of him and pounded him. He staged his first combat to make an impression on an older male cousin from Vera's family he admired, whose regard he coveted. He was terribly afraid and was crying as much as his victim. The beating continued until the other boy squirmed and ran. There was no joy in the win. The backyard victory, the showing off for his cousin, was a matter of luck, not ability.

Funny, the stuff a person can recall as an adult, beyond the intuition and dreams, inside the cache no therapist can unlatch, those few slices of childhood experience that are seared-in, permanent, the ones that escape taping over when the memory bank requisitions space.

Like that one day when he was in the yard with his cousin Bobby and some poor kid with the bloody nose.

And that other odd day in San Francisco, the same year, in the house that faced the street in the middle of a tree-shaded block, its living room with leaded glass panes sparkling light that danced on the walls. Vera cuddled the boy in her arms on the couch, humming, both of them drifting. After awhile she unbuttoned her blouse, crooning quietly, rocking in rhythm, giving her femininity to him, a woman needing child, a baby needing mother.

Burt remembered this moment as vividly as when the air roiled with her angry bellowing and his replies of noxious rejection.

Doesn't matter if it actually happened. If he found peace in the memory, that peace was a thing apart from its realness.

Bouncing back to the Midwest, destination Detroit by silver-streaking train, Marilyn and Burt were rattle-standing on the rear platform of the last car as it screamed through Rocky Mountain tunnels, screeching a child's surprise with the sudden passing over creek bridges and past dark tree stands and small-town water towers, sooting up their white travel clothes to Vera's high-decibel frustration.

The New York Times was hiring Bill as a supplier of automotive news and advertising. This new career turn paid enough for an apartment on the seventh floor of a nine-story red-brick deco-decorated building on Seward Avenue, about ten blocks from a large General Motors plant.

It was a hot Michigan summer, with plentiful sun; Bill said the kids looked like Indians. Vera took them for swimming lessons, she was still trying. At a Tigers game, Bill saw Babe Ruth.

They soon upgraded to a nice rented house for ninety dollars a month in the Detroit suburb of Pleasant Ridge, a few blocks off Eleven Mile Road and close to the zoo. They could afford a maid, Sadie Griffith, forty-two and carrying a seventh-grade education.

The kids stayed in touch with their grandparents, the late Charlotte's folks Nina (called Nana) and Louis the doctor. Burt, at eight a precocious young master of cursive writing but not the grammar to go with it, wrote them notes about the Christmas gifts he received, including a tool set, a pair of "skies," a fire boat and the "electro set" Nana mailed him, and his plans to have seven friends over for his January birthday party.

On another penciled note to Nana, Burt signed off with a line of X-O's and, with a whimsical flare of prognostication, a two-inch drawing of a boat with portholes, like an old sailing ship minus the masts, the silhouette of an LST landing craft that wouldn't be in general use until the war around seven years later.

While Vera was off with her relatives in the spring of '37, Burt sent his stepmother a letter after listening to the coronation of King George VI on the radio. He claimed some pride in not spilling food in his lap at a restaurant, and that he'd joined the Cub Scouts. He included a presumably original poem, "Maytime." *May is here. It brings good cheer, And every one is happy. Your in the west. And we feel best when mammy's home with pappy.* What a suck-up.

Bill's salary afforded vacations, and off they motored into Big

America: to Hershey, in Pennsylvania, with its hotel swan boats in a lagoon and the ever-permeating smell of chocolate from the factory smokestack regardless of the wind, and Washington, D.C., in one of the early "motels" that accommodated travelers with something between a hotel and a cottage camp.

In New York City, there was a trip to Jones Beach to visit Bill's friends, because he had friends everywhere. They passed through clustered neighborhoods where the summer streets stank, poor children splashing in spewing hydrant water because, as Vera instructed, "They are poor and that's the only place they can play in the water." Once they reached the beach, they spent all their time in a fresh-water swimming pool instead of the ocean, the damn big ocean right there, the reason being, Burt thought, "parents are stupid."

Bill, along with Vera's adamant vote, engineered Burton's send-off to a military school when he was twelve. They told themselves some story, how it was for his own good, what with the old man moving around. A solid education would be Burt's stepping stone to West Point. And by his own later admission Burt was incorrigible back then, self-centered, vain, irritating to those around him, lonely, pathetic... it was time to get straightened out.

A man came to the house in Pleasant Ridge, had a projector and screen, showed them a place owned by a fellow named McFadden, publisher of the popular magazine Liberty. Castle Heights Military Academy was just as the movies portrayed those sorts of places back when Mickey Rooney played the student. It was old school polish on more than two hundred acres. Stone buildings, young men dressed up, flags flapping in the north Tennessee breeze. Impressive.

In late summer of '39 the couple drove Burt and Marilyn down a two-lane road past Stonewall Jackson's house and on into quiet Lebanon.

His folks stretched for some sentiment, but the drop went down with a lot less feeling than the departure scene in *Ocean's Eleven*, when Richard Conte does the "sorry, kid, you'll like it here" with his tearful, saluting little boy and goes off to make one last big score to afford to get his son back.

Under a wide-brimmed military hat far bigger than his head, Burt displayed no smile, only resignation.

Marilyn waved to her big brother through the back window as her parents rolled out of the tree-lined driveway.

They left him to join a mix of boys from broken homes and the wealthy ones where parents were content to ship off their sons and let someone else educate and discipline them, plus South American and European kids from striving families. The grass was trod left-right-left-right over the years by the future rockers Gregg and Duane Allman, the eventual General Wesley Clark who would run NATO for a time and impress Western values on Serbia, and the guy who started the Cracker Barrel highway eateries.

Far from home, Burt was among patriots and schoolyard bullies and boys from next door who were all dealing with being dumped to one degree or another. Twenty boys to a dorm, sharing a typewriter room where all were expected to bang out weekly letters home, and a study hall that hosted the "inquisition," the regular review of the boys' talking out of order, tie crooked, shoes unpolished, brass not shiny enough. Just outside its door was a worn dirt circle, the "bull ring" where a demerit was worked off by a half-hour of marching. (That sure was better than paying off demerits by holding one's ankles as a teacher-officer applied a three-foot-long paddle with drilled holes for painful effectiveness to a boy's posterior, and it had better be withstood in silence. Burt, a record-holder for insubordinations and indiscretions, yelled a lot, disgusting the paddler-in-charge who thought the little soldiers should take it all without noise.)

The instructors were mostly retired servicemen, some in cavalry attire, older and beyond the range of recall to active duty as the world heated up with the Werhmacht plowing across Europe. They smacked and insulted the kids into line, as how it had been done to them.

The 6AM reveille would push you out of cold, inhospitable barracks for formation in scratchy wool uniforms and white shirts and ties, slick and tight for daily drilling. At the flag parades across the grounds on Sundays, townspeople would come out to watch and applaud America's future finest.

Burt's seventh and eighth-grade life was of forced-march campouts in the Lebanon woods, strappings by instructors bound to the traditions of male power, and hazing of the young or the dim or the marked, set to humiliating tasks or displays by the old and the clever and the payback-seeking.

There was loneliness and hurt. His father left him and his mother instigated it, and now he had to eat salad every day. There were no pillows, no condiments, relief found only in the dessert selections and unlimited cold milk in steel pitchers. The only tactical retreat was to the Butt Hole, the one weedy spot where you could sneak a smoke.

Castle Heights imbedded its rigor with the Browning Automatic rifle and Springfield 104's. Grenades went off in the distance. You had to be of a certain age to handle the weaponry, so all Burt got to carry were little wooden rifles.

He did well in football, yet despite his constant summer practicing back home, he didn't make the swim team. Turned himself into the fastest typist in the platoon, though.

When she was around twelve, Marilyn sent a letter reassuring the brother she'd always looked up to, in the way that pre-teen girls bask in the protective, older masculine force, that her life was happily grounded in school plays, thrice-weekly dances and a girls' basketball team slowly gaining in the standings.

It didn't last: Bill and Vera packed Marilyn away to a girl's academy in Gainesville, Georgia.

As the Motor City crawled out of the Depression, DeSoto, Plymouth and Oldsmobile and all the other outfits kept on building cars, while their fights with the unions made for a lot of pushing and shoving at the factory gates and in Washington. What was good for automakers was good for the country, so said the car companies and occupants of the White House alike, but all that static needed buffing and focus. Bill Mason had skills in that arena. He could tell a good story, he knew the auto-corp culture, the gladhanding and drinking and favor-exchanging, all practiced at the Elks Club and the Masonic lodge. This was the dawn of the corporate public relations executive, the character who promotes, smooths over, glides past and spins the alchemy of regulation-adherence, imaginative corner-cutting and consumer-conning.

Bill was perfect for General Tire and Rubber down in Akron, and they made him an offer in 1941 to take over P.R. for $35,000 a year (much like getting $600k eighty years later). He'd also have his expenses covered, and public relations has a lot of out-of-pocket. He and Vera rolled down to Ohio, nestling in a house on Market Street, the primary thoroughfare through the Fairlawn section northwest of the city, two brick stories with Tudor gables, a protected arched entryway and an attached sunroom off to the left. Coming in from a side street, a roomy driveway led to the garage.

One day Vera watched a tow truck clunk Bill's car down in the driveway with the entire front end bashed in. Bill suffered a broken rib and a bruised chest from what he called a "minor mishap." No doubt some of his torso was already somewhat delicate since the last time he clumphed into a steering wheel when his approach to motor vehicle operation proved no match for the laws of physics.

At certain times of the year you just know, blindfolded though you might be, you're in Provence, one of the floral hearts of France. The lavender fields waft their herbal delicacy across the countryside. Even in the middle of Valensole the fragrance drifts through the bus fumes and deep-fried courgette flowers at the street stalls.

Akron was no Provence, but you knew where you were.

The smell of Akron was everywhere, part of the landscape, particularly in the neighborhoods around South Main and Wilbeth. It was as if the fuliginosity of a coal-gloomed Welsh village was sown onto an American city. A city resting amid otherwise placid farmland long connected to Cleveland's gate to Lake Erie by twenty-some meandering miles of the Cuyahoga (the same river that in its industrial decades famously caught fire a dozen times, contributing to the creation of the Environmental Protection Agency).

Akron smelled like a Rubber City would, and the town's tourism talkers would prefer you didn't discuss it. It was the toasting and bubbling of rubber stripped from countless millions of plants from tropical nowheres, the stretching and molding of it, that forcefully relinquished a smell that got in your hair and followed you into the store, that sank in like rain on an un-Scotchguarded cloth coat.

Firestone was on the south side with three smokestacks like the exhaust pipes of a *Titanic*. Goodyear Heights commanded the northeast with a towering clock. These plants, and others, supplied the rolling parts when everybody hit the road out of the Depression, more than a hundred million vehicles by the mid-Thirties. After that came the demands of war, and then in the Roaring Fifties the national highway system expanded and commercials extolled the virtues of "seeing the U.S.A. in your Chevrolet."

At General Tire & Rubber in the 1940s, Bill Mason busily promoted the Dual 8, the Dual 10, the Super Squeegee (said to take more than three hundred nails without losing air) and the aircraft tires, plus the company's first factory down Mexico way.

Bill was one for big ideas and splashy stuff, an exuberant booster of Akron and its industry. He rubbed elbows with the mayor at the Rubber Bowl, a football stadium that hosted the Cleveland Rams on occasion. After Pearl Harbor drew the country into international conflict, he coordinated efforts in the rubber factories for a national bond drive that financed wartime expenses. That went so well General loaned him to the Treasury Department to conduct the same appeal to get steelworkers to donate ten percent of their paycheck for bonds.

Serious-looking, wearing plaid shirts and a large Stetson, Bill's dour countenance masked a fast-talking teller of funny stories in a Scandanavian accent, an inflection picked up during his army service where ninety percent of the men in the 135th Infantry were of Swedish origin.

One day he called Akron City Hall to Swedishly complain, as "Bjorn Turnblatt," that his group of distinguished visiting scientists were at the train station waiting for an official entourage to greet them. A coterie of officials scrambled, and while Bill and some friends were laughing somewhere, folks from City Hall, having come up empty at the station, were unamused.

Many a businessman spent hours at a West Side bar on the receiving end of his raucous stories, with or without the accent. Bill was named Toastmaster of an American Legion post, the official guy for glass-raising and "but, seriously, folks" guest introductions.

He posed in a wide-lapeled gray pinstripe three-piece, sitting in a dark walnut executives' room, examining a newspaper ad for El Producto cigars and smoking a seventeen inch-long pipe, perhaps for something ceremonial like an honorary induction into the Leprechaun Society.

Mason impressed his peers as the personality who would just as soon spend all his time playing poker at the National Press Club, where he often won or lost thousands of dollars in an evening, as anyplace else. His command of "smoking car songs" from the long-distance travel culture, such as "Gentlemen Will Please Refrain," about the warning signs on the old trains advising against inconvenient behavior, was exceptional.

When General Tire opened a plant in Texas, Bill and Vera moved along with it to Waco and what was for them the new frontier. Famous as the birthplace of Dr. Pepper, Waco was now bursting with wartime purpose, trying to accommodate eighty-four thousand people after its airfield fueled a fifty percent uptick in the population. To promote production efforts by the rubber, steel and oil companies, Bill ferried forty newsmen around in government-provided planes for two weeks.

In a town called Goose Creek near Houston, a writer in the local Sun observed, "He isn't much to look at, being just another overfed mid-westerner." But Bill's promotional event for the industrial-at-heart, American Made Rubber Day, impressed the columnist. "If the big rubber companies have chemists on their payrolls who can do as much with their test tubes as Bill Mason can do with a mouth full of banana oil, the future of the nation is secure." A nice compliment, although the fruit in question seemed geo-incongruous.

General Tire also paid an executive visit to Mexico, for interest-inspection and bigshot-influencing. Each night had a dinner for reciprocal back-patting and alcohol-infused intelligence gathering, and the guests, including two dozen newspapermen, sat through Spanish speeches by their Mexican hosts. After too many incomprehensible talks, the group of visiting diners asked Bill to translate a speech for them into English. Not knowing a word of Spanish, Bill did it anyway and gave the audience a half hour of jokes, while the Mexicans were unamused. But Bill found he really liked Mexico City.

His influential friends in Washington enjoyed his company enough to wrangle him an invitation in 1945 to the White House Correspondents Dinner, the annual fundraising event for journalism students. Soon after, Bill watched President Truman and radio comic Jack Benny entertain in a piano/violin duet at a cocktail party that was "loads of fun, as all dignity was parked at the door," sitting alongside two "nice fellows," Supreme Court Justices Hugo Black and Robert Jackson (later the chief prosecutor at the Nuremberg trials).

After Castle Heights proved not to be the ticket to a remarkable future his father had hoped, Burton and his parents were looking to give public school and home life another shot. He spent a few weeks in September '42 hanging around an Akron bowling alley, knowing how uncommitted and unachieving he was (as did his parents).

Then he took off alone for where he began his life's journey, the San Francisco Bay.

He made it to the bus depot at Seventh and Market (where the Civic Center is now), where he found a hole-in-the-wall hamburger stand called Scotty's. It displayed an early version of those later-ubiquitous signs bragging about having sold an impressive multiple-thousands of burgers. Three employees wore Scotch-like bonnets and Burt talked his way into one. They paid him thirty bucks a week and a free lunch. The place sold small cans of cold "apricot nectar," which he swiped to the tune of six or more a day without reimbursing the Scotty's register. (Another *Strange Snick*®, as a decade later Burt would cross paths with another "Scotty" on the other coast.)

One day in the shop, in the fall of '42, he met the guy who steered him to join the merchant marine. To Burt, "He was a solid queen." Apparently Akron had been "full of them," not that anything happened there. He met one "gay blade" while hitchhiking from Ohio, a middle-aged, pot-bellied truck driver with a two-day beard, handling an automobile carrier in Oklahoma. For these characters who popped up from time to time, Burt understood he had a certain appeal: fifteen and fresh, rosy Eastern cheeks, soft hands and "dumb as they make 'em."

Then along came the customer at Scotty's with both a come-on and advice about a fellow finding his future at sea.

Sitting on the tip of the Cotentin peninsula, Cherbourg was freed from German control a few weeks after D-Day in 1944. There wasn't much left to the port, and viewed from the air most of the grand old French city was the crumble atop a Dutch apple pie.

Cut off by the sea and, to the east, the Americans from the Normandy beachhead, the German garrison destroyed the city's resources in an effort to cripple the Allies' push to Paris. The harbor was replete with mines; it took minesweepers eighty-five days to clear them, not without significant losses. Power plants, bridges, submarine pens and wharves, everything of military value had been wrecked to rubble by the Germans, determined to hold fast and make a mess in the process.

By the time Burton came in that summer on his Liberty ship, the relatively inexpensive tincan supply vessel used for transatlantic convoys, Cherbourg was for the most part secure. The adventure provided him with tales to tell. Some of them, maybe most, weren't true.

He enlisted in the civilian merchant marine in February of '43, a month after turning sixteen, propelled by a cocktail of patriotism and adventure, by a need to be something, forget something. Or to get away from his father's drinking or the difficult woman who wasn't his mother and found him in the way. To trade his Scotty's bonnet for a more grown-up look.

The merchant service, overseen by the military but not part of it, was pressed for manpower during the war and signed him up *sans qualms* along with plenty of kids like him, still a lightweight at five-nine and a hundred-sixty.

He was a messman making coffee and swishing mops on *Lyman J. Gage*, a four-hundred-plus-foot freighter with little uncrammed space, pressed into war service from a Gulf of Mexico steamship line called Waterman and mounted with guns. *Gage* handled a Pacific run over to Brisbane, Australia and the island of New Caledonia.

From a nook in a bulkhead in the late spring of 1943, he responded to his sister Marilyn's "not altogether illiterate" letters. A bunch of his shipmates admired a photo she'd sent of her "lovely phiz." Among them was Ed, the group humorist, engaged at nineteen to a hometown girl, and tall Allen, who played the drums and had just turned eighteen.

While warning his sister about the would-be Ohio Casanovas that might pursue her on trips home from that academy in Georgia, Burt also expressed regret about a girl he dated in Akron. "Please keep trying to get

Laura to quit thinking I am a heel. Even if I was one, I don't like people going around thinking about it. Especially out loud."

Later in the letter he mused, "I am going to need some feminine company after 6 months down here. The local beauty prize winner looks like this," followed by a crude sketch of a South Seas islander with a ball of fuzzy hair, giant lips and stretched, multi-ringed neck, like a tribal extra in *King Kong*.

He denied being seasick with the "horrors of the Briny Deep" and, confident of his qualities, announced an intention to publish his letters when he returned from the war.

After a time he tried enlisting in the Navy but was rejected because of a mild bout with malaria.

In an August 22nd note to a family he knew in Oakland (from, as with many of his letters, "Some where in the South Pacific"), Burt expressed some of that frustrated optimism of war: they "thought we would be home by June... now it won't be by Thanksgiving." He mentioned that *Gage* was a "Jinx ship... everything happens to us," but out of caution about the military censors or the worries of those at home, nothing was specified. It wasn't until *Gage* reached a port that the letter was microfilmed into a V-mail (the system that shrunk forty bags of mail into a space-saving single sack, for later reproduction back to paper) and postmarked in San Francisco on the 31st. Burt and his letter probably came to town at the same time.

A year later on D-Day he was an ordinary seaman crossing the Atlantic from Oran in Algeria aboard the *S. S. John Fiske*, making port in New York on June 9. By the time Cherbourg had been secured in late summer in the aftermath of the invasion, the tanks and supply pallets offloaded by the thousands, he was still a kid making coffee and mopping.

As 1945 began he was back in Akron on a holiday leave. He met up with his sister, still a bit teenage-chubby, spouting her poufy-haired, floral-printed likeness to her late mother Charlotte. That's when Burt related an adventurous, even bombastic travelogue to a newspaperman. It was a colorful yarn, based on things that didn't really happen to him in France, as he conflated some of his actual activities with an oversized memory of things he couldn't have experienced.

Burt claimed to have been just blocks away from incoming German V-1 rockets known as buzz bombs. But the enemy's few remaining operational launch sites in western Europe after D-Day were firmly restricted to London targets, so none of them threw V-1s at Cherbourg. The only remaining organized Luftwaffe was far to the south in Brittany, and the Allies controlled the skies over Normandy. Burton may have been exposed at a distance to some sort of shelling, but it wasn't the "robot bombs."

An unarmed teenage seaman would never get past the security perimeter encircling the Cherbourg docks to see much of the landscape, and the Army controlled all access beyond the wharves. The streets had thousands of booby traps and stinking dead animals; any hospital still standing was a pit of corpses. Restaurants, hotels and the captured German headquarters were full of enemy booze, bacon, octopus and canned food. The Army drank everything in sight. If you got in line before the 9PM curfew, you could make new friends at the two unofficial brothels.

Ah, well. A young man sitting in the bleachers might sometime magnify his exploits as if he'd been on the playing field, particularly to a girl, or a reporter. Understandable. Maybe he was simply a *farb* (what they call someone these days who shows up for historic reenactments but pays little attention to authentic costume or equipment).

The impressions of foreign affairs Burt offered the Akron paper were likely gleaned less from experience than from French longshoremen and other civilians.

He said "the Germans were lenient with the French in the coastal cities" to make the expected Americans seem less attractive, even as liberators. He passed along an elderly English-speaking woman's opinion that German rations were better than the Yanks' and that "people blamed the Americans for the destruction of their homes."

Even more pointed, "The French girls wouldn't have anything to do with Americans. The girls said they wished the Germans were back." A bold observation.

The reporter had only Burt's word for any of this, as would anyone in Akron reading it. He might've been confined to his cabin that entire summer for mouthing off to an officer, as far as anyone knew. If Burt had been through it all, he'd know there were no V-1's hitting the harbor. The story was a big bunch of "maybe yes / probably no," that foreshadowed a life's pattern.

Soon after seeing France he was on a run connecting Durban, South Africa to the States, where he docked on August 6, 1945, the same day as the big noise hit Hiroshima. Three days later his wartime contract with the merchant service expired, as did Nagasaki's lease on life. He packed into his duffel his Merchant Marine emblem and service bars for the Atlantic War, Pacific War and Mediterranean Middle East War Zones.

Burton watched to see if life on the water in peacetime made sense long-term. In late October, he worked his way from Antwerp back to New York in the crew mess on the *S.S. Joseph Hollister*. Next stop was in Cienfuegos, a key sugar-shipping town on the southern coast of Cuba, then he cooked and cleaned his way to Brunswick, Georgia and New York on the freighter *Tag Knot*.

But he was eighteen and tired. Time for dry land and some decent pancakes with his dad and to try getting along with his stepmother. Enough with the water already. See what his sister's friends were up to.

To the regret of General Tire and a contingent of hard-drinking Chamber of Commerce guys and perspiring reporters, after the war Bill left the company and its expense account to start his own consultancy. "Wild Bill" was enamored of Mexico. He'd met a lot of influential people while handling a PR campaign in the U.S. to support Presidente Miguel Aleman, Mexico's first such officeholder who was reasonably civilian, non-military.

The couple's Mexico City jaunts made several appearances in the syndicated "Washington Scene" column for big-city newspapers that featured colorful characters buzzing in and around the halls and restaurants of influence. Stories about Vera were always welcome, such as the one about her "unswerving policy" to park a car in a no-parking zone and toss any tickets. Mexico City being just another town, she threw away a short note in Spanish tucked under the wiper. Unfortunately, the local *policías* also removed license plates until a fine was paid. The tossed letter being the ticket, the tag went unretrieved. The couple drove without a plate and Mexico City cops stopped them every few days. But Bill had an "out" stashed in the glovebox: a picture of Presidente Aleman presenting a medal to somebody, and off in the background with a head sticking out was Bill, thus bestowing some officiality that impressed policemen. It always worked, so Vera had no impetus to be more law-abiding.

In the Mexico City Herald, a paper for American readers, "Around Town" columnist Dorothy Neal described how election day in July '46 was quiet despite the tanks roaming the streets. "Ohioan Bill Mason and his charming wife Vera remained in their suite through the day, receiving a few of their own and daughter Marilyn's guests."

With Aleman successful, Bill saw an opening in early '48 to represent Mexican industry in the States, in a grandiose strategy for offices in New York, San Francisco and Washington, D.C. It came to pass that some well-intentioned, if not well-devised, plans by some businessmen bubbled into a sketchy, multi-million-dollar advertising and sales scheme. People around Aleman got a little itchy, then steamed with the *norteamericanos corruptos*. While it would be gracious to assume Bill wasn't one of the insiders in the scandal but simply, as always, the upbeat public face, after he took one particularly pointed phone call, he deemed it judicious to throw some shirts in a valise and Vera in the car. Without stopping to collect his money and other valuables from whatever hotel safes they were in, lest the move alert somebody keeping watch on foreigners, they broke for the border a few hundred miles off.

At Laredo Bill and Vera found a crossing with a large enough American presence to fend off any hassles with open-palmed Mexican officers or some politician on the phone with Customs eager to keep Bill in the country as a source of embarrassment for Presidente Aleman. They were alone for this adventure, if you can call it that; Burt was briefly working in New Mexico, while Marilyn had grown up fast, got married real young and headed for a life in Connecticut.

The couple pulled over at the first newspaper with a job opening, the San Antonio Light. In Texas, a place Bill always considered hospitable, they could start restructuring their lives. And avoid the ribbing he imagined waited for him in Washington or Akron.

In July word came of a position at a smaller paper in a more manageable town, the Echo & Banner in Alice, tucked into the far southeastern corner of Texas. Bill saw Jim Wells County almost as a new, undeveloped country where he could take life a little slower. Maybe write a book.

In some respects Bill fit in with his new surroundings. At fifty-one, two hundred pounds, his face was tugged a little long with a second chin emerging, a little gap between the upper front teeth as if a permanent souvenir of adolescent tussling. Still had the tousled waved-back dark brown hair, now under a broad-brimmed hat just short of a cowboy's ten-gallon, similar to the Stetson he donned on the streets of Akron.

"In Mexico things were bad," Bill wrote to his daughter Harriet at 5:30 one morning. "I came back discouraged and beaten and feeling I was just too old to start again."

The Echo job, he said, "will never pay much but I am enjoying it. I have taken over a little daily and am trying to build it into a real force for the community."

Along with his general duties as editor, as the Echo wasn't a hefty operation, he took on a "Street Scene" column about local people and activities. To cover sports, he wrote as Lib Nosam. After Nosam asserted an Alice high school football team lost to a better squad, someone else's brick-sized opinion crashed through an office window.

It didn't take long to learn who in Alice made and/or interpreted the law. A whopping town like San Francisco, or small like Alice, it was the same thing, big people and little people. The bigger they were, or fancied themselves to be, the louder and pushier their point of view, their entitlement.

It was his first experience with a small-city media environment where avoiding conflict was a rule of thumb. It dismayed him how the factions in town didn't negotiate resolutions to their problems. In his old world, Chambers and Committees figured it out and things got done, so he encouraged a middle ground. "Hatchets must be buried, and we don't mean in anyone's back."

In one column he complained he couldn't get information about a particular case from the police and said, "We should change the policemen or police chief or both." The publisher, V.D. Ringwald, gave him a dressing-down and his follow-up article that was supposed to further examine the cops didn't mention them at all.

Often taken to task by someone in town for being critical of any subject, he published his commitment. "I will try to be a good boy, but I will go right on printing what I think is news." Supportive phone calls after that gave him confidence, and Burt, having rejoined his parents when they landed in Alice, was all in favor of his dad's display of integrity.

With a pointed folksiness Bill laid out his position: "I am agin 'em when they are wrong. I'm for 'em when they are right. I'm agin 'em when they won't give me information."

That autumn Ringwald was assaulted on the street by some guys from the sheriff's department loyal to George Parr, the unelected "Duke of Duval" whose influence stretched into neighboring Jim Wells County and beyond. To protect his wife and children, Ringwald insisted Bill lighten up and lay off.

By year's end, Mason felt he could no longer practice the dictum to "be fair to all, do good if you could, but publish the truth even if it hurt someone." Time to hit the road again.

In his last column for the Echo, on Christmas Eve of 1948, he wrote, "If I can't follow that creed, I leave... we learned we could not follow that creed here. We are all right as long as we do not tread on certain toes. We have. We can't print anything that steps on those toes. We are leaving," back to San Antonio.

Then while the bags were half-packed, word came about KBKI, the AM station in Alice looking to replace its program director. For Bill, that would make an agreeable change of venue rather than address. He signed on for the job.

The station was owned by backers of George Parr. If Parr had a hand in approving Bill's hiring, it might have been to keep a perceived challenger on the radar, in accordance with that old dictum about holding one's enemies closer.

The job came with some airtime. *Bill Mason Speaks* was tucked in just before lunch a few days a week, between farm reports and housewives' recipe shows, jukeboxes of local country-western records and national Caucasian acts like Patti Page and Dick Haymes. Mason was a quick hit among mid-day listeners when it circulated how Bill was talking about stuff everybody knew was going on but didn't discuss in nervous company.

Listeners were regularly jolted with "Whoa!" moments when *Bill Mason Speaks* began poking at the region's sore spots. They weren't accustomed to this sort of tree-shaking on local radio or in the papers, with most Southeast Texas media more vested in bland continuity than controversy.

Selling advertising for the show wasn't always easy; a prospect knew they might ruffle someone's feathers by paying for Bill's airtime. What was less difficult for the show was attracting legal noise and anonymous threats.

Mason once charged a county engineer with corruption on a sewer line project. It seems someone else had done the reporting and Bill used it on the air without confirming the facts. With a lawsuit threatened, Bill heard out the man's complaint and apologized on the air for the error.

Then there was the day in March '49 when Bill was in a bowling alley. One of the workers told him two guys were in the parking lot to talk to him, and those guys were the sheriff, Hubert Sain, and a deputy, Charlie Brand. When they got Mason aside, they proceeded to smack him around, what Bill called a "token beating." Even ripped his pants off.

Bill hung his torn pants on a lamppost at the station and said on the air that anyone who wanted to see him or throw a punch could meet him "under his pants." Brand was fined five bucks for simple assault.

(Such intimidation and violence were portrayed in the 1955 film *The Phenix City Story*, based on the noir crime scandals in the varietally-spelled Phenix City, Alabama, and a mirror image for Alice. In the movie, an attorney and his son are reluctant but driven crusaders in a humid Southern town where a czar of the red-light district stops at nothing to maintain his profitable, thuggish control. It's replete with requisite blue saxophones, overheated mood swings and real-life locals in small roles while the known actors – Richard Kiley long before *Man of La Mancha*, Edward Andrews and John McIntire – chew the scenery. One version of the film includes a fifteen-minute introduction with real-life journalist Clete Roberts interviewing courageous citizens and the widow of a Phenix City man murdered for standing up to the gang. In his closing the reporter offers, "I return you to... *your city*," as if such political terrorism could occur anywhere if good people relinquished their vigilance. Which, of course, it always has, because they still do. For its investigations into the wide-open Phenix City corruption, the Ledger of nearby Columbus, Georgia, took the Pulitzer Prize.)

Burton would proudly relate that story about his dad and the pants for years. He wanted to be a journalist, too. He'd done some scut work for papers in Waco and down in Uvalde, and when Bill went south for Mexican trade promotion, Burt spent a little time in southeast New Mexico, reporting for the News-Sun and the Flare in Hobbs on the Texas border.

When Bill and Vera retreated back to Texas and settled in Alice,

Burt, twenty-two, joined them to embark on the next phase of a life that had become adult too soon. There had been an abundance of growing up too soon for hundreds of thousands of American boys who'd been fighting a few years before. Boys who learned to take care of themselves, looking out where dragons be.

By this point Burt had become accommodated to the unsettled, the unbalanced, the unfair, from far back in the years in California when he was small and needy, bearing the raw rip of his mother's death in front of him when his father couldn't handle a curve.

The end of July is sweltering at midday Thursday when office workers gather in front of the fan on someone's filing cabinet, the luncheonettes ricochet with clattering plates and housewives tidy up the remnants of their kids' peanut butter sandwiches. And the guy on KBKI who's always yammering about some crap is on. He showed up as many as five times a day, depending on what other programs were on the docket. He taped his reports before going out on his morning rounds, using a single-track recorder that had been around since the war days. Sometimes he'd be on hand to read his copy live.

"Eat hearty, folks, while I tell you what's going on… with a few more questions to ask." Bill's regular opening.

He mentions his wife Vera, always affectionately referred to as "the gadget" (perhaps adopted from the nickname for the first atomic test bomb). He also includes Julia Picard, the couple's close friend and regular vacation partner who just arrived from San Francisco. Then he runs through some copy for the sponsor, Alice Market and Delicatessen, with its "rarest cheeses."

Bill segues into a riff on meat ordinances, promotes adherence to the rules and advocates that all meaty businesses, the deli's, slaughterhouses and café's, each get a meat license before the week runs out. His approach to this kind of issue is that everybody's in the same situation, we all eat the local meat and a bum steer spoils the burger. It's not a populist stand, necessarily, more of just speaking up for the public because he's on the radio and they ain't. A reporter as opinion columnist is a careful mix.

In a brief turn down an editorial side alley, Bill mutters a line or two about a suspect's questionable identity in a widely publicized New York holdup.

Then Bill reinforces his willingness to "take the gloves off and start swinging."

The prostitute situation, been told I shouldn't pick on Hungry Hubert Sain, any of you can spend an hour on the south side and see the suffering and misery caused by the operation of the dance halls, nightly violations of the liquor control laws, dance hall girls work on the property of Sam Smithwick the deputy of Hubert Sain, every night the world's oldest profession is plying its trade, heaping dollars into the pockets of the proprietor of the place.

"I charge here today that Sam Smithwick knows what is going on. I charge that the taxpayers in Jim Wells County are paying wages to a man who is permitting the spreading of vile diseases. Disrupting homes, endangering the lives of children, yet unborn. I charge that Hungry Hubert Sain knows about these things."

Threatened over the phone early in the morning, better shut up or else, dismay that advertisers were advised to avoid me, keeping faith in George Bell Clegg (the chief of police) to pick up the girls like he said he would, hot potato is in Sain's lap, dereliction, malfeasance, what things he has done besides sending another deputy to tear my pants off, imported harlots, nefarious diseases, impeachment, yes there is some way of getting rid of him. A chance for church people, form a committee, send people out to these places, don't take my word…

"I have tried to be accurate. Give me your support on this and we'll clear it up. If you don't, no matter whether you like other things I say or not… you are not the kinds of people I think you are. I'm leaving it up to you."

Then Bill gives out his phone number again, 2144 (in a time when a few digits identified a telephone), "in case any more of you want to threaten me."

As he'd done before, Bill wraps up with "This is my answer – this is my challenge. As long as a situation like this is permitted to continue, I shall blast it every time a new fact comes to my attention."

Around nine the next morning, Friday, Vera picked up the phone. A woman told her, "I just overheard a conversation, your husband is in danger."

Before Vera could clarify, the caller whispered, "Someone is listening, I have to hang up," and did.

Burton later said, "The family didn't pay any attention to the warning as Daddy was being threatened almost daily." This may have been hyperbole from a young man already practiced in swagger, or a reflection of actual menace, but, still, the house was infected with tension.

Heck, anyone could reach Bill Mason, giving out his phone like that despite the crosshairs that abounded in Jim Wells County where the men making the fortunes gave badges to Mexican-American brownshirts to hassle the peasantry and violently enforce political policy.

After Thursday's *Bill Mason Speaks*, maybe Sam Smithwick saw no further value to telephoned intimidation. Maybe it was a cultural thing, Mason having misjudged (or not caring) how the deputy might react with his mix of macho Latino and combative Irish. Or it was real personal, Sam might've heard a rumor Mason was going to connect the questionable dance hall to one of Smithwick's older children. Could be that Sheriff Sain was shoving his finger into Sam's gut, too. In any case, on Friday Sam was fed up and pulled his gun on San Felipe Street.

The script Mason taped for Friday's pre-noon broadcast had less perspiring copy than Thursday's entry, a rolling up of the window shade to grab a spill of light, change the whole damn mood from yesterday's grim show. With another "eat hearty" for his lunchtime audience came a social note on attending Hap Holcomb's barbecue the night before, accompanied by "the gadget" and the visiting Julie. At Hap's a groom in an upcoming wedding received shower gifts from his buddies, and Edna the harmonica player delighted all with some prize yodeling.

Then Bill spoke of new equipment to improve cotton baling, and how farmers' checks would get a boost not only due to better mechanization but also the government's poking in to establish some standards, which was okay by him.

Next, the struggling Alice Monarchs would take on the Brown Bottlers on a lamplit Friday night, followed by a Sunday trip to the Eagles' diamond in Benevides. There was an ad promoting the air-conditioned comfort of the Flamingo Club over in San Diego. Don't miss the calf roping contest tomorrow night, male entrants only, and the women at the Methodist church will be scooping up an ice cream supper, all home-made, cake too, twenty-five cents a plate.

Then because Bill just couldn't help it, he was back to the dance hall girls, the implications for the tourist courts just outside of town, the wrong business undertaken in the cabins, the owners should call the cops, get rid of the disease-ridden women.

And with that last burst of combustible opinion, that was it for the week.

The Friday tape was due for airing at the same time Bill was in the wagon from Moyer's Mortuary.

Mid-day, Vera got a call from some lawman with news about her husband. She didn't believe it. Another ugly prank.

The air was humid and hostile in Alice late Saturday. Every city patrolman available was called in to make sure street-corner pushing didn't escalate. Three Texas Rangers disseminated a "stern warning" about public order.

The sheriff's *pistoleros* were out as well, Luis Salas among them, applying their pretense of representing the law rather than political thuggery. They tended to stay out of the Rangers' way, though. Mexican cops rarely went looking to provoke the white wiseguys who got their badges from the governor.

Plenty of people were steamed up, pro and con, about Rancho Alegro, what with Mason's turgid editorializing as to how "No possible good can come out of a situation where young girls are exposed to drunken men... there can be no excuse for trafficking in the souls of kids."

Rancho Alegro had been wisely closed up. So none of the cops were around at eleven-thirty Saturday night when five men approached in two cars. Either to blow off steam at the current level of Texas immorality on behalf of a law-abiding and frustrated citizenry, or to send a message to competitive panderers of booze and girls, they shotgunned ten blasts into the walls, popping out three lights and shattering an electric meter. The next morning barbed wire was stretched across the driveway.

Ranger Ben Krueger insisted again they'd tolerate no "street justice" and Captain Alfred Allee came to town to supervise. Meanwhile, Deputy Smithwick, denied bail by a pipe-smoking Justice of the Peace, Brown Fuller, was spirited off to a jail forty miles away in Corpus Christi for safekeeping. "Everything is being done to bring a fair trial to the accused," Kreuger said.

The local district attorney, Samuel Reams, wisecracked, "I think if I were Smithwick, I wouldn't mind staying in jail for a few days." Reams didn't specify what the defendant needed protection from, a pro-temperance mob or some corrupt crowd wary the hot-potato suspect would spill somebody's beans.

Sam was a father of seven who barely read or wrote English (although he could speak the language of his British great-grandfather if he "wanted to"). He also had his hand in farming and ranching. In his younger days he was a renowned brush popper, the guy who'd go into dense scrub to recoup a wild steer. Sam was recorded as purchasing the land for Rancho Alegro from a couple named Boyd in March '48. When the structure went up a few months later he hid his connection by enlisting one Biterbo Flores to slap a legitimate name on the beer license.

Defending such a suspect was prickly, like picking a sizzling fatty ribeye off the grill with just fingers. One firm of lawyers in town turned away an offer to handle the job; rumbles of a special prosecutor from Dallas didn't make it any more attractive to others. To help pay what a prosecutor would need to investigate the crime properly, the San Antonio office of the American Newspaper Guild, where many members had worked with Bill, pardner'ed up with the Texas Independent Broadcasters Association to organize the Bill Mason Memorial Fund to "insure that justice is done."

It was all tricky in a place where most everyone was breathing George Parr's air. George had learned how to operate a political empire at his father's knee. Archie Parr knew how to handle opposition, like the time an appeal to unlock Duval County's financial records hit the state Supreme Court, where Parr lost the decision, not that it mattered because before the auditors could access the county courthouse it burned to the ground and took all the records with it. Archie arranged for his son's election as a judge at twenty-five, not too difficult in that George was the only name on the ballot.

George's control over affairs in southeast Texas could sideswipe the businessman who wouldn't sign a shipping agreement, or light a match to a man's county support benefits for mouthing off about Parr in a tavern. A critical shopkeeper would find deputies blocking his parking lot and his customers arrested for being drunk and disorderly. Oil companies and road contractors were either Parr pals at a price, or didn't get contracts. If a drink cost more locally than elsewhere in Texas, the extra went into Parr's pocket. When the American Legion tried to improve Duval County's literacy rate, he retaliated by dismantling a veterans' training program.

In the "Land of Parr," where the boss owned seventy thousand acres and a race track and moved around publicly flanked by his *pistoleros*, murders with political angles occurred more regularly than angry spousal shootings or tipsy tavern gunplay. A county doctor once estimated more than a hundred suspicious deaths.

However, Parr was said later to be upset at Mason's assassination. It would just stir up a lot of sand.

The Sunday New York Times again reported the events in Alice on the front page, this time a late-breaking focus on the shoot-up of Rancho Alegro. It continued the story back to page fifty, where the last two paragraphs described the Friday victim's son, his exasperation with local law and his zeal to uphold his father's legacy. (Hardly anyone in Alice had ever seen the Times; if a Sunday edition showed up in town, they'd treat it with a curiosity afflicted by sputtering distrust, as if it were a hissing saucer from outer space cracked up out on Hazey's farm.)

When the mercury hit ninety-seven on a summer Sunday many Texans dreamed of a chipped-ice-glass to the forehead. There was none, however, in the brick First Presbyterian Church on Adams Street over on the east end of Alice. There was only the wisping of handheld paper fans in a crowd jammed to suffocation. Men with jackets in laps irrigated the pews with sticky biceps transmitting droplets into their wives' cotton dresses crunched against them.

By 2PM scores stood on the lawn, stretching for a glimpse through a window as if a limo of celebrities had arrived for a wedding between a local girl and a European prince. Streets were closed for blocks around.

The entire front of the chapel was banked with more than a hundred floral displays. A forty-eight-starred flag donated by the Veterans of Foreign Wars draped Bill's coffin.

Vera wore widow's black. Burt's double-breasted light gray suit was too tight across the middle, the tie wide and flashy for the occasion. His eyelids were heavy, colored as if bruised, worn out. It was his task to hold up his stepmother, a crumpled and soaked handkerchief in her hand, helped by Julie Picard in a dark dress with white polka dots, probably the best she had in her vacation suitcase.

Bill's mother Clara was 72, long widowed, when her son was killed. She stayed home in Minneapolis. His sister Marion, who also lived there, rushed to Texas, as did Katherine from California. Brother Elden was on the road as an executive with the National Blood Bank based in Washington, D.C. He read about Bill's murder in a newspaper, but couldn't make the trip in time for the services.

Burt's sister Marilyn managed to get down from Connecticut. Their half-sister Harriet, Bill's first daughter, now married in Minnesota, had seen Bill a few months before. She didn't come to Texas, perhaps preferring to remember her father from a happier setting.

Reverend Andrew Byers was assisted by two ministers, Episcopalian and First Christian, and the American Legion sent a chaplain. Mrs. Laughlin played the organ and a male trio sang "My Shepherd Will Supply My Need" and "We Walk by Faith and Not by Sight."

"I speak as a man who respected Bill Mason's abilities and courage and did not like his weaknesses," Byers orated. "We know the things of his life that he set out to do and did do, and we know the failures."

The minister poked his finger into the town's chest. "This should be a period of the calmest, quietest, most reflective thinking we have done. Tragedy has stalked our town for many a day."

The local VFW commander folded the flag and rested it in Vera's lap.

The widow planned at first to take the body for cremation on Monday at Mission Park in San Antonio. Word came from Bill's mother that she wanted him in a family plot up north. Instead, a compromise saw Mason buried in a flat, treeless section of Alice Fraternal Cemetery on Gloria Street.

That's where the excavation under a twenty-foot-long tent was surrounded in the manner of a gangster's funeral by the many floral displays transferred from First Presbyterian. The attendees relegated to the back couldn't see the grave, but at least they had something to inhale more pleasant than Alice in summer.

A few hours after dark on Sunday night, with the rest of the population off with their thoughts about the big hubbub in town, Vera's friends gathered in comfort, teary silences, gossip and anger at the Mason home on Presnall Street, a nondescript rancher on a sandy-soiled corner not far from the city's main strip.

The next morning KBKI devoted Mason's usual midday time slot to a memorial review of his life and work, plus some of his favorite poetry. The program closed with what in most other circumstances would be considered the worst of radio: a moment of silence.

Later Monday afternoon, an opinionated person or persons unknown visited the rough-turned soil that mounded Bill's grave. There was no wind that hot day, so it was by a human hand that more than fifty wreaths and arrangements were angrily upended and tossed across thirty yards of the cemetery. Seemed like grudges in Alice could outlast a gunshot. A beauty salon employee named Lorraine gathered up the flowers and returned them to their intended resting places.

Seven hundred miles to the south, Presidente Miguel Aleman, peacefully ensconced in his capital of Mexico City, cut the ribbon on a massive exhibition of a thousand works by the artist Diego Rivera.

As August dawned seventy years later, I sat a thousand miles away, composing the perfect lyric for a Marty Robbins country-western hit about a man who told the truth and was shot down like a lame cow on a back street in a town called Alice by a lawman who ran a whorehouse.

Not many people could say that.

The killing of journalists to subdue their voices and audacity, thought to be restricted to societies less inclined toward the democratic republic model, may have happened several dozen times in American history. In shootings, car bombings, beatings, even lynching, reporters have been silenced, some by executive fiat, others by rogue thugs protecting any number of bosses, schemes and lifestyles. Terminal intimidation has been doled out in an Annapolis newsroom, an Arizona parking lot, a Chicano demonstration in Los Angeles, a Denver garage.

When it's larded out by a guy like Smithwick, a representative of the government costumed as a protector of the people, then you're really getting hardass.

As President in the '70s, Richard Nixon construed the fact-insistent press to be an enemy. Wasn't the first or last time that's been heard in the Oval Office, with virulent aides or downstream partisans or general nitwits responding to what they hear as either direct, specific instructions or a vague call of the wild. The people are thus not well-served by those in authority openly spitting out their Henry II, "Will no one rid me of this turbulent priest?" Someone might think they'd said *press.*

A newspaperman named William O'Neil called my grandfather's murder "a throwback to the pioneer days when hard-hitting editors were often the targets for horsewhips or gunfire. It is easy to picture him in the setting of the little Texas town, disturbing the complacency of citizens and public officials who may have fallen into the habit of taking vice for granted."

The weekly industry magazine Broadcasting led its editorial column in early August 1949: "The shooting of Mr. Mason is one of the first times a radio commentator has been killed because he did his job.

"The only difference between freedom of radio and freedom of press is the manner of 'publication.' Militant radio, like militant journalism, carries with it certain calculated risks. Mr. Mason paid the extreme penalty as a crusader for local betterment. The history books may reveal him as one of the first martyrs in the cause of freedom for radio."

(The morbid *first* killing was that of radioman Jerry Buckley of Detroit, gunned down on election night in 1930 for his probing of corruption.

Then, welcome to a truly *Strange Snick*®: an early, perhaps the first, historically recorded killing of a member of the American press was that of Elijah Parish Lovejoy, a Presbyterian minister, abolitionist and journalist. He was shot in 1837 by a pro-slavery mob as he defended his printing press, a killing condemned by John Quincy Adams as an "earthquake" and which was said to have inspired John Brown to commit to the anti-slavery cause.

Bill Mason's birth father, William Lovejoy Heywood, was a descendant of Elijah's family.)

After a time, a large gravestone was planted to mark my grandfather's repose, paid for by donations, with a prosecutor's sound bite chiseled into it. "He died because he had the nerve to tell the truth for a lot of little people."

Caro Brown at the Alice Echo & Banner won the Pulitzer Prize for Local Reporting in 1955 "for a series of news stories dealing with the successful attack on one-man political rule in neighboring Duval County, written under unusual pressure both of edition time and difficult, even dangerous circumstances."

Brown, who joined the Echo in 1947 and worked alongside "Wild Bill" for a time, wrote about Parr's pursuit of power and profit for two years, even as local officials resisted her requests for public records. The Rangers warned that her life was in danger, so she kept a pistol in the glove compartment of her car. Parr wasn't sure what to do about her; at one point he claimed Brown saved his life by stopping a Texas Ranger from using his revolver to settle a confrontation with Parr.

In the years since the gunfire in Alice, studies and references about Bill's death in academic treatises, journalism courses and the occasional lecture have been sporadic, and usually focused more on the violent political crater administered by the Duke of Duval.

One such examination, by Mary Sparks at Texas Women's University in 1992, "William H. Mason: How a Journalist's Murder Influenced Media Coverage," observed that the episode wasn't mentioned in any journalism history textbooks, only in a couple of volumes focused on Texas politics.

Among biographer Robert Caro's deeply drilled studies of Lyndon Johnson's rise from backwater Texas to the White House, "Means of Ascent" in 1990 made two references to Smithwick's gunfire. Yet so comprehensive were the Duke of Duval's corruptions in Texas, some of which linked to the 36th president, Bill's murder was but a minor factoid for Caro.

In Facts on File (then, as now, a publisher of compendia on assorted subjects and a week-by-week Yearbook of world events) the blurb about Bill was among July 1949's miscellany that included a mid-air collision near Fort Dix, the drowning of a hundred and forty Hindus in a capsized ferry, and a trio of murderous felonies directed at blacks in Florida and South Carolina.

The crime was reported across subsequent decades as a news blip of one degree or another, usually to lend dramatic heft to a story on Parr. Often this was among the many popular weekly magazines that brought the larger world to America's mailboxes, mixing the political and cultural with show business and human fluff. It hit Collier's in its 1951 foray into oil-country politics, "Something is Rotten in the State of Texas." Three years later the killing figured in the Saturday Evening Post and Life, each with their own exposé of the Land of Parr as reform brewed in Jim Wells County. Life threw in a photo of Bill's gravestone.

That same summer, five years after the shooting, those stories in Life and the Post rested in grandpop Edwin's maple reading rack nestled by the parakeet Scotty's cage at the panel of windows overlooking Pine Street, under which a tousle-haired two-year-old busied himself on the floor. But the articles about power and homicide in far-off Texas had no impact on my family in New Jersey. Jean never knew the name of Burt's father or what happened to him.

They also didn't subscribe to Newsweek. In early August of '49, more than two years before Jean met Burt at the Press Bar, Scotty wouldn't have seen its roundup of national news, where Bill's murder (and young Burt's ill-fated intention to carry on in his dad's editorial footsteps) was briefly sandwiched between an anti-prostitution crusade in Gary, Indiana, Communist-hunting in the United Nations by blowhard Congressmen, and a note that New York State would no longer mail unemployment checks to the jobless while they vacationed in the Catskills.

The 79th Texas District Court opened for business on the first Monday in August with a preliminary hearing in a second-floor courtroom. Outside, the Rangers had doubled to six, and they assertively examined packages and patted down attendees.

Sam Smithwick was in place in his cowboy boots, rancher's hat and his favorite tie, with three stripes of white diamonds on a dark background at the bottom and a graphic similar to a large bottle opener running up to his fleshy neck.

Avelino Saenz testified he got out of Mason's car and saw the shooting from that vantage, although in earlier descriptions he'd still been in the car and Sam's shot had hit his pants after plowing past Mason's heart.

At one point, after Saenz had spoken and Dr. Philip Joseph from the hospital was taking the stand, a condenser on a photographer's camera exploded, jolting those nearby and causing Smithwick to go to pale and slump in his chair.

The next day, the judge was figuring to call a special session of the grand jury to unpack the mess. A defense attorney and judge from another county, H. M. Wilder, had been brought in just that morning, so the magistrate gave him a two-day recess to see how lousy his cards were. Then he begged off for a surgery on his acute abdominal cancer and, despite "Duke" Parr's pushing him to assign another local jurist who'd be likely to see things Parr's way, he replaced himself with Judge Paul Marteneau, who had to drive up from Corpus Christi.

A week after the shooting, Smithwick received two checks from the July county payroll, a salary of $156.25 and a hefty $125 mileage allowance for using his own truck to get around. With that payout, the government severed its employment with Sam.

The next week, on August 15th, gasoline-soaked rags and paper were stuffed beneath the rear of the closed Rancho Alegro and set afire. A watchman who lived near the place saw the flames around 2AM and put out the minor blaze before it had charred much beyond some flooring and a few foundation timbers.

The day of the pissant Rancho arson, Elden Mason sat in his Washington office and composed a eulogy for the brother whose burial he missed, either just for himself or some intended audience, with the accomplished dialect of a wizened editor or an articulate pastor.

It was probably inevitable. Anyone who devotes the better part of twenty-five years to blunt challenge of the parasites who infest American communities is highly vulnerable. The jungle is hazardous.

The newspaper from which I learned of his abrupt passing referred to him as a "crusader." He would have protested. He was no "solitary pine on a lonely summit," no "knight in shining armor." He was a newspaper man and a good one...

... Both in writing and verbally he laid bare the sores of the social body, but he did not quit there. He became part of the community, contributing creatively to its concerns. He was not only part of it, but in it...

... He detested the chiseler, the poseur, but above all the vicious parasite. He possessed the quaint conviction that those uniquely favored in our society should meet a standard of civic performance at least equal to that demanded of John Doe...

...he knew that the social and political health of America was not reflected primarily at national and international levels, but at the local level...

The good people annoyed him, the good people who were either gullible or too self-saving to challenge, and if necessary disown, those who exploited their fellows...

... I am sure he preferred to die as he did than in bed after long years of passivity. He would have said, "O.K., some of the boys will close ranks and see it through."

The grand jury would decide what charges applied and if they warranted a trial for Smithwick. A local cattleman named McGill was named foreman.

As long as it was tying up taxpayer dollars, the grand jury was assigned other cases to weigh beside the murder. An ex-F.B.I. man, Kellis Dibrell, spent five weeks looking into power plays in Jim Wells County. His inquiry touching on George Parr made its own noise in the courthouse hallways in the afternoon while the same jurors spent their mornings listening to the Smithwick case.

Judge Martineau, visiting from the relatively big and civilized coastal city of Corpus Christi, had his own perspective on life in Alice and wasted no time in setting the stage. "You will find that if you close up any unregu-lated beer taverns and houses of prostitution you will go a long way toward stopping shootings in your town."

Bow-tied prosecutor Homer Dean tarred the defendant Smithwick as having planned to silence "a man who was telling the truth," to kill a "defenseless, helpless, fifty-two-year-old, fat bespectacled man sitting trapped under the steering wheel."

The now-growing Smithwick team included attorney Byron Skelton, who painted the town as a den of one-sidedness against an otherwise dedicated lawman. To him, Mason was "a viper, a smear artist, slanderer and character destroyer." Sam, on the fatal day, was nothing more than a "humble Mexican" from a little Mexican town, peace and quiet, mind your own business, then this Mason comes along, "a serpent like in the Garden of Eden," and spread insidious lies to "four hundred thousand persons, one hundred miles in every direction."

Skelton accused the district attorney, James K. Evetts, of using Hitleresque tactics. Evetts roared out of his chair, and the judge instructed the jury to forget they heard it, as if.

The defense twice delayed forward motion on the case, and while a trial was unavoidable, they scored a change of venue that moved it way up past Austin to Belton, a small town in Bell County.

Sam had five lawyers by this point in late 1949, led by Henry Taylor, Sr., a smooth, respectable ol' Texas so-and-so. Taylor asked the prospec-tive jurors if they believed in the concept of self-defense, of standing their ground. If they gave the newspapers more credence than actual courtroom testimony. If, in order to enjoy various exercises of citizenship like jury service, they'd paid their poll tax (that income-producer so popular with counties and states, usually Southern, often used to keep poor blacks and whites alike from voting; you couldn't be a good citizen if you hadn't paid your poll tax).

The average time to select one juror was three hours. Eventually it took herding and plowing through a hundred and eight Bell County *veniremen* to find the requisite dozen, plus alternates, a process sliding way over into January.

The prosecution lined up two dozen witnesses and the defense had at least twenty. More than a hundred subpoenas had gone out.

The old stone Belton courthouse was swimming in steel and square jaws, as a company of twenty-five Texas Rangers moved into town. Good thing, too. As D.A. Evetts returned to the house where he was staying after the first day of the trial – he'd leaned over the jury rail and introduced Sam as a sanctimonious lawman who didn't care if there were prostitutes at Rancho Alegro as he "sat out front in his car checking them in and out" – a figure in the shadows of the garage let loose two gunshots that creased the trunk of Evetts' car and hit a storeroom. The gunman ran down an alley.

Bloodhounds were brought in but couldn't hold the scent of the assailant. Guards kept watch from then on at Evetts' house. A citizens' group led by the publisher of an airplane enthusiasts' magazine posted a $1,000 reward for information leading, etc.

Five hundred people, probably more, the largest trial crowd in the county's history, with German and Czech farmers and tradesmen mixed with a few Mexicans, shoehorned into the courtroom every day after lining up since six AM. Rangers searched for weapons. A good number in the audience had lunchbags, aluminum cups and thermoses (and any number of flasks). People prayed for no need to use a bathroom lest they never get back in to their seats. Some sat on apple boxes piled along the back wall. Sitting behind a table of reporters was a group of high school students on a class trip with their business law teacher. During the many less stimulating moments of courtroom minutiae they consulted their smuggled comic books.

The courthouse was being refurbished and audibly smacked around by carpenters' clatter. Tobacco smoke fogged the place and gave the widow Vera a sore throat; she hadn't slept much. A well-dressed family friend, Barton Daily, sat with her. Her stepson sat in the corner of the jury box alongside some reporters and took notes.

Most days Smithwick wore the same dark pants and a sweater. On collared-shirt days that same neon headache of a tie with the diamonds and abstract bottle opener design appeared again.

He gnashed at his gum, timed at eighty chews a minute, as he tapped his right-hand ring finger on the table. His children and a few in-laws maintained vigil in the second row but his wife was ill at home. Sam complained about the cold concrete floor of his cell giving him rheumatism; he'd dropped about thirty pounds on his new state-funded diet, but didn't look it.

Sitting in his cell in the off-hours, Sam still dressed not in prison issue but his own clothes, khaki trousers and pointed-toe hull-heeled cowboy boots. A big pocket watch was stuffed in a short-sleeved tan sports shirt, with a steel crucifix two inches long at the end of the chain.

He had time for Martha Cole, a part-time reporter for the Echo & Banner. "All I want is a fair trial. That's all I want. Just a fair trial." He addressed the change of venue that resulted from the hometown uproar. "I've got nothing to be afraid of down there. I came up here because my friends - they would have put up the money to get me out. But you know, I didn't want to cause them trouble."

He related to Cole his memories of a life in hardscrabble south Texas, herding cows in the brushland, taking the deputy sheriff's badge twenty-four years earlier. He shared the Bell County cell with four others, young guys who had made a mess of a Saturday night. "They don't realize they're ruining their lives, they don't realize what they're doing."

He anxiously played with the corner of his shirt, getting a little shaky as the dismal reality of his position settled in his mind. "I'm sixty-one years old and I've never been in trouble before."

The jailer, Dick Knowles, asked, "You've got some kids, haven't you, Sam?"

"They're all good boys... The three girls are all married and stay with their husbands like good girls." Sam wasn't sure how many grandchildren were out there. "Twenty-six. I think."

It had been just a few days since he was moved to Belton. "It seems like weeks," he told Cole. "But I guess it's because I'm away from home. My wife hasn't been here. She's in Alice and it's far away, a hard trip up here. I miss her cooking."

There was more to this sense of loneliness than not having supper on the table when he came through the porch door each night. "They're nice to me up here, but you know, it's away from home. I just sit, I can't read. I left my glasses at home."

Knowles offered, "Why, I have just some plain reading glasses, I'll bring them to you."

Smithwick said, "Thanks, but I keep thinking I'll be going back home."

That home, all the details of that life, the little normal things like a pair of glasses on a particular chair or the way the vegetables were boiled or the tortillas were warm and right, a creak of a floorboard that he never got around to fixing, the beer he'd drink when one of his sons came around, were very far off from Belton.

Witnesses kept going missing.

Right after the shooting Avelino Saenz went on a hike, didn't go home or call his family. Since testifying before the grand jury in the fall, he again wasn't easy to find.

Once D.A. Evetts' search party finally pulled him in from the big ranch where he was working far afield, Saenz had plenty to say. After all, the bullet was pried out of the car door next to where he'd been sitting.

Willie Chapa was equally difficult to get into a courtroom to recap his grand jury testimony, as he kept disappearing to "go fishing."

Chapa spoke of knowing some girls at the dance hall intimately as prostitutes. Heck, Chapa knew everybody. He'd been a sergeant on the police force before he was fired for conduct unbecoming: his off-hours job as the bookkeeper at Rancho Alegro. Now at the trial he talked about handing off thirty percent of the take to Biterbo Flores, whose name was on the liquor license (and whose wife kept a second set of books), and the other seventy was split between Smithwick and another politically-connected partner.

Two girls whose difficulties with English necessitated bringing in a local grocer as an interpreter said they were regular visitors to Rancho Alegro. The first, claiming not to be employed there, some kind of independent contractor, apparently, was paid fifteen cents for every dance. Twice she went out on dates at five bucks apiece. She didn't get specific about what the guys were buying.

Next was Maria Smithwick, Sam's niece. Evetts asked if she'd taken dates home. "No," she replied, "to a room." She deflected Evetts' pointing finger about charging the men any money.

Flores, the front man for the tavern, said if any prostitutes ever showed up it was only to have a beer. According to his rent receipts, there was only one large room, "no side rooms or beds."

Toward the end of this parade, Baptist minister W.B. Billingsley made the case for the social reforms he and Mason had been seeking, each from their own pulpit.

When it was time for the defense to make lemonade, Taylor's line of witnesses included a wealthy oilman named Smith. Mason had criticized him on the radio, too, and as a result he had been hot under the collar. He could see Sam's point of view. Others blamed the widow Vera for goading her husband into insulting Sam.

(During one peculiar moment in a recess, Vera, in a silk dress with a print that equaled Sam's tie in optical disturbance and a black velvet hat, was at a table alone with Sam Smithwick. They didn't speak. She later complained, "When other women's husbands die they can grieve and not have to go through all this. I wish we could get this over with.")

Several other defense witnesses were said to be ready to testify that at no time did "lewd and lascivious women ply their trade" at Rancho. But they never showed up.

While he didn't have to take any chances, Taylor thought it best to present Sam on the stand to get across how hurt he was by it all. The crime was a matter of degree, not of fact, and Sam's future rested on that degree.

Sam was in this position because of Mason's insistent hammering on the radio and he just, well, you can see he was provoked.

Taylor asked his client how Mason's broadcast allegations felt. "I was ashamed and disgraced."

"Were you afraid? Afraid your life was in danger?"

"Sure," Sam said. Taylor didn't get more specific about the cop's source of endangerment, not wanting the jury to dwell on the image of Bill supposedly getting out of the car to assault a deputy holding an automatic weapon; not wanting to suggest how Sam posed embarrassment to a system of money and power, i.e., Parr.

On cross-examination Evetts went after the deputy. "He's dead and you're alive," Evetts yelped. "Yes," Smithwick murmured, slowly twirling his wide-brimmed hat on his lap, "and sometimes I wish I was the one that's dead."

Everything that had been reported and gabbed and clucked about, Evetts now wanted to get on the record. When Sam got out of his truck and approached the sedan, "What did Mason say?"

"He say,*'What in the Goddamn hell do you want?'*"

"What did you say?"

"I say, *'I just want to ask you, please, to take my name off the radio.'*"

"And what did Mason say?"

"*'Who in the God-damn hell are you, you Mexican son of a bitch?'* Well, when he said that, I pulled my gun. He made a grab and grabbed my gun. I stepped back and fired my gun."

Vera rested her exhausted chin on her arm, eyes tearing onto a gray herringbone cloth coat.

Prior to the opposing counsel making their final arguments, trial judge Wesley Dice outlined the jury's options for Smithwick: death, life imprisonment, prison for more than two years if they didn't agree on the premeditated malice, or not guilty.

Taylor, the lead defender, had his last word, one more opportunity to tarnish the dead man as having destroyed a good lawman's reputation.

The prosecutors wrapped up. "Smithwick calmly and cooly made up his mind to kill a man who was telling the truth," said D.A. Dean. "He made up his mind to silence forever his critic." Dean asked the jury to restore to the people of Texas confidence in the justice of the law of the land. Meaning, take the law back from Parr's *pistoleros*. Then his colleague Evetts said the people of Texas deserved the execution of a "cold and wanton" killer (although no one in Jim Wells County had ever been so condemned).

Then the deputies locked the courtroom doors and covered the exits. No one was getting to that jury. Two rangers at the front swept the room with their eyes as if prepared for assassination.

In less than four hours, including a meal, the twelve farmers, shop-keepers and salesmen emerged from the jury room to speak to Sam Smithwick in his striped shirt with a red, white and blue tie his wife had given him for his sixty-second birthday. They relegated him to confinement for the rest of his life.

Although a crying Vera was heard to say, "It's too easy for him!" she was pleased. "It was wonderful!" she later repeated several times.

Sam told reporters about his sentence, "If that's what I need, that's what I take."

Vera sat for an interview with a radio reporter and expressed appreciation for the way the Belton locals had been kind to her during the circus that had taken over their town.

In the following days as Belton emptied out, the hotels and coffee shops built during the war when Fort Hood moved in watched their business plummet.

At the first hearing in the courthouse, Burton, twenty-two, wearing black-rimmed glasses and a light-toned short-sleeve shirt, stood leaning with stiff arms and palms flat on a table, studying some papers with Avelino Saenz, the man who watched Burt's father get shot a few days before. Without a caption, the grainy picture would suggest a science teacher and student in a school yearbook.

The young man's determined posture, the waved hair and spectacles, the considering eye, were the same as with the fellow captured by the lens years later on a New England wharf cluttered with submarine artifacts, and yet again when someone grabbed a picture of me another three decades on, watching over my little boy in muddied white sneakers at a Bronx pond.

I could have been the guy leaning over the desk with Saenz. Same face and hair, same structure. Seeing yourself embodied in a parent you've known all your life is a normal human experience. When it's someone from another world, who you never gazed at in the mirror as he taught you how to knot a necktie, that's a strange thing.

Vera tried to engage with life during the months of hearings and jury selections, legal machinations and shouted press questions. She spent Halloween with a friend, Mrs. W.A. Swope, whose husband had been one of Bill's pallbearers, then traveled to Dallas to meet other ladies for an ice show and the Ringling Brothers Circus.

Six months after the murder, the society writeup in the New Year's Day edition of the Alice Echo dutifully offered, none too sensibly or sensitively: "Happy Birthday to Mrs. Vera Mason. Not many of us can claim such a widely celebrated occasion as the date of our birth." Certainly not her husband, who would've been fifty-three around the time the trial of his killer began.

A month later she headed to the nation's capital to visit her brother-in-law Elden, and then on to Connecticut to see how her stepdaughter Marilyn was holding up, both in her grief and recent marriage.

Vera ended up in a retirement home bordering a golf course in California, where Marilyn and her kids visited in 1964. Sometime in the mid-'70s, Vera lost her assets to a con man who preyed on the elderly with an investment scam. Destitute, bereft of both quality of life and pride, she filled the refrigerator with food she knew Marilyn liked (knowing they'd call her to come take charge of things), and took far more sleeping pills than was necessary for a simple night's rest.

The eleven o'clock mattress check at Huntsville was unremarkable. The one after that, less so.

A twisted towel strangled Sam Smithwick's taxpayer-funded existence in the state penitentiary, now two years along, just before midnight on April 11, 1952, his considerable girth hanging from the upper bars of a bunkbed. He was alone in the cell because of his medical issues, not to mention that other prisoners might want to shiv the onetime lawman. Official interviews with guards, convicts, staff or anyone who might have seen him in the mystery hour uncovered nothing.

Mrs. Ernest Franklin, filling in for her late husband as the local Justice of the Peace, signed off on a suicide.

People were expected to agree that Sam took his life. It was nonsense to think Smithwick was silenced by parties unknown who didn't want him upsetting an apple cart. How dare there be irresponsible conspiracy-mongering to suggest the sad event was related to the rumored visit to his cell by Coke Stevenson, former governor of Texas, who was intrigued by a letter written by Smithwick claiming he could produce evidence about a peppery primary four years before.

Seems Lyndon Johnson had trailed Stevenson in the 1948 Texas Democratic Senatorial primary by a slim margin. George Parr, favoring LBJ, was known to keep election returns under wraps until he could see how many he needed for his candidate to win. Residents of cemeteries often popped up on his voting lists, along with kids and residents who'd moved away long ago. The Johnson-Stevenson Senate finagle ended in a runoff, with vote tally corrections and shouted claims of varying legitimacy careening around. Johnson was on the phone with Parr every day to ensure he'd be the one to take the oath of office.

That all led to the infamy of "ballot box 13" that popped up in Parr's territory with enough votes to sway it for Johnson. Just over two hundred votes came in at the last minute, unanimous for LBJ but for one or two. In alphabetical order. In the same handwriting. With the same pen. (All attested to by the former F.B.I. man Dibrell, who'd seen the ballots during the brief period when they were around to see.)

Box 13 tilted things enough to result in a statewide net profit to Johnson with a notorious "eighty-seven votes." Then, after another rushed tabulation and zippy official sign-off, those primary ballots and the round tin box containing them supposedly disappeared. The whispered word was that Parr instructed a janitor to burn the evidence.

Denials of complicity in the crude but effective eighty-seven-card stunt came from Johnson, Parr (recently pardoned out of a tax fraud sentence by President Truman) and a lineup of worker bees.

Bill Mason, the old crime-in-high-places beat reporter from San Francisco, wrote about the controversy alongside the national newshounds who trekked to the brush country to see for themselves what was going on in this American backwater. He devised front-page stories that were professional in their balance while alight with heated headlines and *alleges*, careful not to suggest these Texas territories might be predisposed toward a stolen contest. (Some time later a local judge recalled, "bogus voting could be found all over Texas in that 1948 election.")

Four years later, Stevenson still had not cooled off, itching to expose LBJ (who'd won the general election and gone to Washington). The ex-governor's probing for a tired and discouraged accomplice of the Duke of Duval willing to cut a deal had petered out.

Then here comes the mail.

Smithwick asked a prison building superintendent named Sheppard for help in crafting a letter to someone not on his approved mailing list. When Sheppard pressed him, Sam revealed it was for Stevenson. "Sam said he was old and nervous; that he couldn't write good. He asked me to write the letter for him," Sheppard later told his captain. An inmate bookkeeper, Herb Cochran, was enlisted to translate from the Spanish that made up a lot of Sam's speech. Sheppard looked at Cochran's typing twice, got Sam to sign it and then passed it over to Warden Moore. That was the last he heard of it. And because he worked the day shift, Sheppard wasn't around a few weeks later on the night of April 11.

So either somebody looked at Sam's letter in the warden's office, or the warden didn't give a hoot because he disliked Johnson; in any case the letter leaves the prison after who knows how many eyeballs got to it. It had a few errors of spelling, facts and dates, but got its point across.

Dear Sir:

You probably do not remember who I am but I am the fellow who got in trouble in Alice over killing Mr. Mason, something that I regret very much and I am now serving a life sentence in the Texas Penitentiary.

I am writing to you in regard to the 1949 Election in Jim Wells county when you were running against Lindon Johnson as you recall the election box with all the votes disappeared and that is the main cause of my trouble with Mr. Mason as he was on one side and I was on the other.

On June 24, 1949, five days before I got in trouble I arrested Gonzalo Loera, the son of Maria Loera, and Lupe Garcia, the son of Melario Garcia, and from the learned that Louis Salas who was the depot agent at that time, and a bossom friend of Mr. Mason's, had stolen the box and give it to them to dispose of, but I recovered the box from them and am quite sure that I can produce it if you are interested. I could never get in touch with you because I didn't have a chance or anyone to trust to send to you and was never allowed to make bond after that. I intended to get in touch with you, but after recovering the box and getting it safely away, on my way to contact you I met up with Mr. Mason and as you know what the result was now.

If it would be possible for you to come to Huntsville Prison to visit with me at your earliest convenience, I would like to go into this matter in detail with you.

I trust that I will hear from you in the very near future.

Respectfully yours, Sam Smithwick, #118236

Stevenson headed for Huntsville after breakfast on April 12th accompanied by the most famous Texas Ranger, Frank Hamer. (He was the lawman who delivered a hail of justice to Bonnie and Clyde in '32; another time, less than admirable, he reportedly fled from a town rather than confront a white mob hanging a black man assumed guilty of a sex crime). Along the way the ex-governor called the prison to alert them of his arrival, but was told not to bother as his intended appointment had self-cancelled.

Somebody up or down the line knew that Sam was prepared to say too much to the wrong person. Sam certainly had reason to be depressed and fearful of the risk of ratting out the eighty-seven votes. No wonder he'd be so despondent as to commit suicide. *Why didn't everybody just get that?*

This didn't end the fracas around the eighty-seven votes that sent Johnson on his way to history. The whole subject pestered LBJ up to his death in 1972. There was never a visible line from Smithwick to Johnson, but the volcanic dust of Box 13 never left the thirty-sixth President's suit.

In 1964 Barry Goldwater's Presidential campaign bought up a garage-full of copies of "A Texan Looks at Lyndon," a thorny self-published book from back in the Fifties, and "Wild Bill" Mason became famous again.

The author was J. E. Haley, a right-wing businessman and political hopeful who was no fan of *l'empire Parr*. The tome detailed how Bill's murder, the ballot box and a disreputable, tubby lawman were just two degrees of separation away from the guy who was now President, so look, people, follow the dots.

Haley aimed the book at the dot-following crowd that wanted to believe the worst of Johnson, those willing to charge he was the secret showrunner on the Kennedy assassination. Anyone with a distaste for liberalism bought it and with the Goldwater campaign's push "A Texan Looks at Lyndon" became the biggest-selling political book in history. More than five million copies, maybe seven. That's how far Bill Mason's martyrdom reached.

There was, of course, Caro's LBJ bio decades later, giving Bill and Sam a tidbit in the volume's shelf space at Barnes and Noble. (It was to Caro that Luis Salas, the *pistolero* and railroad radioman who was also, quite handily for Parr, a county election judge for a time, confirmed that he'd lied about the results of the '48 election to investigators.) Smithwick was also exhumed in two pages of a messy volume by frothing conservative provocateur Roger Stone, who sought to pin the jailhouse suicide (along with a half-dozen other corpses) on Johnson and his minions.

The most effective recounting of Smithwick's inviting himself to be a rat fink for Stevenson was in Mary Sparks' paper about my grandfather's murder, and in the later "Faustian Bargains" by Joan Mellen, an author and professor at Temple University in Philadelphia. She turned up research on the chimpanzee poop-fight that was Texas politics by veteran Time/Life reporter Holland McCombs that Caro didn't cite in his books.

Even the noble municipality of Alice, in its official 2018 city magazine, was willing to admit to the tarnishing of its reputation in those Bad Years with a paragraph on the Box 13/Mason/Smithwick triad.

The now-closed Newseum in Washington, D.C., noted Bill's killing in the Freedom Forum Journalists Memorial. The still-open Wikipedia relates some of the story.

In 1975, twenty-six years after Bill was buried, George Parr ended up a fugitive from tax convictions, sitting as dead people sometimes do, under a steering wheel, this time in a '69 Chrysler Imperial in a Texas pasture, a bullet in his head and a gun in his lap. The following January, Mike Wallace reported on the Duke of Duval on CBS' *Sixty Minutes.* Opening the report with a photo of Bill's tombstone in Alice, Wallace included among the subject's many alleged misdeeds the story of how Bill ended up on the fiery end of Parr's patience and a deputy's distemper.

In the early '90s Duval County officials organized a tribute to Parr on the second floor of a local museum. The George Parr Room was set to feature Ballot Box 13, but plans fell through when the *objet d'art* didn't show. A facsimile was unearthed but it was the wrong size and shape. The head of the historical commission would only say they were negotiating with someone who didn't specifically admit to having the box. Rumors claimed the little treasure just walked away at a county auction, while one report had it being tossed in the Rio Grande. The George Parr Room was dismantled.

So, Sam Smithwick set himself up for self- or otherwise-induced suicide by trying to cash in his insurance policy, the disappeared Box 13. But this dumbass with a closet of shitty ties wouldn't have needed insurance in the first place if he hadn't gone off and shot Bill Mason.

(Brings us to the next true, can't-make-it-up *Strange Snick*®: I found all this – the misadventurous, multi-married grandfather/P.R. man/ radio announcer, the hauntings of a sour lawman, the corruptions and the crusades, the bum choices and defects of character, not to mention a YouTube of an old TV show – as I sat at a desk in the basement of a middle-class house where I'd lived for fifteen years in a suburban Jersey development laid out atop what had been a peach orchard, just around the corner from Smethwycke Drive.)

Like a guy grabbing wind-swept twenties off the street when an armored truck gets whacked by the falling piano and caroms sacks of bills out the back door, I spent months stuffing my pockets with my grandfather. There was an intrigue with, sympathy for, acceptance of these characters in the family, but not what you'd call love. It was more of a regard and respect for Bill and Charlotte as historical figures, just as I held for my grandma's ancestors in Edinburgh and Glasgow.

It went back and forth on Bill, starting with a sense of ownership, a pride in his not putting up with crap, insisting on integrity where people had a right to expect it. Then it would flip to some unkind thoughts about Bill's taking too many drinks and whatever else Bill might have done in his life (automotive and otherwise) that projected dismal shades across his boy Burt. In turn, I'd allow a gold star for trying to raise Burt and Marilyn after Charlotte died (but not how it happened), then counter with a red check for marrying a woman who wouldn't like his kids and packed them off to Lonely School.

For the first time in my life, I had two grandfathers. The one living on Pine Street who gave me what resources and love the old man could muster. The other was in the grave three years when I happened along. My mother knew nothing about Bill and Charlotte, or that her ex-husband's father was murdered. Burton may have mentioned the man's name to her over a drink that first night in the Press Bar, but nothing else... although that didn't seem like Burt. One would think he'd slowly, cagily lay out such a sympathy-inducing story about his lost father for a wide-eyed nurse as they dated... but, no.

Even if Bill Mason had been alive in '52, would Burt have told him about the boy who didn't exist?

Burton's life subsequent to the Shakespearean burial of a murdered father would challenge most observers to abstain from a sarcasm that could easily drift into sputtered laughter.

Two weeks after the shooting, the night someone set fire to Rancho Alegro, Burt was two hundred and forty miles to the northeast in Houston. That's where three guys beat the crap out of him at 2AM.

Burt was with a woman described as his secretary and/or girlfriend, Flossy Kennedy, a waitress from Dorman's Drive-In who also worked at KBKI. The couple had stopped for a traffic light on South Main on their way to the town of Victoria where the lady's parents lived. The other men pulled up in a convertible and Burt said they "hurled some vulgar epithets" at him. He might've had a minor collision with them at the corner and frankly, his statements conflicted; he either got out of his car or was hauled out. In any case, after a little smacking around the confrontation somehow moved down the street, and the three went at him again until he lost consciousness.

Flo drove him to Methodist Hospital with a mild concussion, a cracked ankle, assorted lacerations and a purple-red concrete skin-scrape across his forehead the size of a movie star's lipstick.

Being temporarily famous not long before, he was again deemed newsworthy, photographed the next day smoking a cigarette in his bed, the times being such that one could smoke in a hospital. "I just want to prosecute the one who kept sticking his fingers in my eye during the fight," he told a Houston paper.

From his bed at Methodist, Burt told the Houston police no one knew he'd left Alice with Flo. He didn't know if they'd been trailing him, but figured the trouble was unconnected to his father's death and more about molesting Flo. Just paths crossing on a Saturday night at the intersection of Cheap Beer and Insults.

The Wednesday after the attack a tipster delivered two names. The captain of the Houston homicide bureau, who for some reason had been making the public pronouncements about the case, said one assailant admitted his part in the ruckus. A truck driver with a violent criminal record was being sought.

At the end of October, a trial was set for Chester Brinkman, 23, a bus driver, the only one of the three guys in the convertible to be charged. Busy with grand jury proceedings down south, Burton didn't show. Brinkman walked.

(Burt was awarded two appearances in Newsweek that month – eleven years before his underwater adventures were described in the periodical. First, he was the son of a reporter murdered in Texas. Then his suffering at the hands of the street thugs rated its own blurb on the "passing interest" page, alongside an accusation that Stalin and the Russians drank water from vodka bottles while wringing concessions out of drunk American diplomats, a report that touring bandleader Xavier Cugat was being paid by the Spanish with olive oil and the French with a free chateau stay, and a slim note on the first woman pilot to fly around the world, named as "Mrs. Richard Morrow-Tait," although her name was Richarda.)

Burt's foray into radio had a limited run. He already had his own vanity show that summer, *Duval Doings,* under his father's tutelage. A lot of Bill's oversight was required; Burt had been the one to play reporter and fed Bill the unverified information that vilified the innocent sewer engineer the previous spring.

Right after the shooting, Burt made sure the KBKI people knew he wanted to inherit *Bill Mason Speaks.* Management, however, thought that "inadvisable," remarking that "feeling was too high in Alice."

Burt moved on, a karma tumbleweeding along Texan Main Streets.

Early on a Thursday in February of '50, not long after Sam Smithwick took up residence in the Huntsville prison, Burton was in the back shed of a Galveston bar called the Gizmo. He wasn't supposed to be there at 1:45AM with brown cotton gloves, a glass cutter and a pinch bar useful for persuading windows to open. A paper sack with ninety-nine bucks from the register was on hand. Also a .25 caliber pistol he'd swiped from a desk.

A passerby waved down detective J.C. Kline and his partner George Rollish. The cops put the pinch on Burt as he crawled back out through the blades on a ventilation fan he'd pried open.

The sudden grab by the police ignited Burt to cry out, "Don't shoot, don't shoot!"

At the arraignment for "burglary by night" and felony theft he had little to say beyond pleading guilty, and into the pokey he went, waiting for a grand jury that wouldn't convene for six or seven weeks.

A judge finally heard Burt account for his actions, mainly that he "cracked up" after his father was killed and he'd drifted, broke, from Alice to Galveston. He assured he'd never violate the law again, having acquired some good sense in jail and also because he'd inherited some money from his dad and planned to establish a weekly newspaper and shopping guide upstate.

Where did that baloney come from? This was months after his father's death, so if there had been a bequest he would've known about it long before he bent the Gizmo's fan blades. Perhaps Vera quietly promised him some cash through his cell door with a false line about it being his father's to avoid injuring Burt's pride. Or there was no dough, it was just his smoke in the court's face.

The judge gave him five years, suspended. Might have thrown in one of those Western "get out of town by sundown" suggestions.

Burton was fed up with Texas, and the Lonestar State mutually so. At twenty-three, he went back to Ohio.

John Rowley was waiting for him.

There was a young woman, Emily, who was raised with two sisters by Dutch/Hungarian immigrant parents on an Akron estate attached to one of the big tire companies. Their father worked for the company's founder, and he'd come home to his wife in the afternoon to report he'd been with the boss and President Coolidge or Henry Ford, Thomas Edison or John D. Rockefeller. Emily and her siblings would chase around amid amply laden tables in the gardens of the estate during Depression summer picnics, and vacation at the owner's Florida mansion in the cold months.

Young, shiny Emily, curly hair flowing long to frame a high forehead and a small mouth, became attracted to the brother of one of her best friends. They were cozy when he was seventeen and home on leave from the war, in his mariner's uniform with a couple of service bars across the pocket and a wide-brimmed cap, she in loud plaid pants and white buttoned shirt with the tails out, perched on the hood of her dad's two-toned '40 Ford.

In November '46 when Bill and Vera Mason were at General Tire's Waco facility, Burt was nineteen when he married Emily. Domestic rituals were set up in a small, nondescript rented house on Mitchell Avenue. As the following summer dawned, about the time the humorist Steve Martin lived down the street as a fussy two-tear-old, she birthed William Rodney, eight pounds and change, named after a grandfather.

Joyous as that event presumably was, it wasn't much of a year for the young mother. Waco wasn't what she was accustomed to, too little green, too much dirt, with Burt's small-potatoes job at the News-Tribune not providing a lot, not to mention the chickens squawking around the place. She relinquished the town and her young mate and took her baby home to the love of her childhood family in Ohio.

Burt headed off to an equally minor newspaper job in New Mexico while his father tinkered with a new business in Mexico City.

In May '49 the young woman finally filed for a divorce, but that didn't sever all ties to Burt's family.

A few months later she received some telegrams. Around 5PM on a Friday, Western Union processed the first message addressed to Ohio.

... care 1255 West Market St Akron Ohio = Rodney's grandfather shot and killed this morning= Burt=

The next one came after six on Saturday:

Em Dad's Funeral 2 PM Sunday Alice Presbyterian Church Sis Arrived= Burt=

A year later, having escaped Texas after his father's death and his own subsequent misadventures, Burt was living in a room at Akron's inexpensive yet shabby Corine Hotel on High Street when overdue support payments caught up with him. He was hauled in for several days in the county lockup. Managing a $500 bond, he promised to show in court.

That's where he butted heads with John Rowley, the lawyer looking after Emily's interests. "She doesn't mean to be vindictive," Rowley said, but the lady needed help. Little Rodney was already two.

Judge Bernard Roetzel agreed and entered a judgement that Burt pay twenty percent of his future earnings to support the child.

Burt did not attend the hearing alone. At his side was Margaret, a delightful nineteen-year-old clerk with a long, thin face boasting sucker-punch blue eyes and poufy dark hair tumbling down to a white sweater, the daughter of an office manager and an advertising and news man. She'd just enjoyed a spring wedding to Burton the month before in Allen, Indiana, north of Fort Wayne.

On the license application for marrying Margaret, Burt left blank the questions if he could support a family, and his likely continuance of such upkeep. Asked if the child from a prior marriage he'd listed was dependent on him for support, he'd written "no," and skipped the next line about any court orders for support in effect. As a profession he claimed *writer.*

To bolster Burt's courtroom outlook, Margaret sought to persuade Judge Roetzel that sending her new husband to debtor's prison helped no one, and ventured "her father might find him a job." Gazing out at the young wife who'd gotten tied up with a man of shifting resources and dependability, Roetzel said, "Remember, you have married an 80 percent man." Margaret smiled at that, but not sarcastically.

In the following weeks and months she enjoyed her new life with the most charming guy. It's not a comment on Margaret, but rather an indictment of the leitmotif of Burt's life, when the Akron police responded to a call one afternoon and found him in an apartment with his glasses on a nightstand and an anchor tattooed on his right bicep, engaged in disorderly conduct. Similarly held, as she was in bed with the suspect, was a short, thin waitress at a delicatessen. The cops duly noted on their charge sheet for court that the FBI had a Galveston record on Burt. The judge handed down five days in jail with another twenty-five suspended and a fine of $25 plus court costs. The girl got away with fifteen bucks and ten days suspended.

With her husband away for most of the month, Margaret didn't give up that day, she kept at it, put in the work. Who knows what Burt promised that she had to consider, what she had to think and do, those things that marriage requires when despite the bumpy road it still looks better than being alone. There were happy days, and soon some glad tidings, but the time came when one thing outweighed the other.

With his merchant marine card, he could pick up work on the east coast, and get away from all the noise in Ohio.

After one trip in the summer of '51, New York to Puerta le Cruz in Venezuela and back, Burt hitched a ride with some buddies down to Philadelphia. They'd soon check in with the union about the next cargo job out of Marcus Hook, an industrial and refinery hub south of the city on the Delaware River. Maybe stay overnight at the Seaman's Church Institute, a large roomer-style facility along Dock Street, one of the many streets of rutted Belgian blocks that reflected the historical authenticity of Independence Hall five blocks from the waterfront. During the wait for the next posting he'd head out for the usual things – bars, movies, maybe some girls and dancing. Late one night six blocks north of City Hall, his little group wandered into a hangout for local reporters called the Press Bar. Workers from a nearby hospital were in there, too.

Thus followed the quick wedding to my mother and a more drawn-out divorce in the spring of '52. After that Burton spent six weeks running between New York and Nordenham, Germany. He was probably at sea the night they found Sam Smithwick with a roped pillowcase around his neck.

By May he was on Lake Superior, a fireman aboard *LaSalle*, managed by the Cleveland Cliffs Iron Company, on tour from Little Currant in Ontario to Marquette, Wisconsin. Whether he spent the last week of July on land or water is unknown. He wasn't in a hospital on a steamy afternoon in Camden when a nurse gave birth to a boy.

Burt wove in and out of several states where he might have been a line cook and meat cutter, a peddler of brass name plates and ice cream, a warehouseman and oil field roustabout. In '55 he christened a new truck-weighing station along a highway in Connecticut on opening day by being the first driver cited for hauling an overweight load. At one point he claimed to have been a policeman; at another, that he'd been in the television business. Claimed all kinds of things.

The way Burton recounted his interest in underwater salvage, it originated at a diner in the late '50s. The seed may have planted on the deck of *Lyman J. Gage* or *LaSalle*, when Burt spent time with old Navy hands who'd seen a lot of ships sink. Or when he was in Cherbourg harbor and somebody was yakking about how much tonnage had gone down from the German mines and what it was worth if someone could bring it back up.

He'd talked his way into middle management at a large New England fuel oil and equipment dealership. That's when he signed up with the Connecticut Underwater Diving Association. He'd never been deeper than the bottom of a swimming pool, but the whole idea of hotshot, long-shot explorers drew him in, attracted by the physicality and economic possibilities.

After a weekly CUDA meeting some members stopped for coffee. That's where one of them mentioned a German submarine site off Block Island. Burton drifted away that night with a "dream of ocean conquest."

Four others agreed to join in a search for the sub as Burt talked it up, some bringing experience (young photographer Dave Trisko had done salvage work before). They got matching windbreakers with an embossed label for *SubMarine Research Associates*. Mason was enthusiastic about gathering information, traveling to Chicago and Arlington to study plans and artifacts, spending so much time the fuel company fired him.

He might have also studied a guy who couldn't be more different from him yet was after the same thing.

Oswald Bonifay was a cartoon-dapper gent with the prominent forehead and arching brows of a hotel ballroom pianist. Bonifay showed up on a Newport dock in 1953 with seemingly unlimited pockets and a focus on U-853, displaying documents purported to be high-level government stuff. He hired men and a fishing boat to do dive after secretive dive. Eventually he revealed the goal was a huge load of mercury; every sub used thousands of pounds of it as ballast.

Right, made perfect sense, sure, the Nazis must have sent their last mercury stockpile to their allies in Japan via U-boat, but without explanation Helmut Fröemsdorf ended up getting it sunk south of Rhode Island after taking a potshot at a coal carrier. What? Was this was the great secret mission Fröemsdorf wrote about in a letter to his mother, what his frightened young seamen told their parents would prevent their ever returning home? Bonifay knew about those letters, the U-boat's blueprints, all of it; he was convinced of the booty and apparently others were also.

(Years later, a German consul in Boston named Lang denied that U-853 carried a "treasure," saying, "Only the normal amounts of mercury maintained for the operation of any submarine, and no surplus amounts, were on the vessel, according to an investigation made into official war records by the German government.")

Bonifay's well-funded guys who asked him no questions hauled up souvenir parts from the U-boat and some propellers (displayed for years on the lawn of a Newport hotel, the Inn at Castle Hill, before eventually winding up at a nearby naval base), and they nearly got killed by the bends and other aqua-bio irregularities. But no mercury. Bonifay's ultimately wasteful quest got some good rumors going around the docks of the region, the kind Burt would hear a few years later while he sat in a diner with some men who dove into the past with hopes of securing their future.

If Bonifay, man of mystery, managed to stay out of jail with his quarter-million in tax debts, his real estate, young tootsie wife and war-surplus PT boats, maybe Burt could live like that, too.

Through the spring of 1960 Mason's "Associates" negotiated equipment and a boat, and an orthodontist whose own craft was in the shop loaned out his captain. On May 6, the fifteenth anniversary of the fatal shots on the U-boat, the team headed out to the ocean. Two of them had air regulator trouble and had to nix the dive. One was seasick, as was Burt. A decade later, he recounted his first meeting with the briny ghost. "I saw the shadow of the deck before the regulator froze up and I had my first 'scared shitless' experience. Dave got about as deep before it happened to him."

Not long after the U-boat dives, Burt recalled to a reporter with all the drama he could muster, "I had to suck on my regulator with all my might to get enough air and it never seemed like enough. My custom-made suit leaked and I grew numb with the cold.

"Hand over hand, six inches at a time, I lowered myself down the wire. I don't know how deep I got. I saw the shadows turn to angles and take form of some kind. I must have recognized that this was something other than the bottom. At this point panic swept over me… it seemed this monster below was crouching for a strike and I was the target…

"The terror I felt could not be matched by the most violent childhood nightmare. I felt I was suffocating. I forgot everything I had been taught and raced for the surface as fast as I could swim."

Thus was inspired the half-page grit-and-charcoal illustration in a New York Sunday paper, berthed beside the headline "Mystery At 20 Fathoms." There was Burt, artistically interpreted, wide-eyed in the hull of a wrecked sub, training his powerful beam down to a skeleton trapped under the tailfin of a fallen torpedo, its leather jacket half-zipped and wide-belted, all flesh dissolved to leave a skull with pleading, fearful eye sockets and a large, fully-toothed Aryan jaw, a bony arm reaching out along the deck, stretched finger, *got... to... reach... my... cellphone... agh.*

While a partner named Bradbury brought up some muddy life rafts that were still in good condition, the instruction labels still plainly readable and the carbon dioxide inflation bottle intact, that was the end of the team effort. Only Burt and Dave were willing to go down again after that. And they needed a better footing. That's when Burt found *Summer Palace*, the has-been Astor yacht with the chintz curtains and a temperamental engine. They "paid for it with a loan from a very nice bank in Stamford."

Burt kept up the homework: back issues of small newspapers in coastal villages, state maritime records, fishermen who might have snagged old wrecks. They pried up objects and metals out of subs like U-754, destroyed by planes off the southern tip of Nova Scotia after the Germans sank a civilian fishing boat and brutally machine-gunned the crew trying to lower its life raft.

In the fall of '62 Burt came across a big prize, not below the surface but at eye level. Amid those famous, atomically tense Ten Days in October, it happened on the day Moscow caved to President Kennedy's public pressure and back-channel diplomacy and began pulling its missiles out of Cuba. A Soviet trawler of the type ostensibly used for fishing but long suspected of carrying electronic spy gear along the American coasts, its Communist hammer and sickle logo painted on the upper deck, was patrolling twenty miles off Nantucket. Burt cruised to within two hundred feet of it, snapping pictures of its Cossack-hatted captain peering at him through binoculars and the Russian crew waving happily at the Yank. The Boston Globe printed his photos.

In early '64 Burt took what would be the last picture of one of his partners, Al Prejean, twenty-seven, out on the boat. Al was, shall one say, very close to Burt's sister Marilyn. The bushy-browed former Army hard hat diver, part of the *Oregon* team, drowned next to the American sub they'd been stripping parts from. Suspicion was cast on Al's breathing apparatus and double air tanks that gave him thirty-five minutes of operating time. After Burt brought his friend's body back to the surface, he removed Prejean's equipment and donned it, going back into the water to test it and it all worked just fine. (Things happened to scuba regulators; Dave Trisko's once froze up from moisture that blocked the air flow and forced a swim to the surface that might have brought on the bends.)

Along came a hitchhiker, Gerald Foley. Much like Burt he'd plowed through a lot of jobs. Gerald enjoyed this new line of work and spent eighteen months diving with Burt off a boat called *Skatte Jaeger*. They worked the site of the "other *Oregon*" (this was a small Cunard liner hit by a schooner off Long Island in 1886) until the day Foley went down and never came back. Burt said it was a great white that took him, and this wouldn't be the only time Mason claimed a shark attacked one of his cohorts.

From then on, Burt went solo, no more business partners: "I never want to go through that again." He once claimed to be grossing fifty to seventy-five thousand dollars a year, but that expenses were higher. So as a matter of economics, he still had to take work with other salvagers, including Nick Zinkowski, who vied with Mason to be the first to locate *Oregon*.

Boats cost a lot to own, lease, operate. There was *Force Five*, a hundred and thirty-five feet of capability he rented out when he wasn't pursuing a wreck. On *Force Five* a hard-hatted crew fitted his diving helmet and gear, and babied a diving bell along the deck. That vehicle was a tubular base fifteen feet long and a ball sitting fifteen high, all with multiple eight-inch windows and an observation glass two feet across at the bow.

One of Burt's successes was in finding *Seal*, developed in the mid-nineteenth century by the submarine inventor Simon Lake, in Narragansett Bay. This was an early prototype of submarine design and had wheels for crawling on the seabed. One of *Seal's* features was the first retractable periscope; Mason lugged it topside and turned it into a lamp for his home, along with a depth gauge that became a clock.

His "art from the sea" career was thus underway, a niche in which he could be the single professional, a craftsman, a unique fellow selling unique stuff.

He set up a shop in Brookline, outside Boston, to craft the Twenty Fathom line of "Art-décor-utility recovered from the ocean floor," as his new business card crowed. He enlisted some students from the Museum of Fine Arts in the city to make up gift items.

Business envelopes had a three-inch tall illustration of a scuba diver jumping into the water, grappling hooks on the belt and a lit-fuse six-pack of dynamite sticks in his hand. Sure was an exciting selling point, as long as he didn't send any to the Coast Guard in Portland.

On road trips, he visited stores like Halle Brothers in Cleveland. The "famous deep sea diver" would sell you a desk barometer on a piece of wood for thirty-five bucks (equal to more than two hundred today), $100 lamps, a vase of metal and wood for $89.50.

In one Yankee Magazine photo, holding an eighteen-inch-wide clock fabricated from a submarine depth gauge, Burt looked like a puffy-jowled jeweler, carrying his father Bill's face, his chin disappearing a bit, a tousle of hair across the forehead. In another picture, set against a water backdrop, with a flop-top mop of hair, razor-cut beard and sunglasses, he seemed more like an Eastern European criminal prankster preparing to fish with a grenade.

One of his ads was illustrated with a photo of him full-bearded and rough-hewn in rubber regalia, along with bits of the 18th-century wood-block maritime art he enjoyed. It boasted how he could "dive twenty fathoms down to bring up fifty-year-old treasures and design them into gifts for dad." Thrilling text about Davy Jones' locker would incite the reader to go to Burt's meet-and-greets in the Decorative Accessories section at Carson's in Chicago.

The ocean was his wholesaler. From the *Onondaga*, a steel-hulled cargo vessel that hit a reef in 1918, Burt recovered ladies' boots, Japanese pottery and English china, meat grinders, perfume bottles and a motorcycle.

He also dove to *Black Point*, the steel collier built in the shipyards of Camden, New Jersey in 1917, longer than a football field, a ripe if ill-timed target when it crossed paths with Helmut Fröemsdorf's U-boat in May of '45. There were plenty of instruments and such lying about the bridge.

And everywhere across the ocean floor there was wood, knarled and hardened, ready for a steady knick-knack hand to bring it back to life.

The grand passenger steamer *Larchmont* handled the run for the Joy Line from Providence to New York City in 1907. Its white wood hull was over twenty years old, the side wheel propulsion powered by steam engines the size of a row house.

In the bitter, shattering cold of clear February nights, the wind across the east end of Long Island Sound churned the water to twenty feet and sprayed up snow squalls. A hundred and fifty people, possibly many more, sat up all night hanging onto the rows of benches in the salon, a seagoing bus terminal, except those bedded in the expensive cabins below. Sick people in both ticket classes made messes on the floor and in what buckets were handy.

A few miles off Watch Hill Point along came the coaling schooner *Henry Knowlton*, a low-slung tub of rocks with sails. The two crews, each surprised by the sudden appearance of the other ship's lights among the swells, kept making evasive moves but still glided into the other's path like two bicyclists magnetically attracted to the same stretch of sidewalk.

Henry Knowlton ripped a cavity into *Larchmont's* port side near the giant paddle box, cutting through the main steam pipes and dismantling all the power. The weight of sea water crumpled the insides and the passengers with money never got out of their cabins. People in nightclothes froze in the seaspray, clinging to ropes and pipes. The deck disappeared into the water in just twelve minutes. Five lifeboats got away, and some rafts. By the time the boats came ashore a few miles away, most aboard had succumbed to hypothermia.

Seventeen, maybe nineteen people came out of it alive, with or without all their fingers. Captain George McVey and seven crewmen commandeered a boat; they stuck to their story of trying to pick up others but not succeeding. Eight survivors were found surrounded by iced bodies clinging atop the roof of a deckhouse that ripped off the ship. Some estimates of the dead went to two-fifty; with no manifest, the count would never be known. The tides deposited dozens of stiffs on Block Island for days. Pictures of them were turned into postcards.

Nothing could have been done for *Larchmont's* travelers even if it had the new, but still basic, radio technology that was being introduced. It went down with an asterisk on the books as the last passenger vessel to sink prior to the radio era.

Fifty-seven years later Burt poured through newspaper accounts of *Larchmont*, well-known regionally as New England's own little *Titanic*. After his adventures with U-853 and *Oregon* and the TV quiz show appearance that garnered him basically nothing, he was living on a salvage ship called the *Gerry Kay*. He spent an early summer's day weight-dragging across an area he suspected might hold the wreck. Then he bumped into a pair of fishermen, two brothers named Roderick who'd hooked the ship accidentally with a net a few years before.

He used their coordinates but got off to some false starts; Burt used the wrong beachside hotel on the horizon to line up with the anglers' estimates. Once that muddle was corrected, Burt and his partner Charley Warren, a diving instructor, used an ultrasonic depth sounder over the recommended spot. *Larchmont* was two hundred and fifty feet long and would certainly throw a shadow. In twenty minutes they got a reading a hundred and twenty-five feet down.

It wasn't until late August that they dropped a line from *Aggie-M* to snag the wreck. Charley followed it down to see what it had grabbed and become the first person in almost six decades to touch *Larchmont*.

Burt followed soon after in a scuba outfit suitable for quick exploring rather than a pressure suit with air hoses more matched to long-term salvage and repair tasks.

Central features of the ship were still upright, the paddle wheels in mid-spin, the starboard smokestack forty feet high, pretty remarkable considering decades of powerful tides. Burt described it: "The wooden hull had collapsed, folding outward like the petals of a flower, and forming a cuplike depression" holding the debris of the superstructure broken down into it.

There were no skeletons, long freed by tiny creatures and swift currents, drifting and becoming beach sand.

Burt was hoping to sift the debris for *Larchmont's* main safe. Construction blueprints he acquired showed the purser's office with the safe behind the port paddle wheel. That part of the structure either crumbled straight down or pitched forward into the collapsed center of the vessel.

Marking the position topside with buoys made from beer barrels, Charley and Burt went down numerous times and brought up a fire extinguisher, some crockery and boxes holding more than a thousand eight-inch metal files. Burt went out with that teenager named Earl and found a small private safe with some coins. (One career-total accounting of coins retrieved was less than ten dollars.) Still, Burt said he never failed to locate a wreck he wanted to find.

Okay for a guy who never finished high school.

Burt often went all Hemingway about his attraction to the ocean. "The sea is the one place where man is an independent unit, the lesser power in an unequal struggle. The sea does not like to give up what it has claimed. Whatever I recover is brought up in constant battle against an ocean that tries to keep what it has won."

Aside from the recording of Burt on *To Tell the Truth*, the only way to hear Burt, to discern him, is to read Burt. One had to wonder if magazine reporters in the '60s were getting it right. Why did the man talk like a press release, like a rehearsed set of note cards at a CUDA convention, toned like a motivational speaker? That's how he sounded when he was a teenager in that newspaper account of being under fire in Cherbourg (assuming his cadence and structure were quoted correctly along with the words). Maybe that's all he really had to relate to people, some situational performance art, to inhabit a role as the "underwater expert."

He confessed to Lawrence Willard, a writer for Yankee, how that coffee in the Bridgeport diner "cost me my job, my credit rating, and what had been heretofore a comparatively normal way of life."

As if Burt's life was anywhere near normal even before his responding to the sea's siren. Burt didn't tell Willard everything, all the rank details of a confused biography. Just the grand philosophy and enough background to stage the romantic underdog who's ready to take it on.

"Everyone may be equal, but only until the umbilical cord is cut, after that it is dog eat dog. Once you set a goal, fight for it until your last breath. To quit before you succeed is to join the sheep which compromise the majority of humanity."

Being sheepish about anything was never Burt's style, unless it was in front of a judge.

The tale was told endless times. It was described in newspapers and passed down in family lore. The one Burt often related to a reporter or someone else who needed to be impressed with that man-against-nature ideology. The one about how his diving partner was trapped on U-853, caught by a hatch in the conning tower that had collapsed on the poor guy. In the first version of the story it had taken three half-hour dives across as many days for the partners to pry up the rusted steel plate, only to have it finally fall like a beartrap on the buddy's flipper, which Burt lifted enough for a tense escape. By the following year's recounting, they had only fifteen minutes of air left and it took them twelve minutes to free the man from his twisted fate under the plate, and with their scant remaining moments of oxygen they managed to reach the surface while avoiding the bends of decompression.

The story was even more traumatic and ick-worthy when Burt related it to his own family, with the ugly details he hadn't admitted to the various news guys. That the partner couldn't be freed, forever caught by the collapsed hatch, that his air ran out, that Burt had to leave him with his own supply diminishing, and when he returned for the body, the sharks had done their sharky thing and all that remained was the piece of leg sticking out of the rusty trapdoor.

That's why nobody heard ever again from Dave Trisko.

Trisko was the other guy who shared Newsweek ink, the dive partner I read about when I was fourteen, so often described in tabloid accounts and adventure magazines but never actually quoted. Wasn't likely to, what with his demise in the deep.

Except Trisko didn't see it that way.

"Let me tell you something about Burt. He never went down to the sub."

Trisko would know. Dave, enjoying a retired life years later in a sunny clime with all limbs accounted for, had his own memory of being caught by the falling plate on U-853. Extricating his leg took him but thirty seconds. He had tanks with eighty-four cubic feet of air, enough to dive for two hours.

This assumes he spoke the truth, a credible, vivid truth that would match the facts reported by other participants or witnesses. Then there could be "his truth," that singular license we all carry, what he experienced about his partner both on earth and in deep water, where what you see of people and behavior is immersed in a defiant dark fog made barely gray by a blary lamp that still didn't tell you which way was up.

Yet Trisko's little adventure in the conning tower, once translated into Burt-speak, took on a life of its own, repeated every time Mason wanted to dramatize the risk of the heroic diving life.

Trisko was born in Bridgeport in 1935 and began diving when he was sixteen. By twenty-two he was experienced with the adrenalin of hazardous exploration, throwing technical confidence against the whims of the sea. As a member of the Connecticut Underwater Diving Association, he wound up in a volunteer team dragging a Long Island harbor for a member who drowned, and took minor jobs including the cleanup of debris in the Housatonic River that paid him fifty bucks or so.

At CUDA meetings he met Bob Anderson from Wisconsin, two guys named Teddy and Pete, and George Swindell, a machinist from Bridgeport who had a family and taught a scuba class Burt joined at the Boys' Club. They'd stop at a diner after meetings where George, who was developing a new style of helmet, got them interested in a German U-boat designated on local charts with "unexplored depth charges 1945."

Part of the allure was the possibility of finding a design of acoustic honing torpedo developed by the Germans late in the war. "It followed the propeller noise of *Black Point*," Trisko said. "The witnesses who were saved from *Black Point* saw the torpedo make a turn and come right up the stern."

After the long assault that finally put the sub out of action, the Navy sent divers down. Trisko knew they wanted identification of the pain-in-the-ass boat, but suspected there was something else on board – an Enigma machine, the early computer the Germans had used to cipher-talk their military (without knowing the Allies, meaning some Polish mathematicians and, later, Alan Turing and those women in Bletchley Park, had broken the code and used it to track and suppress the Germans for years).

On an Easter Sunday, Swindell, Trisko and the rookies in the initial group dove on the U-boat in thirty-eight-degree water. It was on a subsequent dive that Burt came down, his first and last as Trisko knew it. This guy wasn't a diver; the man Dave came to know was a grandiose talker, a promoter.

"I made about sixty-eight to seventy dives on the U-boat," Trisko recalled. "Burt made one dive. Might've gone down around sixty feet, swam around a bit, then went back up. And after that he made a plan to make an enterprise out of the deal.

"That's when the light went off in Burt's head. Like everybody else, he thought there was a ton of American currency, all kinds of crap on the sub."

Dave demurred at these plans. He didn't buy into Oswald Bonifay's exotic theories, but was content to bring up standard artifacts in hope of a decent price from nautical trophy-seekers.

In the postwar years, Jacques Cousteau's invention of a self-contained underwater breathing apparatus achieved deep-water diving free from hardhat gear, the weight, the air tubes. Scuba's independence benefited the experienced, cautious and wise. It also attracted the unrestrained and imprudent.

"We got all kinds of bozos sitting around thinking of ways to raise this sub, a dead weight, right out of the ocean," Trisko said. "It's got torpedoes hanging in their block and tackle ready to go into the forward tubes. I don't know if those torpedoes were contact or pressure, but if they were pressure, and the pressure changed when you raised the sub, we're all in deep yogurt."

One day two guys showed up seeking an outfit to do the hard work for their respective purposes. One was a rep for David Susskind, a New York producer and host of a public affairs show that was often a cage match for irrepressible points of view. His company "Susskind Presents" did notable work in television drama and bankrolled the films *A Raisin in the Sun* and *Requiem for a Heavyweight*.

This assistant wanted film of U-853 for a Susskind documentary on the Battle of the Atlantic. His appearance on Burt's dock signaled legitimacy, the payoff from a TV quiz show and Newsweek exposure. A reward for the branding, the attention-seeking, the stretching "I'm your man" confidence he threw out at potential partners and reporters looking for the authentic story on men and the sea. To get a top gun like Susskind in your corner would elevate you, propel you. Only thing better than that for a scrapper would be coming across a suitcase of hundred-dollar bills wrapped in plastic, abandoned in some recent wreck nobody would've reported because the seacocks were open and there were little holes in the hull.

The second man who came to see Mason and Trisko was a suitor from Freedomland, an eighty-five acre theme park in the Bronx designed by an ex-Disneyland executive. He was packing an offer to put up the money to raise the sub because U-853 would make a helluva attraction for the ninety-thousand-plus visitors a day. (The park opened in 1960 and closed four years later due to inadequate public-transit access, rampant mosquitoes from the landfill it was built on, and its proximity to the new, super-attractive World's Fair over in Flushing that had its own historic displays and thrill rides.)

The two visitors' inquiries weren't competing, so Burt, doing all the talking as usual, could entertain both proposals. He could be a technical adviser for a bigshot TV producer and also fulfill the grandiose mission to capture history for future generations in the form of a submarine eighty yards long, leased for display at whatever rate of economic consideration could be negotiated.

Dave recalled he might've actually spoken with Susskind on the phone just once, but had no idea what the business arrangements were. The roles of the Mason/Trisko relationship had long been accepted, routine: Dave and a couple of helpers handled the tough stuff underwater and Burt stood on the dock and gave instructions, collected retrieved objects and took the money. "In the very beginning he suited up maybe once or twice. I hate to knock him on this," Trisko said, but he didn't credit his partner with achieving much in the water.

"The only time I saw him was when he was on the dock jumping and screaming, 'how come you guys aren't out in the water? How come I don't have more film? Blah, blah blah.' "

Trisko recorded their adventures with a sixteen-millimeter Bolex. "No one else knew how to use it, so I never appeared in any of the pictures."

For still shots he used a German-made Rolli-Marine, a big lump of green iron housing with clamps and levers that looks like it's supposed to join pipes on an oil drill. In addition there was a pair of thousand-watt lights to wrassle with, powered by a thirty-five hundred-watt generator up on the boat.

"He'd pick up the film, five or six rolls that I'd shot, bitching and moaning," Dave said. "I was the one who laid out the plans about who was going down, who would hold the lights, what we'd do that day, and we'd go down and do that part of the filming. I shot all the film, which I never saw after that, believe it or not. He sold the film to somebody."

The crew "got no money from it. We had to beg to buy food sometimes" from others on the docks and around nearby Old Harbor.

Trisko witnessed the widely reported confrontation over the U-boat with the German government. "We had a luncheon one day, it was Burt, myself, another guy I can't place, and a U-boat commander from the first war, an old guy in his sixties.

"They wanted us to sign papers saying that if we found anything of value on the sub, the German government was going to get half, or a percentage. The argument ended up with Burt talking about how they're not going to get anything unless the Germans put up money to do the work. So we never got anything. Zip."

In his press narratives, Burt laid claim to details from the sub's interior, the way an officer's paraphernalia lay about, and how German pinup photos still hung in the crew compartments. As if paper would still be flapping after fifteen years in the water when uniforms and bodies had decomposed.

At the meeting, the old German officer "asked what the sub was like inside, where this was and that was, and Burt couldn't tell him. I had to tell him," Dave recalled. "The names scratched on the torpedo tubes were that of the sailors, not their girlfriends or actresses.

"What paper was still there was in a big roll of charts that I brought up, of everything about American waters off New England, the shallows, the buoys, all that. It stayed compressed in a sealed tube, only the edges were wet.

"I had it drying up on the boat one day when we were tied up at Block Island. I had a big pair of German binoculars, the kind that would be mounted on a tripod. Somebody stole it all. We were away from the boat or down inside working, and every artifact we had, somebody took it. Never showed up again."

Trisko could not, or would not, speculate whose fingerprints were on that episode.

Burt would one day remark that only with a bank's help could he afford the motor cruiser *Summer Palace*, priced at around $4,200. He convinced the Old Stone Bank it would gain grand publicity benefits from supporting the U-boat explorations. But it wasn't Burt who took out the loan.

"I signed for buying the damn boat," Trisko said. "Some years later when I came back (from the U.S. Virgin Islands, where he'd been in his own business) they were waiting for me with a subpoena for the remaining money due on the boat." The note went unpaid by the partner handling the cash flow, so Dave got stuck with it. Not the boat with its old chintz curtains and a Chrysler flat-8 engine that did more harm than good... just the debt.

Dave got fed up, stopped returning Burt's calls, packed up his gear and left the pier, the work, the ego and the annoying nonsense behind, as did George Swindell, as did most people Burt vacuumed into his big, airy plans. (George headed for the Gulf to make a business of his adjustable, fiberglass Swindell helmet and became a leading diver in oil exploration. He died in a fishing boat sinking in 2005.)

Trisko headed back to the Virgin Islands having never seen *To Tell the Truth*, or the many published accounts of Burt's adventures. In St. Thomas he met June, a delightful brunette secretary from North Jersey, married her, continued in the boating business and started a family. In their later years they lived in the South, not all that close to the water, but content with a quieter life, hooking good-sized fish on short trips to warm waters. He still has the Bolex and the Rolli-Marine on a shelf.

On one point Trisko ventured an opinion. Considering what he knew of Burt at the time they parted ways, was his partner capable of learning what it would take to dive deep, the skills and courage and instincts? Would he be the one down there doing the actual dives, *Oregon, Larchmont,* all that? A serious scrapper?

"Absolutely not," Trisko said. "I'd fall out of my chair."

"He was always very nervous. He didn't have time to do anything. He had this business, heating and air conditioning, and that's all I heard from him. That he had a family to take care of and complaining about us guys moping around… like he was paying us."

And yet, in those years after Dave kissed him off, reporters invited out on the boats for real-life observation would watch Burt put on the scuba gear, flop over the side and disappear into dark water, emerging with quotable insights and the occasional evidence from some wreck, like a fistful of wool or a captain's clock that would make a fine lamp base.

One way or another, Mason turned himself into a diver.

Just like everybody who knew my father, Trisko offered *some* truth as verified by others, and he also held *his* truth from his own experiences with his U-boat partner.

His truth was specific: "Burt was a diver as long as he didn't go too deep."

Many men in the business of risking and conquering in dark water didn't have the time or temperament for a stable domesticity. Guys like that were always away. Always committed to something out on the water, or just out. That's where they could do that masculine thing, in the company of those who could be trusted (usually) with your life, like foxholed soldiers. Working close on the boat like that, these guys were preferably lucid, wary and practical, away from society's eyes and opinions, where they understood everybody.

According to an experienced, seen-it-all New England diver who knew about these guys, "There was a distance between the scrappers, the gypsies, and their families.

"Of all the divers I knew," he said, "most never led a typical life. They were extreme at almost everything they did."

Including Burt?

"He was obsessed. Cost him everything."

Younger by a less than a year, Burt's sister Marilyn was looking for her American dream. Meet someone nice, get married, get out of the house if you could, take command of your life and call it your own without the parental wings always flapping around you. Burt had gone off with Emily when he was still in his late teens. Marilyn's ticket to a new life as she entered her twenties was Pete Krones.

Pete was a Philadelphia guy, an engineer and a decade older, working for Pan American Airlines. He had a stop on a business trip in Mexico City and in a hotel elevator he bumped into young Marilyn, who was visiting her folks when Bill was working on Presidente Aleman's campaign. Back in the States they pursued a romance and married in South Philly. His career led him toward the marketing office of the aircraft company Pratt & Whitney, and the couple set up housekeeping in Manchester, Connecticut, near Hartford.

It wasn't long before she was off to Texas for a funeral.

She loved her brother because little sisters usually do. Still, since the Akron days after the war and up through his quick second marriage to Margaret, Marilyn had seen how her brother viewed and treated women. She was, if not just plain disgusted, certainly upset enough to write a letter to my mother in New Jersey, sympathetic to the nurse ensnared in Burton's ever-enlarging web. (Jean kept Marilyn's letter in a drawer for a few years, a sodden bandage for a painful wound, and eventually discarded it when the time came to unload most of the remaining detritus from her life's biggest setback.)

While a son and a daughter with Pete brightened the relationship, Marilyn was partial to drinking and partying. One day Pete returned from a trip and found Marilyn had walked out. Enough was enough for Krones, an old-fashioned Catholic. After a decade of marriage, Pete filed for a dissolution on the grounds of "intolerable cruelty," the basis for many divorces in the state at that time, synonymous with today's popular "irreconcilable differences." He retained custody of the kids; Marilyn took them out on Sundays and was, to some degree, a "fabulous, fun, if non-traditional mother."

While still known as Marilyn Krones socially, my aunt also reverted to her old self, Lynn Mason, for some situations, not all of which went well.

When she was thirty-three, Lynn was living in a two-story apartment building on Marion Street in southwest Hartford. She had a job a few towns away in New Britain managing an Arthur Murray Dancing Studio. This was one of the franchised chains of the mid-century period, perhaps the most well-known, that would prepare a customer for a daughter's wedding, weekend nightclub outings or perhaps simply some living-room twirling. They offered instruction in waltzes, foxtrots or, for advanced students, the vaguely lascivious tango.

The studio's owner, Bill Nickel, began noticing discrepancies between what a new student said he paid for two sets of lessons and what was on the books. Marilyn found herself charged with being slippery with a few hundred bucks, and pleaded guilty to a slightly less malignant charge of obtaining money under false pretenses. The penalty was six months' incarceration, suspended, plus a fifty-dollar fine and one year's probation.

That was too much of a close call. She couldn't let Burton's life become hers. She tried to find normality with a dentist. That marriage lasted five years.

Four more marital tries were waiting in the wings. As was a change in her outlook on life, if she was going to be a female reflection of her brother, or something different.

Since the discovery of *To Tell the Truth*, for a year and a half I shared some of the more dramatic "you won't believe what I found today" revelations with Melanie. She encouraged my further search for the chapters of my life heretofore lost to the ages.

I didn't tell anyone else, save for my mother on that day when I prepared her and shared the video. Not even my own two kids, whose only knowledge of their dad's father came when they were adolescents, when they heard that thing about how there are different ways to make a family, and their dad's family was just Jean. They didn't ask, they weren't told, not through all those years when the other side of their world, their mother's family, was a raucous, nonsensical mob of aunts and uncles and a grandmother with three husbands and a bunch of spittle-dampened cousins and holidays with a decibel level approaching *Guardians of the Galaxy*. Their life with the mom's clan was a scene quite different from their toddler visits with Grandma Jean in the well-tended, tasteful house she owned for a few years, a subdued, uncomplicated milieu, with only Casey the barky terrier scrambling circles around the backyard to interject any hullabaloo.

A few friends knew what was going on, the stuff about the German submarine and then how I found the YouTube and Number Two. I admonished them to keep my silent confidence, fearing if I told somebody, and they told somebody, and that one told a tech-savvy busybody, my existence and quest might somehow leak from behind my curtained secrecy, for which the medical term was probably *paranoia*.

Only I knew when I'd be ready to part the scrim, for my children, for anybody.

As far as the writing pursuit was concerned, I was willing to let go of the short story, wrap it, entertain somebody, without solving the question of the multiple Burtons. The Known B. was certainly a capable one-man tsunami of hurtful crap. In New England there was still an alternate Burton, a real *modoki*, looked the same, sounded the same, but whose provenance had leaks. And Burtons were all over the phone books from everywhere, shloshing around the investigation like so many *Fantasian* marching mop buckets.

The last page would have to support the resolution, which was no resolution, an unsolved mystery leaving both the reader and the author cliff-hanging about which of the two or three Burtons was what/where, and the one who belonged to me, like it or not.

I didn't yet have a Wild Bill and a town called Alice, the lineage of the Hosters and some judicial humor about an eighty-percent man. Or the other factoids emerging like bones in a graveyard of warming spring soil, such as when an old cabinet of marriage documents spilled a secret for a helpful Waco clerk. Or how I could divine my being four degrees of separation from an American president.

Names, clues, attachments, an address semi-confirmed, another colored string pulled taut to link the three-by-five cards splattered CSI-style across a white posterboard.

Tenuous threads, aggressive assumptions, confusing coincidences and cynical conclusions. How to tell a half-illuminated truth from a half-baked mistake?

I would've let go of all this months before, had my father been just some guy in an office or a farmer or a dental equipment dealer in Palookaville. No, the guy had to be a troublemaker, a wheeler-dealer, a hop-skip-and-jumper who got his name in the papers, a fella with no forwarding address who still got to be on TV because he was an "underwater salvage expert."

So I pulled up the YouTube page again. Checked the viewer numbers to pontificate on their meaning. Scrolled down past the video screen one more time for no particular reason, except perhaps to find an ending to the story I had to write, to bring to market, to amaze someone. Just to look.

Added to a couple of old, innocuous comments about Golden Age TV, there was a new one. Somebody not only really enjoyed the segment about the divers on *To Tell the Truth,* but also knew Number Two.

III

THE ONE WHO KNOCKS

Fate is a strange mistress.

At seventeen I'd mastered a few things. I was really good at geography and history, being a bigshot on the school newspaper, taking guys' money in a seven-card poker variant called Sonovabitch, and acting. I was the most serious actor in school, meaning the one you could see going on to an actual thespianic career. It had been that way since landing the lead in the sixth-grade play about a boy who dreams of meeting the nine Parts of Speech, with the clever Conjunction and wisecracking Article that sang and danced their way into his head in time to score an A on the big test.

In my day, only the large regional high schools were putting on massive musicals. In my little burg, for the junior class play some faculty pill picked out a silly bucket of pee called *Shy Guy*, in which I played a cigar-waving TV producer. Not even close to *The Good Woman of Setzuan*, much less *Streetcar*.

The next year the school cheaped out and combined the senior and junior theatrical event, and the Illuminata selected *Enter Laughing*. The play was adapted from the TV pioneer Carl Reiner's story about a young guy who stumbles into show business to pursue an actress. Rather than press-gang a teacher to run the show, they hired an outside director, Dolly Beechman, who I knew from her summer improv class for kids at the big-tent playhouse in the park back when I was twelve.

Mrs. B. was a local theatrical powerhouse who'd say things like *noli timere*, meaning *fear nothing*. Picking up on my sense of timing and a hidden mass of energy bubbling under my sedate nature, she cast me as Marlowe, an imperious stage director who can't fathom being reduced to the unsophisticated scripts and actors he must contend with. Alan Mowbray played the role on Broadway opposite Alan Arkin and Elaine May, and in the film version Jose Ferrer sank his teeth into it. This Marlowe lineage was virile.

In the second act, the lead character David performs in a play-with-in-the-play, ineptly. At a crucial moment near the end, the young hero exchanges dialogue with an older advisor who's trying to wrangle his hands onto the family fortune. played by the hammy Marlowe.

David: Before you open that envelope there is In Existence... another document that may alter the terms of the will.

Marlowe *(snarls)*: I don't believe it, you're lying. *(pauses thoughtfully)* Fate is a strange mistress. *(collapses, dies)*

Blackout. Curtain.

So I was going to have a big bit, the splash to close the second act, a stage-magic moment the audience would talk about, my mom and grandparents and all those students on Saturday night dates plus a few hundred other people.

For the collapse, in rehearsal I improvised a Victorian arched hand to the forehead leading into a full-360 twirling spreadeagle faint to the floor just before the lights went out. Got surprised laughs from the student crew, and Beechman appreciated initiative, so I kept it in.

Thing is, the script supplied by the popular play publisher Samuel French didn't have those words. Maybe there was a young-adult version of the play for high schools in the Sixties, rewritten out of caution that the conservative or Catholic markets wouldn't buy the dangerous original with fate and mistresses and all that. The dialogue had been altered.

David: Before you open that envelope there is In Existence... another document that may alter the terms of the will.

Marlowe *(snarls)*: I don't believe it, you're lying. *(pauses thoughtfully)* Why should anyone believe you?

David *(faces audience, triumphantly)*: Because ... I am secretly...
your younger brother!

Marlowe: *(gasps, gestures, collapses, dies)*

Blackout. Curtain.

Laughter, wild audience applause. Fantastic faint, both shows, a
triumph, a lifetime memory.

Also, pretty cool, a secret brother.

On a May evening, reading a comment posted by a stranger on a
Web page, I became literally different. It was if I received transfused blood
and could feel it running warmer, or maybe saltier, flushing through my
system.

A person changes (not just evolves biologically and/or intellectually
across time) in very limited situations when they were "one person" in a
moment and self-recognizably "another" in the next. The arrival of the
infant that turns a non-parent into one; the accident or crime that permanently befalls; you awake to the surgeon's assurance of a second chance as
long as you swear off the double-bacon cheeseburgers. Those are genuine
moments of change. Lotteries and lays, however glorious, do not qualify.

A year and a half before, I'd experienced this kind of Richter shake
from the diver's national prime-time appearance, watching Burt win a few
hundred bucks and a carton of cigarettes and maybe a celebrity autograph.
The unexpected video reincarnation, those few moments sitting alone with
a YouTube, brought a transformation that muscled its way into my life like
an obnoxious old-days buddy taking advantage of an insincere invitation to
look me up sometime. Burton appeared and then wouldn't, couldn't leave.

I'd stumbled across a cognate, like words with common origin that
evolve into similar or varied or even opposite meanings while always sharing letters and sounds. *Eodem diversi*, the same but distinct.

Nineteen months later, another change. Some woman sparked it with a comment posted to a massive electro-bulletin board. While all that I had been before, the personality, the capabilities and defects, the politics and paunch, were of course untouched, on this night as a living, experiencing person I just felt… different.

At first I wasn't seeking such an episode born of surprise or investigation, no more than I sought a return of *petit mal* epilepsy. It had been a half century since my mother unpacked the Newsweek articles suggesting Burt had more than one child. Longer still since the mechanisms of my emotional self began their quilting, like the crackle-pattern of frost building on a window, the neural auto-responses to protect me and diminish the volatility of being cheated, deprived, angry.

After all that time I felt no impetus to dash off a letter or grab the phone, to pack a bag and hit the road. No interior fuse-lighting to charge into no-man's-land.

And if Burt's other kid, or kids, had waited so long to appear, let them hang on a few more weeks. Or months. The fog would bound burn off eventually.

Besides, I was busy. Now that I was different, there was finding out more, finding enough, all that getting ready to get ready – the early absorbing curiosities and then the firecracker of *To Tell the Truth*, followed by the immersion, now punctuated by the jab in the ribs of a comment from somebody who seemed to know Number Two.

I remained adamant I wouldn't contact anyone unless absolutely certain of their identity and relativity. No taking a chance on wrong numbers, shadows of doubts, unreasonable anything. I couldn't stand having someone's "uh…. sorry, no," a return email that I'd made a mistake, wrong Mr. Anybody.

But in the outside world people were falling all over themselves to find family. Locate your grandmother's uncle's ancestors and see what percentage of You is Shawnee or Estonian or from Mauritania or really descended from Spanish royalty.

Stock prices for spit-tube genealogy soared, with millions of kits being sold every year, leading to a whole raft of "Excuse me, but I think you might be" letters. (Although two percent of those tests came back as "not the parent you expected." That's twenty-five thousand possibly distressing surprises a year.)

A best-selling memoirist checked the DNA and uncovered that her lifelong father wasn't a biological relation. In a startling documentary, triplets rudely separated at birth back in '61 discovered each other as college men, in joy and then wrenching pain as the reasons for their split-up became clear. Two women, twins also divided for "research" later revealed to be revolting and unethical, wrote a book about discovering their identicalities. A presidential speechwriter learned he wasn't his dad's son, but belonged to one of his mom's professors.

A researcher contributed a rich review of the DNA testing explosion and how it's affected those who previously assumed they knew what they were made of. The media bubbled with experts chiming in about nature and nurture and percentages of each in separated twins and triplets and four-plets and halvsies. Old cold case mysteries started unraveling as armchair detectives tracked genetic links toward new suspects and law enforcement slowly admitted such techniques had efficacy.

A television series took celebrities on a DNA ancestral tour, while a U.S. Senator did herself little good stumbling over her one-bitsteenth of whatever tribe she laid claim to. A popular folksinger and the daughter she gave away found in their reunion, first, an initial comfort in the face of debilitating illness, followed by recrimination. There was a happy portrayal of a guy in Philly who found a half-brother in California and a third bro fathered by a now-dead man in the Midwest and maybe a fourth and it turned out they all loved cheesesteaks.

On the home front I remarkably had more than one acquaintance who shared a story of discovery of separated siblings. They'd each been set out for adoption by a young mother stricken by poverty or insecurity, and thus they'd been severed from the other kids born later and retained by their mutual parent at a more confident time. For them, the results upon reaching out to and meeting the newly-unearthed relations had been delightful.

There was the nurse minding me during the epidural to calm the L3-L4 sciatica that wobbled my left leg and icepicked my hip, whose husband found an unknown brother on a people-finder website.

And really close in, a longtime friend of Melanie's found out about an unknown half-sister after her father's passing – people in town kept saying there was a girl who looked so much like her – and that opened up a whole closet of not-good stuff.

Most folks, though, seemed so pleased to find the long-lost they'd suspected were out there somewhere.

I didn't know how I'd feel, if and when a solid lead revealed itself. Grown and aging, reliant on intuition, only I would know when I was ready to make the Big Thing happen, the call, the letter.

Learning as much as I could about Them was a way to feel safer somehow. Not rushing would further prepare me for the radical change I expected to confront, celebrate, endure, when another Son of Burt picked up the phone or said hello to the mailman. When the stone rolled away.

What's the *operandi* when you find out you have biological family in the distance? Assume you'll all feel the same upon the revelation? And aren't you supposed to now spend every available minute on it? Quit your job, quit it all, and undertake the chase, storm toward the turnpike?

Or breathe deeply and sort your mental three-by-five cards, Zen it? "Whatever the result, I'll be okay."

You spend a lifetime trying to control the approach to anything and the rule becomes "When I'm ready." All imbued with a curated cynicism about what lies ahead, and about maybe being turned away, ignored, black-sheeped.

Now it all began again, not just looking for Burt but for another child of his, the one more than hinted at by a comment on a YouTube page. The who and where and what, a secret brother, and as I probed there were guys of the same name and age in the same state, in the same friggin' line of work, no less. Multiple Burts and progeny and accompanying multiple anxieties.

It was a bag of marbles scattered across my Pergo floor. The legal pad scribblings and copies of internet documents approached kudzu level, Matryoshka dolls nesting in another. The puzzle was a constant stick-poke at some feeling that hadn't even been on my feelings registry before that October night with YouTube.

I was tugged and egged forward by an insistent child to the roller coaster that spun three ways at once, c'mon, c'mon, c'mon. By a *mapinza*, the wanton won't-shut-up kid, curious and demanding to know what was really going on behind the tall people's silence, why there were voluminous records of one Gordian strand of the knot and almost no trace of another.

Marbles rolling everywhere.

Melanie understood why I hesitated. She knew only I could command how hard I pressed the accelerator, to reach out to someone who looked like my first, my next, my probable new living relative. Or relatives.

It had been more than sixty years. I had to be prepared for a second Change, and I was the one to know when to open the curtain, hit the doorbell. What's the rush?

Okay, yes, well, there's that one thing. People die.

Emily hadn't been particularly looking for a ticket out of Tiretown. Life was good there, but she's a teenager, things happen when attraction and excitement grabs your life, when love is a *mapinza*. So she moved with Burt far from home, married him because, well, that's what you did.

But it wasn't long after birthing a child that she gave up on the Texas sun and dirt and drawl and especially the guy Burt turned out to be: an erratic, self-aggrandizing, totally charming rogue who came back from the war with dramatic stories and temptations for young ladies who sought in their evening companions a sophistication and elevation from their normal bland circumstances.

As another Burtonic wife would do in New Jersey a few years later, back in Ohio Emily raised her son with the help of her open-armed parents. She wanted for little, materially, but still, no husband for her, no father for the kid, a pretty empty space for a young woman and a toddler both emerging into the world.

My mother didn't know a lot about what hit her, except to be smitten by an enterprising fellow attracted to what Highland wiles she possessed. Some of the man's tale surely would seduce, what with Burton's confident puffery and wartime exploits. Yet Jean was unaware his mother Charlotte had been killed in a crash, his father murdered in Texas or that he had a previous spouse when he was nineteen. And a child.

It wasn't that Jean simply ignored the track record of her first great love; she didn't get a fact sheet to judge by. Still, how could she, why would she, hmmm, did she *have to*? (No.)

She simply had the bad luck to run into the guy at the Press Bar, and he just went about being the man he'd become, who covered up his pain and longing and empty spaces with what he termed his "energetic dynamism," what he'd absorbed from his early experiences when, deserted by one person or another, the vacuum was filled by becoming larger than life so as to command a room, an audience, a reporter or a child-woman. Be Clark Gable, John Barrymore, fill the screen.

Now, Margaret, she was more aware of what she was getting into. Somewhat.

Let's assume she was looking for the best life had to offer, and willing to do that work. At nineteen, she stood by her eighty percent man while a lawyer squawked about some lady with a shoeless kid.

Burt was no picnic, that's for sure. He could swing and sway a girl. The open question would be how long they'd dance on, enchanted and swirling, before waking up.

It was a dicey period, with the spring wedding followed by the hotel noise in August. Maybe she had a dream that it would be different for her than it was for sad Emily. Until it became the same.

She gave birth to a girl; that part of life was excellent. But there's so much more to marriage than kids, and the end came the next summer. In response Burt did what he did so well, took his maritime union card and headed back to sea, port to port, and on to a midnight bar in Philadelphia.

Thus came the third episode of Game of Burts, lasting only into the spring of '52 when he was unmasked and reviled by an infuriated nurse on a Delaware River pier. A few months later he was leaning on the rail of *LaSalle* on the Lake Superior run, deciding what he needed most and if he could find it back on familiar turf.

Burt returned to Ohio a wounded man, penitent to Margaret, never should have let her go, he was such a dumbass, they have a darling daughter. And if she ever caught wind of his East Coast mess, then *Honest, honey, there was no kid in Jersey.*

He relied on what he had the most of, confident charm. Margaret succumbed and remarried him. Ah, my.

Let's all refrain from assumptions about the girl; to judge her is to judge my mother, sort of. Yet, sitting with our contemporary vantage, we see how histories crash and argue, waves on a rock from multiple directions. The questions of uncautious timing, whether Burt was totally untied from Marge when he married Jean, or totally untied from Jean when he remarried Marge. There were no databases in those days for a clerk to research marital integrity beyond collections of index cards in out-of-state capitals. The fog did dispel, eventually; everything about Burt's down-lows had been on the up-and-up, so one less humiliation for Jean and Marge alike.

Margaret and Burt settled, not the right word, into an uneven life in three states. He wasn't always in town as she delivered happy packages. Five more half-siblings for me.

Like most American spaces in Eisenhower's emerging suburbia, Rodney's backyard had a swing set and petunias. Also an Italian garden and sprawling golf-cut lawns, the fountains, plazas and *accoutrements* of a millionaire's estate where his grandfather worked.

It lasted until his mother remarried to a stable guy from the truck-sales industry, which is when Rodney's last name changed.

At age ten the family struck out on its own, moving not far from the grand estate to a plain house in a tract bounded by some train tracks, Mount Peace Cemetery and the Little Cuyahoga River. Then came a farm way over on the other side of the city, and finally a house near the big reservoir lakes that bordered the southern stretch of the urban sprawl.

Rod rolled around the backyard on a bike, and like his unknown younger brother in the Garden State, he was a Boy Scout. He found his enthusiasms, grabbing high school track records that held for decades. There was work at one of those middle-American roller-rinking, whirly-twirling, car-bumpering amusement parks called Fallon's Kiddie Land, and later at McKeever's Chicken Farm, famous for fried food since 1933. He developed a focus in the precision of carpentry, crafting a finished product to use with your hands or raise up high for everybody, like the houses and apartments he helped build in his late teens.

When the time came for Rod to make more of himself, his grandfather pulled enough money together to send the lad to Morehead University in Kentucky for three years to study history. He came close to graduating but it just... trailed... off. He ended up back home and picking up a route for a Canada Dry distributor, to drive what Ohioans referred to as a pop truck and deliver handcarts of ginger ale to grocery stores.

After a few months of slinging cases of soda, Rod pondered how this life could be improved upon. He was smart, energetic, muscular. Where could that get him, in those times before a college degree was society's demarcation between the upscale and the great unwashed?

He double-parked the pop truck in front of the police department to go in for an application. They mutually liked what they saw.

Rod did well at the training academy, and was first assigned to ride traffic control with another newcomer, Wayne (another *Strange Snick*®:

I also traveled about and engaged the post-school years with a best-bud Wayne). Rod quickly jumped to the motorcycle squad, as it suited his outdoorsy personality. Sinewy, mustachioed Rod was one of two officers on the force who could ride standing on the seat of a motorcycle with arms outstretched like a massive Brazilian Redeemer.

Being uncommon, finding a way to elevate himself, the fast and firm move, was Rod's style. At a training exercise for gaining entry to a building, Rod and another officer threw a third man through a window so their squad could take credit for getting in first. Once achieving the detective's badge, he drove around town with partners from the *French Connection* casting office. They blended in with many middle-class American men in 1974 coiffed like wide-lapeled disco princes.

He worked his way around, with the vice squad that laid into the drug dealer, car-trunk gun trader, pimp or other rep of felonious intent; following that came the property crew, where he tracked down a long-gone TV set, a link to the world for a developmentally disabled man, and pried it out of a crackhead's hands. Then came an elevation to homicide. In a disheartening episode, he helped take down one of his own commanders, Douglas Prade, for the infamous murder of his physician-wife.

Cold Case Files came to the city in October 2006 to recount two girls who were sexually violated and killed, with a prime suspect who at first was released for lack of evidence. Rod and his colleagues recounted for cable TV how they kept at it, tying their man to an unsolved similar murder and putting him away.

It's said a cop can go an entire career without drawing a weapon, much less using it. Rod's experience was different. He became an expert marksman, one of the smoothest, steady-handed men on the force. In tough situations when gunfire was anticipated, Rod was radioed in. He co-founded the SWAT team that busted in dangerous doors, and also started the water-rescue dive squad.

There was the noisy day when Rod took down a guy with a famous old Western hip shot, an inaccurate poke which hardly anyone in the old

West actually did except in movies, but at which Rod was pretty good. If he'd taken an extra blip-second to raise his gun, the other guy might've fired first.

There were a few times when it was worse than that. Even the lousy day when a cop has to go home after a run-in with a dumbshit with a gun, when it was him-or-me, and talk to the union counselor and take restriction to desk duty for a few weeks, and despite how absolutely clean it was, cleared by internal affairs, he still has to find a way to talk about it at home or not talk about it, and pack it around, and it was a long time ago, and it was always just yesterday.

More than one officer said Rod had no enemies, that criminal suspects were okay with him, praised him as fair and square, he never hit or threatened them, never played the bad cop, never bragged about the tough stuff he had to do. One colleague, a motorcycle guy and not a little squirrel himself, said, "Rod was very intimidating because of his size and presence. Once you spoke to him, you realized he was humble and never badge-heavy."

In '74 Rod hitched into the Army reserve for four years of weekend duty and extra money. With Vietnam on its last legs, he managed, like me, to avoid that run through the jungle. Although when he was forty-six a woman plowed into his unmarked car under a red light. Couple of rib aches from that.

Eventually Burt and Marge plunked in Trumbull, a suburb of Bridgeport just north of the Merritt Parkway that swooned down to New York City. This was in the same county with a farm parcel owned by the late submarine inventor Simon Lake, whose early undersea craft Burt would discover a few years later in Narragansett Bay. In Trumball, Burt had his SubMarine mailbox, in a plain house on a long hill with a damaged-grass front yard. (From the *Strange Snick*® file: the family's modest bungalow was at 33 Pine Street, while at the same time my mom and I resided in a modest bungalow in a Jersey town at 132 Pine.)

In flannel shirts and khakis, Burt watched lawyer shows on TV where the story always tied up with a surprise guilty plea, along with the Alfred Hitchcock thriller anthology and America's shared Ed Sullivan culture. He didn't watch sports, preferring to spend weekends tinkering with his salvage art and writing about diving and maritime history.

He did offer some positive fatherliness, the knee-bouncing, tickling, ball-tossing, park-walking, jump-on-daddy moments. Yet, on balance, in all the stories from so many directions that began to pile up about Burt, the tendencies became clear.

With him around, not around, off on the water or just plain away, the older girls would come home from school to their mother half-napped on the sofa with a cold washcloth draped across her eyes, calming herself before heading out to one of three jobs. She faced the depositions of the bathroom mirror and the faces of her kids. Keeping food on the table was rough sometimes.

Naturally, six siblings, like witnesses to an accident each from their own age and vantage, had differences in memory and how they processed their past, what they could confront and or bury.

Said one about her erratic father, "He didn't raise us, we didn't grow up with him." But she didn't carry what might be a child's expected guilt or self-blame. "I never felt like it was my fault." Of course it wasn't.

"I know who he was. People loved him. He was just that kind of person, when he walked into a room he just lit up the place, people gravitated to him. But every child this man had ended up in a crazy life. I felt like I was in survival mode since I was four."

Their dad dropped them at the local theater for Hitchcock movies, *Psycho* or *The Birds*, which would scare the bejeebers outa them. One girl was stranded on a boat for hours while Burt dived; another, very young, was deserted on the beach for an afternoon and the sun scanned her paint-red before for her dad retrieved her.

There were barely any photographs of birthday candle-blowing in the boxes and closets of their lives. For some of the young ones with no image of a father in their early years, it wasn't until they were adolescents that he started showing up like a bothersome uncle.

The stories about Marge and her six youngsters as related by those who were in the room swung across all temperatures. I wasn't there. I found Burt, figuratively speaking, thumbing through a medical dictionary: devoid of empathy, disconnected from guilt, with a penchant for moving on, the sociopath. The one who could cooly appraise a situation, an opportunity, in his fired-up prefrontal cortex, in the judgy dorsolateral, yet without igniting the nearby medial subdivision of the brain which, in most people, injects emotion to complicate and influence their analysis and action.

By virtue of slick talk the sociopath could entice a woman from a moribund life to the precipice of danger or convince a closed wallet to open. Seduce with soul-mateness or sex or profitable partnership, be *The Music Man* or *The Talented Mr. Ripley*. The life of the party who could size up everyone in the room and figure out who, and how, to manipulate, twist, win over with wit and compliment, and later dismiss without stress. (It didn't mean going criminal, necessarily, if a properly wired amygdala would steer its host away from the illegal and maintain course in the simply selfish.)

Maybe Burt saw himself in his kids, the child he hadn't wanted to be, needy, difficult, packing the weight of loss and betrayal. He'd been driven off to a military school for reform purposes and thus was no stranger to the concept of what to do when one's children become overwhelming. So he did the same; at a time when Marge was weakened by responsibility, economics and exhaustion, he deposited them in a Rhode Island children's home.

Margaret found some strength to battle her circumstances, the ones imposed by her health, her finances and state regulations. She scrounged an apartment in Bridgeport and started collecting her children from the state dormitory. Her dad visited from Ohio and donated some furniture. Slogging through paperwork, processing and interviews, she retrieved her oldest daughter and youngest son from the children's home, and then another pair, and the last.

At one point she was in Trumbull again, where the kids shared two rooms of bunkbeds and twins. At least there was a backyard, and over on a pond called Boot Hill, swimming and fishing. A few blocks away was Aunt Marilyn in the home she'd occupied with Pete Krones and her two kids for play dates. Marge got a job for a restaurant association, teaching classes on dining service.

Of course, it had to end. After the second divorce from Burt she had to sue for support several times, and at one point a Rhode Island court slapped him for contempt and $3,000 in overdue support payments. A sheriff's sale at Tommy's Garage in Bridgeport would dispose of an Olds station wagon the bank had reclaimed for nonpayment.

For Burt, enough was enough. Screw New England. Time to make some better luck.

Margaret gave marriage one more run with a man she met in Trumball, for family and stability. Again, she tried her best, and the guy didn't.

New England, these men, the illnesses and the winter cold, wore her to the nub. Marge collected the children, piled them atop mounds of clothes in the car, their heads bumping against the roof, and drove back to Ohio. Her mother took them in until Marge found a little house she could afford, enough room but with too many summer bugs. She tended bar and managed a Howard Johnson roadside diner, but always had presents under a Christmas tree and did something special for birthdays, six times a year.

Amid the "shambles" onboard the tug *Barney* at the end of 1973, Burt drove one day from the New Orleans wharf where the tug was tied up over to Richards Boulevard. In what was then a rundown office building long before they rebuilt the neighborhood with gleaming business towers and hotels, he sat for an interview at a business called Video Court Reporters. As the tape rolled, he answered questions about legal action he'd undertaken against a local guy, Bud, with whom he'd collaborated in a business called (and about) Atmospheric Diving Systems, and Bud's wife Penny.

Burt told the lawyer about a diving bell he'd helped develop, along with tools, hydraulic fittings and a variety of equipment which had gone missing while the couple had control of it, and at the heart of it all, a patent. "It's a damn shame we have to go through this. Bud is such a phony bastard. He can wreck someone's life and then sit back and play cat to my mouse. And never have to pay for what he has done."

It would never occur to Burt that he also might have acted in such a fashion with anyone.

He enlisted the services of a young attorney named Koerner, who chased Bud and Penny and their lawyers through the system. Burt wasn't an especially impressive specimen to Koerner, but the attorney didn't have a problem with the guy he viewed as a "square shooter," who "was smart, honest, personable. He inspired confidence. He was always straight with me."

Yet the lawyer, who by training could summarize people and their capabilities for harm or good or compromise, perceived a gap in Burt's totality.

"People have many qualities, but the one that completes them, he didn't have it," Koerner said. "Some people you meet seem to have every good gift but one. I couldn't identify what it was about him, but he couldn't seem to pull it off," meaning actual success in life.

Chasing Bud and Penny (who Burt called "a vile woman" for her manipulative arguing), Koerner finally got a win on the patent dispute. His wallet being pretty slim, Burt paid Koerner for his services with a nine-teenth-century partner's desk he "had in stock," so to speak, the kind where two lawyers or accountants sit facing each other. Koerner still uses it.

(Months later one of Margaret's sons engaged Koerner to handle the paperwork for the young man's divorce. As cash-strapped as his old man, the fellow made a partial payment to the lawyer of a bay laurel tree, costing probably ten bucks at the time, which now towers thirty-five feet above Koerner's house.)

While awaiting further resolution of the patent entanglements, Burt went off on that Caribbean job "under protest" about a list of maritime irregularities, hoping the captain had the navigational skills to avoid cross-ing Castro's Cuban radar.

A letter in mid-February from a patent attorney named Feldman brought a dollop of better news, approval on one of his patent applications. Maybe something would come of that, a profit from his ownership that no one, not the elusive Bud, not one of the marine or oil or drilling companies, could take away.

However, it wasn't enough to inject much immediate cheer. He was again unhappily sitting in a New Orleans shipyard, in the birthplace-of-jazz parish called Algiers. His current predicament was dim, as was the state of affairs at his current home address on the far side of Lake Pontchartrain.

"A real drag. Sitting here alone is bad medicine," he told himself. "My mind races from Bud and his poisonous wife and their foul deeds... to why a forty-seven year-old man who is not a complete dummy is wasting his life aboard a battered, ruined old tug boat."

The boat he was newly assigned to at the end of February was under repair and the galley was flooded due to plugged drains. The crew spent a day or two pumping fuel out of problematic tanks and swatting at a heavy bug infestation.

Beyond the wharf, Mardi Gras was getting underway throughout the city on the twenty-sixth. Burt was anticipating a week off, as the boss at the maritime company told him to get some rest before a ninety-day voyage to South America. He'd wait until his relief came in around nine-thirty the next morning.

The causeway across Lake Pontchartrain is twenty-four concrete miles, one pair of lanes to the north and one southbound, allowing two-way traffic should one span be knocked out by a hi-speed spinout, an errant barge or a pestilent storm. It's straight, always, a zinging sunset in your right-side vision or a gray rain front slashing straight at you, miserably.

The speed limit is sixty-five and cops tuck under the signs at the crossovers between north and south. There are two drawbridges mid-lake, but ships can't pass between six and nine on weekday mornings. Most of the two spans are only fifteen feet off the water.

The northbound lanes spill into six miles of freeway that feed a crossroads, absorbing and fanning out the traffic coming up from New Orleans. That's where Covington, the municipal seat of St. Tammany Parish, is situated just off true north of Bourbon Street.

It's a regular size town, built on river branches and old trails, spreading into bedroom neighborhoods and warehouses. Covington had seventy-five hundred people in the mid-Seventies, not many more now. Framed by old trees, famed for a farmers' market, this was the boyhood home of musician Stephen Stills, and later a retreat for basketball's Pistol Pete Maravich and some movie-making with Jim Carrey and Samuel L. Jackson.

It's where you go to see a contestant for Largest Statue of Ronald Reagan, a looming sixteen feet of magnetism including pedestal, not that he had anything to do with the place.

One little asterisk on the town is for the man who changed the world with three rifle shots (supposedly all his own) and then had a *follow-up act on live TV* – Lee Harvey Oswald, who spent some scant months in first grade at Covington Elementary. No plaque there, so don't go lookin'.

North of town, the road up to the humid nethers of Louisiana, that's Lee Road, Highway 437. That's where Burt and Nancy Ruth Ross bought a house on two plots of ground.

He'd dated Nancy in New England while he was still attached to Margaret, and after Marge chucked him forever he quickly did what he'd done before, with a woman younger than he and predisposed to the ol' charm.

She was twenty-five and studied at Syracuse, Julliard and Columbia. Burt thought it a good idea to tell her New England family he'd attended U.C.L.A. after his stint at Castle Heights Military Academy. To ice that cake, he added that his father, the late Bill Mason, was a resident of Newport. You know, the Newport Masons, remember, you must have met them at one of Binky Herringbone's parties...

Nancy was even thinner than other women Burt was attracted to. Her elongated face perched upon a stretched neck and bony shoulders, presenting a contrast to Burt, relatively a boyish marshmallow.

Once his legal connection to Margaret was finally severed, save for the child support (cue laugh track), Burt and Nancy married in January 1964.

The wedding was certainly the richest Burt would ever take part in, held at Boston's Sheraton Plaza with Rabbi Samuel Perlman officiating. Nancy's sister Eleanor provided her fiancé Frederick to be the best man, what with no friends to stand up for Burt, or at least none who could afford a suit, or perhaps none who could be depended on after a few drinks to not spill the beans about his wharf rat lifestyle or marital parade. (Ellie and Fred married two months later, same hotel, same rabbi, nice package.)

The society sections of the Boston Globe and the Jewish Advocate puffed up the affair, but did not specify if Burt underwent any religion-specific surgery or academic regimen to lubricate his acceptance into a fine Brookline clan overseen by Bill and Martha Ross, who'd found success running a large laundry concern. The well-heeled parents sent them off to Mexico to honeymoon.

The couple started out on a small, pleasant tree-lined street in the suburb of Newton, in a house like many, a shingled single-entrance duplex with apartments top and bottom and a shared two-car garage at street level.

The couple's domestication started hitting a few snags as his realities bubbled to the surface. The seagoing career foundered, partners unwilling to invest in him or drown for him, and the ramshackle attempts to earn a living from his Twenty Fathom crafts didn't carry much pizazz. Five years into the marriage he was still casting about for help on projects, advertising in local New England papers for "deckhands for salvage operation... age no barrier... know diesels and or machinery." Applicants had to be free of the military draft for at least a year even as Vietnam raged. He'd provide wages and a bonus, plus room and board (probably in some flophouse, although prospects might have believed they'd be treated to a more upscale opportunity, as they were to inquire for him on a Sunday at the Viking Hotel, a fancy, historic Rhode Island establishment).

Burt saw potential for improvement down south, not to mention better winters. Where the warm waters of the Gulf met the spiderweb of the Mississippi delta, there were navies of the diesel boat engines he knew how to operate and fix, and sunken ships ranging from historic Civil War blockade runners to storm-battered freight hulks.

In '68 they bought the house in Covington, the second built on the plot since the Thirties and fairly new, with Ross money.

It was set back in some trees, and at the head of a long driveway were stone-brick columns holding a wrought-iron gate. There was a big porch for enjoying the leafy canopy in summer and a stone fireplace for winter. Out back was a barn with room for horses.

The house was a double-wing structure in a U-shape, with an enclosed hallway between the main sections. The wing to the left held the kitchen and storage areas, the other a lounge and secondary bedrooms on the first floor and a master bedroom and library upstairs, encircled by a large porch. A small separate section in back of that had other living spaces and storage. Actually, every extra square foot in the house was packed, including the connecting hallway with its bathroom and laundry. There was no getting through the hall without smacking a knee or elbow into furniture or boxes of shipments from France or other sources of culture and vintage sophistication.

It was all Nancy's stuff. She was passionate about antiques. She established her adult life down in the Covington house, away from the stuffy Bostonian snobbery, doing business at New Orleans antique shows and in a little operation at the house for restoration and sales. At the end of the driveway, dangling from an iron-pipe goalpost, was her sign, six feet across, *Mason Antiques*, topped by a plaque of an Edwardian buggy and team of horses.

(Burt was mildly interested. He had plenty of antiquated things, leftovers from the Twenty Fathoms line. There was that desk he'd eventually use to pay off a debt to a lawyer, and somewhere he acquired a cane that belonged to the prizefighter Jack Dempsey.)

The house, valued at $35,000 (around two hundred grand nowadays) held well over a hundred thousand dollars' worth, maybe up to a hundred-sixty, of rare furniture, bric-a-brac and collectables. There was a lot of value sitting on Lee Road.

Nancy was also dedicated to what had become her primary purpose in life: Adam, her only child, born at the tail end of '64, less than a year after the wedding. Burt always had been one for quick pregnancies.

For almost a decade, Nancy was settled and old-fashioned in her own way, and if he was supposedly out on some stupid boat, she'd put up with it. She had the business to thrive in, or get lost in, and she had a son to raise.

In February of '74 the daytime high was 64 degrees while the overnights sank to 24. There had been little rain that month, ten days and sporadic.

In the crisp overnight of the last Wednesday of the month, Burt was down on the tugboat in Algiers and Adam, then nine, was staying at a friend's house and fighting off a cough and cold. Nancy had a houseguest named Reginald Carrette, forty-four, visiting from London for around two weeks to see the Louisiana sights and discuss a long-term relationship for consignments. Burt wasn't altogether happy about the friend, had some suspicions about his wife's mixing business with pleasure. She might've taken Reg down to the city that evening to her favorite nightspot, the clarinetist Pete Fountain's French Quarter Inn. Burt was expecting his imminent departure.

Dawn was still an hour away when, almost explosively, sound and light rollicked the house. Nancy hurtled into the first-floor guest room to rouse Carrette. Smoke was billowing through the entire residential wing, and Reg could see flames in the center hallway between the halves of the house.

In the foyer Reg held his hostess as her hysteria ballooned, her face bearing shock as adrenalin pumped its flight response. By the demands of a Gothic script she broke loose from him, said she had to get the little dog that always kept her company, and went back upstairs with her robe flapping with warm wind. Carrette tried to get up to the second floor to bring her back but coughs of fire through the upper hallway walls backed him off and he tumbled on the stairs.

The heat in the lower connecting hall blocked his escape to the front door, so Reg went into a side room that was just starting to catch. He broke a window with some piece of furniture and crawled through, the pain coming up on his hands, lacerated and burned. Out on the lawn, his British composure collapsing, the third occupant of the property met him.

Willie Haywood, a twenty-five-year-old Black caretaker, awakened by the noise of crackling destruction, ran from his bedroom in the small rear section toward the kitchen and saw the blazing central hallway. He headed out a back door, circled around the house and found Carrette standing outside the bedroom wing. Reggie pointed up where he thought Nancy had gone.

Willie then clambered up onto a low roof to try extracting Nancy from an upper window, but the extreme heat beat him away. It was never established whether Carrette or Haywood could get to a phone, depending on if it was in the kitchen over in the last section of the house to catch fire or the living room that was already being consumed. Maybe it was dead, the wires emerging from the home melted out. In any case, Willie ran out the driveway to Lee Road.

He flagged down a passing driver on his way to work and directed him to the old firehouse which, luckily, had someone in the office making morning-shift coffee. That guy got on the phone to the volunteer fire department that had moved a few years before to 26th and Jefferson, ten minutes from the scene on North Lee. A full-time dispatcher, funded when the new station was built, pushed the button on a general alarm.

Some volunteers' homes were a few minutes from the station, but naturally it would take a longer time for others to scramble out of their beds and drive over from points around town.

A firefighter named Galloway arrived first and found the blaze chewing through the center hall and engulfing the living-space wing.

Once the trucks arrived, the hoses needed clamping together to run a thousand feet to the nearest hydrant, draping over a wire fence and then crunched through a wooded lot.

By then the entire two-story building was engorged. The chimney spewed volcanic flares, the upper rooms were devoid of any recognizable structure, doors and walls carved open revealing sheets of flame beyond. The first floor along the front pushed its conflagration outward before it boiled vertically. Copper objects and building parts melted into blobs; other metals oxidized and flaked. The fifty-foot pines surrounding it all didn't move a muscle. They were a cold green fortress, resistant to the arc of fireworks that settled on their branches.

As the sun finally brightened southern Louisiana, the house was a smoldering caldera.

Young Adam, getting ready for school at his pal's house, was in the bathroom where a little squeaky radio crackled its signal from a small New Orleans station. The local news report at eight was headlined by an early morning fire north of Covington. A place with an antique shop. A woman was dead.

Thus it came to Adam, the stun, the ripping. Came to him as it had for his father, the child on a bad turn on the highway south of Napa. A unique bond of father and son.

Burt evidenced both a love for and annoyance with Adam, depending on what conversation you monitored, letter you read, or tantrum you witnessed. He was no longer emotionally involved with Adam's mother, if ever this sociopathic candidate truly was. Burt left no record attesting to, nor did anyone witness, whatever crying he may have done.

It was left to the playmate's mom to hold Adam the rest of the morning and try to learn something on the phone.

It took awhile for the firefighters to start poking through the remains of the disaster. At noon there were still hot spots spitting up little camp-fires. The only upright features were the central brick chimney, an exterior wooden staircase to the back structure and some downpipes from the rain gutters staggering skyward like war-blistered flagpoles without their banners.

In the afternoon the bones of a torso were picked out (gruesomely, without limbs or the skull) and the coroner went to work identifying Nancy. The Tammany Farmer led its evening edition with "Probe Smoking Rubble For Body Of Woman In Antique Shop Blaze."

Neither Police Chief Bill Dobson nor the head of the fire company, Jim Grogan, knew enough to make any immediate statement about the cause. They knew only from the fireman Galloway that it seemed to have started in the center hallway section, with the laundry area jammed with furniture that eventually would reveal a small gas-fueled space heater, whose control knob was in the open position that night, parked under a table.

The way Burt told the grim story, around eight-thirty someone rang up the shipyard's customer office, and Burt was called from the tugboat to the phone to hear Nancy was dead. An electrical contractor named

Rappaport, whose business was close by, picked him up and they zoomed across the causeway. Arriving at Lee Road just before ten, smoke was wisping and curling in the stench of wet ash. Firefighters repacked tools and equipment. He was standing on the front grass by the trees when what could be found of Nancy's remains were brought out.

Years later, some people who knew Burt in Covington had no trouble imagining he wasn't actually away from town the night of the fire. That instead he was hovering in the woods. At least, that he was capable of hovering.

But when you don't really know nothin' you can't say nothin'. The state fire marshal's investigation turned up no incendiary evidence aside from the gas-fed heater with a faulty knob. "Accidental" was the final keyword.

If there had been actual suspicion on the authorities' part, the final report would've mentioned if Burt was or wasn't aboard a tugboat at the Algiers drydock far from the pluming smoke on the far side of Lake Pontchartrain. But he wasn't the sort to go off half-cocked in a drunken, vituperative stupor at three in the morning, even to commit a foul deed. But he was, indeed, somewhat alone, in emotional estrangement from his wife, who in turn was alone in the home with a British gentleman caller Burt was real interested in seeing go away, and knowing his kid was staying at a friend's house. But this. But that.

Cast Burt as the villainous insurance arsonist? Doubt it. That really stretches the profiling.

C'mon, really, how much horror can follow one man across the breadth of his life?

A normal day in pleasant Gary, Indiana in the mundane mid-Fifties. Population one hundred and fifty thousand, twice as many as today, a town imbued (as a setting for a popular musical of the era) with more enthusiasm than modern life might reflect.

Margaret and Burt left Fremont, Ohio, with their first two kids for a Gary district called Aetna, a few miles from the southern tip of Lake Michigan and close to where the Jackson Five were growing up. Not long after, the couple transplanted to something less expensive and sulfurous on the south side of town. Gary made steel, and as how steel smells like bad eggs, the farther from the lake, the less of an odor, unless the wind was from the north, in which case you still got a taste until you were halfway downstate.

They tried normalcy as best Burt could construct it, normalcy as best Marge could manage in her remarriage to Mister Mercurial, teetering as it might on any day considering his temper, his willingness to zoom around life and pick up speeding tickets, or his penchant to stick her with the now-three girls they'd compiled and go out who-knows-where.

The house on Kentucky Street was in a line of duplexes, two-story suburban tract homes glued together with garages on either side and plain concrete driveways, beige siding, big yards. They were still a bit shiny from their postwar birth but in years to come would falter into the dismal, overweeded state that Gary would acquire once the steel mill economy disintegrated.

Young Boomer kids and tricycles commanded the sidewalks. A few houses over some neighbors had a girl, eighteen months, a pre-pre-toddler figuring out as all kids do about life, the home, the limits, what worked and what they could manipulate, where the freedom was.

She was out in the late afternoon the Tuesday after Memorial Day, warm for the spring at eighty-five degrees under clouds, content to roll around on the grass with newly practiced motor skills in the secret garden of childhood, her folks in the house or maybe a few doors down talking to somebody about the White Sox. Across the street, more kids, more noise, screaming their *daddy-daddys* to breadwinners coming home.

Burt, twenty-nine, shoved his keys and wallet into his pants pockets, no cell phone in those simpler times, and announced (or maybe he didn't) an intention to run over to Morningside Drugs on Broadway and pick up some photos, or to see if anything at Goldblatt's would fit him.

Or perhaps he just slammed out of the house as he often did, to screech away and let the engine and tires speak for him.

On his way to wherever, he stopped briefly at another house on the block and pulled up the guy's driveway by the scrappy lawn. While he was in there, the baby from the other half of the duplex plopped down at the right-rear of the car, a tiny object in relation to the bulk of the auto. When Burt emerged he had no reason to reconnoiter, he just started up the big, puffy '50s car, saw nothing notable in the rearview mirror over the dashboard if he looked at all, and tugged the gearshift on the steering column into reverse and rolled the sedan backwards and compressed enough of the child's body to crush the blood vessels and muscles and bones and leave it a quiet, bereft shadow.

It was an odd, what-the-hell seismic rumph Burt felt in his seat, as if he'd backed over a tree limb.

The older kids across the way banged back into their houses and their moms ran out.

Then there were police cars and ambulance lights and small, quietly murmuring groups along the block. Children stopped running and yelling.

When Burt got back after sundown, rehashing the mess with Marge in the living room, he whimpered a bit, atypical for his personality, stretching empathy to his limit. He went over to the neighbor's house, where by then the father had put away all kinds of alcohol, and there was no calm in that conversation.

The cops never charged Burt for what was deemed accidental, as involuntary manslaughter wasn't a thing back then in Gary.

So there it was, the specter that followed Burt across his life, sometimes packed into his duffel and carried with him to the next port and the next opportunity to escape it, and at other instances just sitting close by, unseen and waiting for another moment to bring the pain. In those stretches when it seemed Burt might've really desired to shake it off, he couldn't because it attached to him like a goiter, always to be a part of his being, like the curse of an offended witch.

Over the years there wasn't much talk in the family about the baby from down the street in Gary. Nobody wanted to revisit it, really.

The little girl taken from life by heedlessness was from a family named Scott. Same as Jean's in Jersey a few years before. Different hurt, far more terrible of course. Only Burt recognized the coincidence of the Scotts, two families to whom he'd brought the apparition, separated by seven hundred miles. He kept that to himself.

Bill and Martha Ross left Boston the afternoon of the fire, along with their daughter Ellie and her husband Fred. Along with shocked parents of Adam's friends and some colleagues from the New Orleans antiques community, they attended services Friday at the Schoen Funeral Home. Nancy's vague remains were cremated at another Schoen facility in New Orleans. On Monday, her parents took her ashes home.

Two days later, after fitfully sleeping on somebody's couch, Burt rented a small house on the south side of town near the Tulane University Primate Research Center. He retrieved Adam from a playmate's sympathetic parents and moved him in with almost nothing to wear, to play with, to eat, but plenty to remember and dream.

Chief Grogan and state investigator Bill Roth arrived at the fire site for an appointment in mid-March. Burt was already there, sifting through the lumpen ashes where his wife's torso was discovered. He said he was trying to locate other parts of his wife's body; in Roth's words, "he would rather find the remains himself rather than have somebody else come onto the property" and "not take the proper action." Burt told one of his kids years later that he'd come across Nancy's shoe with her foot still in it, maybe just to get a *Ewwww* out of them.

The officials asked Burt why Nancy would have run back upstairs into the inferno. There was the story about the loyal, affectionate dog. And one about a gold watch Burt said he'd pulled from the wreckage, one that his father Bill Mason had given him. Burt's pained guess was that Nancy had returned to the master bedroom and library not only for the pooch but for sentimental items, a lady's watch and a ring he held in his hand. In a small pile to the side Burt stacked some salvaged undersea artifacts.

He "advised" the investigator that any rumors about a large sum of money in the house were unfounded.

There would be money, though, coming later. There was the thirty-two thousand bucks from Continental Insurance. This was a lot of money in 1970s cash when gas was fifty cents. Oddly, there was no coverage on the hundred-and-a-half-thousand of antiques and business assets, at least that Burt mentioned to the investigators.

Some, if not all, of this compensation was in Adam's name. Naturally, a boy his age couldn't be expected to handle anything beyond an allowance. Gaining power of attorney through some paper-shuffling, Burt would manage his son's sudden cash assets along with the child's grief. Maybe an encouraging token for a magistrate in an underfunded parish court expedited Burt's getting approval, but that's just more of the speculation that was the *lingua franca* among those in town familiar with Burt's tendency to slip and slide.

By the end of March, Burt was cleaning the property with a bulldozer he'd borrowed from a friend. It was slow work, and he contemplated burning what was left because moving ashes was easier than decrepit lumber. On weekends he kept Adam busy at his friends' homes, and at the movies with Kurt Russell and Bob Crane in *Super Dad*.

Burt's sister Marilyn, long divorced from Pete Krones and now living in an old cottage in a cul-de-sac in Walnut Creek, California, over the mountains east of Berkeley, flew down to Louisiana with her son for a visit. Burt put him to work hand-clearing the fire scene, burning off the wood and scrubbing down the stone porch. It took three loads in a dump truck to move blackened and misshapen iron, copper and brass to a local scrap yard.

Eventually Burt set to rebuilding the house with help from some locals and the carpentry skills of two of his post-teen sons who'd driven down from New England. The home had a log cabin-styled interior, with a balcony overlooking a main room with its wagon-wheel chandelier, wooden barrels and jukebox installed with the intention of leasing the place out to a money-making commercial use such as a restaurant.

Atop the detached garage Burt managed his business dealings from a desk commanded by a large stained glass window. He planned a pool.

Even though his marital relationship with Nancy was emotionally diluted, he had some fondness for her still. He was happy to get some old rolls of film back from a local camera store to find six good photos of her riding Joe, a horse they'd kept for Adam. He also hoped some images from eight-millimeter home movies shot by Reg Carrette a day or two before the fire would turn into pictures worth framing.

One Sunday in April, Burt tried to get Adam away from all the stress. He took the boy out with Marilyn's visiting nephew and some adult friends on a houseboat owned by the family Adam had been staying with the night of the fire. After the road-and-water trip everyone was pooped, but Burt stayed up past ten that night watching the TV news with one of the friends, Gerrylynne Cooley.

Jerry, as Burt spelled it, was by most accounts a nice, pleasant, Southern-country woman of thirty-six, easy to laugh, a jokey sort with a wide-dimpled smile. She was thin, a little more than a hundred pounds, six inches shorter than Burt with a long neck, a bit of a bump to her nose and medium-red wavy hair parted on the left. She was a secretary for L'Oreal Cosmetics out of its Houston office.

Back in mid-February Burt had just returned from a quick trip up to Memphis when word came that Jerry was in a multi-car crash on a rain-washed road a hundred and forty miles northwest of New Orleans. She suffered a severe laceration to her lower lip and other cuts, along with a totaled car. Burt, who hadn't been staying on with Nancy and Adam all that much, immediately drove that distance up to attend to Jerry's physical and automotive health.

In the spring Jerry moved to Covington and rented a small, basic house for a hundred and twenty-five bucks a month. It was conveniently around the corner from where Burt and Adam had taken an apartment.

Once Burt had her in his sights (or perhaps it was the other way around), she was regularly at the house during its rebuilding. Jerry became a fixture at parties Burt hosted there with a wide social circle that encompassed both exotic and gay inclinations, plus plenty of alcohol. Years later there would be, as often happens, a mixed bag of memories on the part of family members about just how rampant things were.

During the day there was another woman around, with non-partying intent. Lois was from the family of the contractor who'd helped Burt the morning of the fire. She signed on to be Adam's tutrix. This was a designation in Louisiana similar to a guardianship with authority to manage money or property on behalf of a minor.

Burt's having another adult with legal sway over Adam's upbringing or financial concerns may have been at the court's insistence and/or to demonstrate Burt wasn't entirely a callow, grasping character, agreeable to enlist an objective parenting participant.

After all, Covington was a small community and the chattering class cast some suspicion on Burt for the fire, Nancy's death, the insurance payouts and all that. One woman in town who remembered the fire four decades later said she thought there was something fishy about the whole thing. As the well-meaning Lois felt sincere affection and sympathy for Adam, bringing her in as the boy's tutrix might've served to chill the tongues.

It was December of that tough year before Burt was on the serious water again, this time as a chief engineer on a big supply boat for Marathon

Oil. Seven days on, seven off, taking cement and construction fill-mud to an array of big-rig platforms a hundred-fifty miles into the Gulf.

Jerry had become quite the fixture, and she and Lois looked after Adam, a spare one hundred pounds at five-one, who got calls from his father whenever he was on dry land or had radio access. Meanwhile, wires, plumbing and wood stain had gone into the reconstructed house.

Mid-month, with his right hand hurting from recent cuts, Burt started getting panicky. On Tuesday the seventeenth, he planned to get picked off the supply boat by helicopter, but foul weather and a bouncing boat with several broken anchor links negated that departure. The next day his relief engineer had a car accident, missed the first chopper from the mainland, and barely grabbed the last flight to meet Burt chugging toward Port Arthur.

He managed to get back to his pal Ted's house in Covington on December nineteenth. That's where, ten months after the fire, in the company of his son and witnessing friends, he married Gerrillyne Cooley.

Please mark your scorecards, adding to previous entries: Emily 1946, Margaret 1950, Jean 1951, Margaret 1953-ish (record for multiple), Nancy 1964 (record for duration, record for most traumatic conclusion). *Please allow additional space for any further information.*

No time for a honeymoon, it was back to work, an unsatisfying, dim future, constant distractions: patent fights, keeping his mitts on his diving bell, the U.S. Marshals from Mississippi trying to chase down the slippery Bud and Penny, pestering the Coast Guard about a chief's license, the thicket of details about Nancy's insurance.

At Sabine Pass, a deep water port in Texas, came attacks from massive swarms of mosquitos, nature's deep drillers an inch and a half long and mounted with half-inch blood-extracting stylets capable of doing organ transplants if you weren't careful.

Except for Jerry and Adam, there was no longer much good about this part of the world.

But there was some money in England.

Getting to Ekofisk is a real pain. Staying put is a bitch.

Pretty much mid-distance between Britain and Norway, the Ekofisk waters cover nineteen square miles. After two hundred exploration wells were punched into the crust, in 1971 Phillips Petroleum began pulling dinosauric petroleum out of fields with Ikea names: Cod, Tor, Edda, Embla. They pumped Norwegian crude through pipelines to England, then shipped in tankers back to Norway, either for technical reasons or maybe to jack up the prices.

With more than two dozen platforms and plenty of other infrastructure, Ekofisk is expected to keep producing natural gas and oil until 2050, assuming the planet doesn't burn up by then.

One reaches Ekofisk by helicopter or boat, depending on one's rank or budget. Burt ranked fairly low on the transport chain.

Robin Towing Company of Harvey, Louisiana, signed him up at seventy-five dollars a day, including room and meal expenses for when he wasn't yet out on site. The contract was for ninety days to start, working twenty days on and ten off, the off times presumably back on English soil but not necessarily.

"If I can stand it, I will go for a year," Burt said. He needed the cash.

A year after the Covington fire and two months into his sixth marriage, Burt touched down at Heathrow from a Miami flight on National. He took a train north out of London's Liverpool Station in a second-class coach car, with double seats facing a center table and a spotless bathroom down the aisle providing soap and towels. Outside the windows on the path to Yarmouth, a fishing town at the eastern tip of County Norfolk then becoming co-dependent with the emerging deep water oil industry, was a countryside of roughly-flailed hedges and gently tumbling sward still winter-rough and not yet gold-green.

Burt looked out across an expanse of water not of the pale blue he'd seen from the air that lapped into the rocky crooks of western Ireland, where the Gulf Stream still flourished and landed the seeds and sheaves of Bermuda palm trees, but more of a traditional forest-plaid green that pillowed into blue only when the spring sun bloomed plankton.

It relieved him to see calm waters. "I don't relish trying to get my luggage transferred in a North Sea storm."

Beyond the industrial odor of the harbor, the water screeched at various decibels with Atlantic puffin, black-legged kittiwake and the gray and white fulmar diving for shrimp and fish. Seals graced green-slimed rocks and harbor porpoises teased the traffic approaching the anchorage. Kelp and knotted whack drifted along the shoreline, but in those days it was not yet being harvested to improve one's iodine intake.

His destination was *Robin #8*, a support vessel for a derrick-mounted barge, *Hugh Gordon*, owned by the marine division of the giant Brown & Root industrial corporation. At one hundred and twenty-eight feet, *Robin #8* was still the smallest supply boat on the North Sea, stuffed with men. Two of them spoke English. The Scandinavian, Lithuanian, Spanish, Greek and Bulgarian contingents all spoke only to their comprehension group, with Anglo-based seamen's terminology supplemented by a lot of shouting and pointing.

It took a few days for the crew to get organized and make its way out to *Hugh Gordon*. In foggy air atop placid, cold water they set about transferring fuel from *Robin #8* to the barge.

Relatively peaceful, so far, but of course subject to change. As was the simmering pot 'o mess Burt left back in Covington.

He wanted to invest in repairing the house and to keep the antiques concern rolling on the strength of Nancy's name in the New Orleans market. After all, the big *Mason Antiques* sign was still out on Lee Road. He'd arranged for another couple named Carty to finish construction of the house and live rent-free while the wife sold antiques, but they kept drifting in and out of the deal.

Adam's tutrix, Lois, legally obligated and personally committed to assuring the ten-year-old's security, had engaged an attorney named Jones.

Seems that Burt used some of the insurance money designated for Adam to buy antiques in order to restock and revitalize the old business. Lois thought he should pay interest on the funds.

Alone out at *Hugh Gordon*, Burt steamed out his "clarified thinking" about Lois and Jones; Burt was "enraged by Jones's scoffing mood." He was also ticked off by an influence from another angle: Nancy's parents were also seeking Burt's paid interest on the diverted insurance money.

That's when Burt set his mind on changing his will, writing as to how money was "too hard to make (I really hate this life at sea) to have to give it to Adam at the order of someone else...

"I shall probably keep the house. Cut Adam out of all other property and insurance until he is eighteen, at which time, or later, I shall decide what to give him outside the court."

He penned a half-dozen ideas to solve the problem, from asking a judge to approve the use of insurance money to rebuild the house and shop, to removing Adam as beneficiary of Burt's patent rights or property holdings, get the boy to sign a "quit-claim" for his rights. He asked Exxon and Citgo to change the payees on life insurance still in force from when he'd worked contracts for them.

If Adam was to get anything it wouldn't be until he was eighteen, "based on his progress," and then he would get what he earned, "when we shall all sit down and talk it out."

Based on what progress? The kid was getting B's and B-plus at Covington Elementary. Maybe Burt wanted to hold all the cards until he was sure Adam didn't blame him later for the fire, for losing his mother. Perhaps, as with his other children, Burt wasn't good at parental schematics, only the wielding of authority.

Early in the morning of the first anniversary of Nancy's death, a barge from Rotterdam delivered blocks of modular living quarters to one of the drilling platforms. The *Hugh Gordon* crew was using its crane to lift all six hundred and thirty tons' worth without spilling any of it into two hundred and seventy-five feet of water.

Close by on *Robin #8*, Burt had a fierce cold and was concerned about the weight he'd put on during the party months with Jerry.

"Trying to cut down on food. No coffee, no milk, almost no bread, eating a lot of fruit, trying to reduce that, too – must be down to 240, or below, by now. Would like to see 210 again.

"Diving was more fun and more money."

On the days when he could forget his financial furies, and as the coughing and sneezing allowed, Burt found some moments for his human self to breathe.

"Seems like forever, much harder on me this time than ever before. Miss Jerry and Adam so damn much, and feel guilty about being away from Adam."

March barreled across the North Sea with gales rushing the deck at forty miles per hour or better. The barge rode it well enough, but the constant shifting of its center of gravity, the rolling tools and stuff falling off shelves, was hard on everybody's nerves. An experienced hand could accommodate the motion, but this was no rockabye drift that put a kid to sleep in a car seat. Swells of fifteen feet and twenty came off the yawning green sea and then, hitting more narrow blue depths, backed each against the one before it, mounding up and heaping some more.

That's how it always was on the edge of Dogger Bank, a shallow section of the North Sea that had once connected Britain to Scandinavia in a bygone epoch. Burt, the salvager of water-logged history, got a kick out of sharing a blot of sea that hosted German and British warships blasting at each other in the First World War, as well as the "Dogger Bank Incident" of 1904 when the Russian Navy took potshots at British fishermen, thinking they were Japanese invaders, which is a fairly odd place to believe Japanese patrol boats would wander around unless somebody had their map really turned inside-out.

While squalls churned the sea, "the Mason clan is up to its ears in lawsuits." Jerry's letters brought him updates on the list of problems, including the second lawyer Burt hired to deal with Bud and the diving bell and now was "trying to collect $4,500 for no work." Burt countersued "for zillions on malpractice."

Reginald Carrette, "that drunk Englishman who allowed Nancy to burn to death" wanted money because his clothes, and an "alleged contract with Nancy," had been lost, and to compensate for his personal injuries. Burt was more interested in Carrette paying him for some unspecified irresponsibility.

The "death trap," as Burt called the Hampshire House apartment building where he and Adam had moved, sought back rent while Burt yelled back over safety violations.

Each dawn looked the same.

The crew's general despondency over the constant rolling, with not much solid material between them and eternal wetness, didn't brighten when a helicopter went down about forty miles away. They spotted an infrequent search plane in the gray distance. A supply boat recovered just one man, the others lost to time, trauma and temperature. Everyone, commercial or military or recreational, knew the rule, that no matter how prepared you were, this water would wipe a man out in an hour. Or minutes.

The ocean was an awful place that no one conquers, only borrows time on by avoiding the wrong step on a slippery steel-plate surface, evading a tip-over of a thousand-pound piece of equipment. While there was no danger he'd overtake Joseph Conrad, in his notes Lord Burt described the negative realities sloshing amongst his fabulist possibilities.

"3/29 I have been sick for 3 days, constipation, severe stomach hurt, horrible. Got some medicine from barge's meagre stock, the boat has nothing. Pity anyone seriously ill or hurt out here – no doctor on barge and yet over a hundred men. A most dangerous situation.

"3/31 Had a "seafaring" experience today. One of the anchor buoys from barge got stuck in our "suitcase" wire – seas were pounding, decks awash. I went out into this maelstrom with a torch and cut the shackle that caused the trouble. Got very wet and cold.

"Thinking about divers on the barge in saturation tank," (a long-term, pressurized environment that reduces exposure to nitrogen narcosis). "They couldn't work for two weeks, can only lie in bunks, limited exercise. At $450 per day a body can stand a lot.

"4/3 We are about out of food, been about 3 weeks since it was ordered. Have been bumming bread from the barge. We do have some biscuit mix but the cook evidently does not know how to make them and can't read English well enough to understand the label. Fixing hydraulic steering system without benefit of instruction books, parts views, schematics.

"Bounding away, day after day, on Ye Olde North Sea. None of the dashing adventures of those of years past, when we were engaged in marine salvage, diving to the depths of the Atlantic sea to wrest treasures from the sea floor. Too bad all those books burned up – I am going to try to reconstruct some of those events in a new manuscript.

"Am writing a little now on my notes for 'A Story,' which is simply a narrative of all I can remember of my life since I was born. It might have some literary or historical value someday. At the very least it will give my son Adam something of a picture of how things were, the generation before him – my part in it, anyway, which I suppose was a little different than the life of Mr. Average America – I hope so."

In April Burt rode back to solid English ground for a nine-day stretch. He hiked around Yarmouth and took bus rides to outlying beach and market towns, to Beccles, Acle and Loewstoft, deep into the counties where the gentle landscape still allowed the smell of the sea to drift. In the evenings, he sat in local pubs drinking Scotch (a practice his children in New England and Ohio never ascribed to him), drafting memory for whatever audience there might be for "A Story," his *memoire magnifique*.

"And looking at ladies. Did not "make out" with any – a pity – maybe it's my old age catching up – or maybe I'd rather been home."

True or false. An man's pride for his masculinity waning as his body and his appeal traipsed down the road. A revelation in a diary to show off to a wife one day to prove marital loyalty, or that might hide in the bottom of a duffel on assumptions no one would ever see it. Maybe after a life of working the gimmick (the pro wrestlers' term for how they project their flamboyant persona into all their public appearances, even outside the ring), enough was enough.

One of the Robin Towing managers had a 1965 Hillman Minx for sale. This was a boxy version of a Ford Fairlane or an old Dodge, although some two-door models had a little more pizazz. Who knows where or when Burt expected to drive it, but he bought it, perhaps thinking he'd store it in a garage until Jerry and Adam moved across the Pond to be with him.

At the end of one leave Burt found himself on Borkum, an island on the German/Netherlands border. He met Boris Doncic, movie-star handsome and twenty years his junior, whose father was a hero of the Yugoslavian resistance in the war. Burt enjoyed his company before Boris quit and/or was fired in a dispute over Robin Towing's hiring or non-hiring of foreign mates.

There was also a Norwegian on the crew they dismissed because he refused to go out and pull anchors in heavy seas, having already been washed overboard twice, and was on a tug that sank the year before and was thus, medically speaking, nervous.

In May Burt's back was in constant pain and his stomach not much better. Negotiations for the next contract with Robin didn't go well. By mid-month he was back in Covington with some goals: to finish rebuilding a house he "inherited," promote an antiques business he'd equally taken over, advance his patents and convert mechanical ideas from pipe dreams into moneymakers and publish authoritatively on maritime history and his own unique life.

In a crisp, yellow buttoned shirt and rust-red pants, with wire-rimmed glasses half the size of his face, Adam marched with trumpet in hand in the high school band. He stretched his muscles and spirit at a karate school and constantly hugged the air hockey game his dad got him one Christmas. Weekends brought out the dressage helmet and boots, as he still enjoyed the horses Nancy introduced him to. When more noise was called for, he and his friends Naveed and Rommy went out on dirtbikes.

Jerry became Adam's second mother when she formally adopted him in late '75.

Lying around on a coffee table was a two-page manifesto, "Advice to a Young Man." This was Burt's rundown of the six steps necessary to assure success at college football (not that Adam seemed destined to pursue it). Its lofty objectives included zeroing in on schools that provided tutoring, plus national TV and newspaper coverage, and that even if he got hurt on the field, they would "guarantee you a job while in school, sufficient to keep all financial responsibility off your parents." (Although if college proved too burdensome after an injury, there was always trade school). "Advice" recommended Adam ask for promises in writing, or at least "have them say it in front of witnesses."

There was a P.S. to the recommendations: "Negotiate, Bargain, Negotiate. Don't lay down the law. Do not be influenced by personalities, vague promises, etc. Make your final decision based on pure 'business' factors."

Burt didn't want his boy to be a sheep.

When away working on the water, Burt went on and on about his inner love and generic liking of his young son, treasuring the letters from the boy in the infrequent mailbag on a supply boat. If he was actually being honest with himself and not just composing for some unknown future reader, these notes appeared as sincere, authentic gestures, empathy for his youngest, as they'd both lost a mother's guidance, the stability unique to the maternal heart.

But behind all that was a darkness easily swept in by a raw moment. Burt could feel sorry for himself, his pitiful situation, the failure and insecurity. He cried when a car hit his dog but barely drew it up for his children, if he dipped in the well for it at all.

A relative who spent some months around Burt observed with a visitor's perspective a "gregarious person" who yet was a "terrible father." A guy who was "a lot of fun in small doses," who could be a "fabulous companion" on one hand, yet "overwhelmed by an insecurity complex" and a "cataclysmic" temper. A man who "had no wish to accept or acknowledge any of society's mores with regard to behavior or anything else."

Once Adam blipped onto the radar of the Ohio and New England half-siblings, Marge's gang welcomed the young teenager into their lives. His new siblings all shared warm feelings about the boy. "He was a sweet and beautiful soul," said one. "I loved and adored him."

And over time they all came to see just how difficult it was for him.

Adam could be whiny, effeminate, with a measure of dyslexia, spoiled his mother. Nancy was his defender, and the fire took that away. Now the new wife Jerry succumbed to Burt's dominance and kept her head down when the rage erupted.

When Burt committed violence upon Adam's body and abused his emotions, sometimes brutally, as he had the others up north. Once his half-siblings visited their young brother, they witnessed the wrath pelting down.

It's true that, as his children grew to adulthood and recognized they could claim something of their autonomy, they unhooked from Burt's ability to control, defeat or ignore them. And not always incrementally, as when one of his New England sons recalled, from how he held his truth, about a visit to his dad and Jerry during a Southern business trip when he was in his mid-twenties:

"I'd always been in fear....Always. I didn't realize who I was.

"I stayed with them three or four days. One morning I'm up early to go do things, and he's sitting at the table and goes off on me. Normally I'd acquiesce. But for the first time ever, I confronted him physically. I leaned over and said, 'If you want to get your ass up right now over here, come over here and I will whip your ass, and you will never, ever intimidate me again. You've never been anything but a bully and a piece of shit.'

"He didn't say a word, sat there with his mouth hanging open. Then just like he would normally do, like I'd said nothing, he looks over to his wife then and says, 'Do we still have any of that vanilla ice cream?' That was the last time he ever talked crap to me and the first time I took my power back from him."

Adam, still young, didn't have that much power.

Burt got his weight down from two-fifty to a bit over two hundred. He'd quit smoking three years before and switched from coffee to tea. The back was still hurting.

As was his wallet.

Bank Americard was going after him for about $1,500, part of the outlay on materials he'd bought for Bud when they were working on the diving bell. Several local banks were in pursuit for a mortgage he'd taken on the Lee house while shuffling money and business names like Omnimart and Monitork (this was an invention that evaluated diesel engine efficiency and cost $25,000).

The IRS chased him for his 1973 taxes and a list of all the antiques in the house that burned in '74. Burt called it "Justice-crap," and ruminated how "bureaucracy will ultimately drive this country to ruin or revolution.

"The justice system of the USA is sick – of course, the entire nation is sick."

A few antiques were sold for operating capital, but Burt couldn't afford any more patent fees for Feldman and the push-button ballast system, the automatic heading control for submersible chambers, the underwater pincers and grapplers and all the diesel engine improvements he was designing.

He bemoaned "the greed of our lawmakers, and the lives of the ants who work (about 2.5 hours a day, according to latest reports) for government, and who try to tell me how to live. It would be more beneficial for me to spend the sums to locate in an area where there are fewer leeches – no doubt this is a cry on the wind."

There's no mystery why Adam was conflicted about the old man into his early adulthood. Burt had stripped away Adam's self-worth and the money, what with the fancy papers the boy was pushed to sign, his affirmations to a judge's questions with Burt's shotgun smile against his back. Or maybe the teenager read his father's seagoing notes and learned of the machinations Burt undertook with insurance and interest payments, the will and the supposed affection and good intentions.

In March 1987, when Adam was twenty-two, Burt sold some parcels next to the house, unimproved land along Thirty-Second Avenue, to a couple by the name of Ellis from over by the Alabama line. Of the sale price of a hundred and seven thousand dollars, forty-five went right to the First Bank of Covington to pay off old debts, and after the agent's commission there was fifty-three grand left (like a windfall of a hundred and twenty thou today). Adam signed his agreement to the sale. There's no telling what he got out of it, but to hear other family recount it, the answer was mostly "nothing."

With the physical abuse inflicted upon Adam, you couldn't blame the kid for whatever he felt. Adam also confronted his own special reckoning as his gay sexuality emerged. (One of his half-sisters was convinced that

Adam's identity, which she felt the boy was aware of as early as seven, to the degree he could be, was not a factor in Burt's violence toward him.)

Late in his teen years Adam made his way across the causeway to New Orleans and found in that beaded, festive community a spare cot, a compassionate embrace, an assurance that he'd left the judgement of others back in Covington. The football macho encouraged at home was left behind for the music, the dance, the twirl, the realness, for the acceptance by a new community of those he could openly love. Eventually Adam and a life-partner with whom he shared a flamboyant French Quarter life had an unofficial ceremony that even Burt attended.

Adam grew long, thin wheat hair and a square jaw, was slim with a casual posture, comfortably modeling a blue and yellow striped Nautica windbreaker at a miniature golf course in the Maine woods when he visited the sibs. They delighted in his company and defended and celebrated him. There was peace in the trees and lake water. There was family, solace, dependability, hugs from people who meant it.

For me, Adam is a far-off figure passing through history, like a photograph of some proud kid who helped his mother around the farm and then stands in gray wool looking out at the world, and you know he's going to march off to die in the rout at Chancellorsville. The connection for me started out as simply genetic, a product of Burt's seed-spreading, okay, fine, we're related, I get it. But the love Adam earned from those who knew him passes through to me as well. I've adopted the sadness and disappointment, the anger at his circumstances. Any child of Burt carries that for all the others.

Across a span of forty years or so, around seven hundred thousand people in this country, mostly young adult to middle age (along with some children and old folks) – either innocent medical recipients of donated blood, but mostly those attracted by or propelled into an uneducated and unprotected and oft-times exaggerated lifestyle – absorbed a human immunodeficiency virus, an acquired syndrome and a fungal disease and other shit, and Adam, the who-he-was and what-the-world-made-him, contracted

209

it and by its indiscrete hand died when he was twenty-eight.

The rebuilt house on North Lee is still there, and the stone columns at the road remain along with a more recent rolling gate. The *Mason Antiques* display was long removed and now a no-trespassing, beware-the-toothy-dog sign warns the visitor to cross the street. About fifty yards back under the trees the driveway curves around to a similar gate with old columns on 32nd Avenue. The barn's intact, as is the pool sunken into the north patch where Burt's older sons swam at the end of hot afternoons of rebuilding, with a lawn chair patio by its side. For a long time, a small business owner occupied the house, with the company name in white paint glaring up from a roof overhang at the Louisiana sky.

None of the current neighbors at a large day school, a pair of homes and a "wellness center" with a health food store and offers of therapeutic massage have reported Nancy's ghost at an upstairs window.

Once upon a time, to announce yourself at someone's home, you had to whap your knuckles on the door. A hand, a weight, upon a door is to allow emphasis, introduce a story, the way a landlord pounds for overdue rent, or the light tap vamps an uncertain blind date.

Electricity changed that. Now you push your finger onto this indented crystalline bar or a round button of faded white plastic or faux bronze to make a noise on the other side of a wall. A chiming, buzzy proclamation to generate instantaneous Pavlovian recognition, and every visitor becomes neutral, all news-bearers and guests sound the same.

So someone's finger sticks out from a half-fist to press the button trumpeting an arrival, invited or not, something postal too big for the slot, or an Amazonian expectation or IRS surprise, to proffer a ticket to a solar-panel deal or the Policeman's Ball, or ask, "You the owner of that Corolla parked on the corner?"

Some visits you just don't want. A bench warrant for all those parking tickets. Or a young man with glasses and wavy hair on the doorstep, "You'll never believe this, but do you remember dating Sally who ran the flower shop on Fifth Street twenty years ago? Well..."

I ascribe to simple luck of the cosmos that I was never challenged, confronted, surprised by such a living leftover.

Yet I spent a long time considering the potent results that might ensue as I crowbarred my way through the lumber nailed across the mineshaft of another person's past.

What would happen if I pushed the button, contacted a cop in Ohio? Might get an embracing welcome and coffee cake. Or a complete get-lost and never darken that driveway again.

Was I "dad's mistake"? Automatically *enfant maudit*?

I might be the scion of Satan, a dark prince born of Burton the Maleficent. *La oveja negra de la familia!* Could produce an outright rejection as Mr. Impossible. Even if a meeting ensued, it might bring barely a dank mumble at a banal food court on some neutral turnpike so as not to spook a bunch of grandchildren.

On the lighter side, a family out there might have spent their lives with the same curiosities about another boy left behind due to Burton's bad manners with women. Or a box of photo albums and detritus in Rod's closet might hold everything the Seeking Man sought, all the unanswered loose ends just waiting for an appearance by The One Who Knocks. Or, in modern parlance, Chimes.

In charge of local security for the spiffed-up, overwrought events at a country club, where ex-presidents and cabinet officers and sports stars gave dinner talks to dressy audiences, Rod coordinated the local police with the Secret Service and got a few handshake photos. With a woman who managed the club's events, he enjoyed hallway talks and backstage flirtations and similar stories about life's adventures and odd turns.

One Friday morning in '92 after the regular roll call in the Akron detectives' offices downtown, a reserve officer who was a minister at a local mission house called the cops to attention and somebody started a cassette tape of a familiar processional on a small boombox. At the podium in the middle of the hall, the pastor was joined by the detective and the captain. Before the cadre of tough investigators, in walked the lady grasping a bouquet, all dolled up with her bridesmaid. By nine the couple was declared officially a duo and the family of officers were eating cake for breakfast amidst yellow crime-scene tape decor. A sign on the door of an interrogation room read "Honeymoon suite, do not disturb."

That day in February – National Tell a Fairy Tale Day, to make of as one wished – went along as many of my days when I wasn't scheduled at the bookstore job. While I made tea and perused the newspaper (on actual paper, a habit since I was eight), beyond the kitchen-sink window the sparrows brunched on the seed barn hanging from a black iron shepherd's crook punched into the grass. The clouds were a thin overcast, but the sun would come through and some winter blue nestled high to the east.

Headed for the warehouse office of her family's company across the river, Melanie left me sitting in the billowy brown, fuzzy-faux-luxury robe my daughter had gifted me many Christmases ago. At the breakfast table was the sealed, addressed package I'd completed the previous night. As she opened the door to the garage, Mel called to me with encouragement and spine-stiffening determination, "This is the time."

I clicked on the TV, which was not a morning habit for either of us, but it was a special mid-week occasion. A onetime lawyer and problem-solver for Donald Trump was speaking to a congressional committee about what he thought of his ex-boss.

I slouched on the couch, puttered, did upstairs business and then back to the congressional logrolling on CNN. I checklisted for departure, filling the pockets of an oft-wounded black leather jacket with the tools of my modern life that lay about the table. My forearms and wrists were palpably weak, trembling as if through blood loss.

Out on the curving driveway I put the car in neutral, not reverse gear, and coasted back down the gentle slope as was my habit, checking both side views to avoid dog walkers and zippy kiddies. But I didn't relate to directly behind, which is where the Italian lady across the street was backing out her white SUV. Only within bare inches of crappy, crunchy results did a sudden flash in a mirror spark my jamming the brake before two perfectly good bumpers took to tribbing. The shaken woman profusely apologized for her own rearview error as I lowered the window to reassure her of my inappropriate fuzziness. Mustn't let one's mind race and distract from Safety First.

The post office was a zoomy ten minutes north up a six-lane highway. In the large parking lot facing an old graveyard by a Methodist church, I found a space away from everybody.

I sat for a while like a skydiver in the door, awaiting the green light overhead to signal it was time for me to exit the craft with a hope that my emotional parachute was properly packed.

A rhythmically sonorous, emphatic soundtrack of Strauss's Waltz Sequences One and Two from "Rosenkavalier" played on the Philly FM station where I'd spun jazz on vinyl at that time of the morning thirty years earlier, long before they imposed an all-day classical format.

A sudden sun beamed down as the Strauss Sequences harrumphed and swayed to a close. High noon on a Wednesday at the end of February, two years and four months since the Video From Outer Space invaded my basement. Nine months since the appearance of the Comment. Gestation complete. The green light blinked.

Walking across the brightly painted lines of the asphalt parking lot, with no one around, my mind was idly wide-open to the weather and a humming quiet, while also pin-dot focused on what I was carrying. It felt like a long establishing shot for a film, and once I'd gone through the first glass door of the building I'd hear a distant "Cut!" and come back outside to do medium dollies and a few covering angles.

Inside was postal cacophony. A conveyor belt in a cavernous back room punched a rhythmic racket. Seemed like everybody in line had a package to slap down. A guy with a deep Portuguese accent was trying to explain options to a customer.

Then my envelope lay on the gray scale plate. I stabbed through the details with the lady at the counter, when will it get there, who can sign for it, if the guy's not home does he have to go over to his post office, what a big bother, he'll get all pissed off for having to go through all that trouble and then to read this nutty letter…

Poking a fingertip on the card-scanner screen, I affirmed assent to the name displayed, the intended recipient of a package that would bring about someone's Change. I felt wobbly-certain about the address; I'd found it on multiple internet references, used Google Earth's streetview to peer at their house, nestled down a driveway into the trees up off the creek. A green receipt clicked out. In that I didn't grab over to retain the envelope in a tug-o-war, the woman lobbed it into a canvas bin to await pickup and pipeline. Good as gone.

Machines binging and phones toning and bags crunching followed me back to the lobby, and out the glass door.

I could have undertaken all this in what the casual observer might see as the easy way. C'mon, why didn't you just Do This? Track down some Facebook link or an email, because everything's on the internet, click and you're in somebody's face, following, befriending, leaving a message along the lines of "guess who?"

It certainly was trouble to search, pin it down, be sure of myself and of all of them, from my hiding spot, my culvert at the edge of the woods. Preferring double-down cautious, those long-held rationales about who was let into the fort, I wasn't on Facebook in the first place. (Well, I did start an account so that I could peer at others parading the stuff of their lives, but it was one-way glass.)

I probably could never live in Iceland, not just to avoid resorting to breakfast cereals like "Arctic Char N' Bogberry Crunch" but also because ninety percent of its population is on Facebook. Put up your page there and who knows what unsolicited "komdu með okkur" huggery comes one's way in the volcanic-steam grotto. No, thank you.

The Saturday after my trip to the P.O. I was off work, and aside from preparing my dainty self for a dinner at Melanie's friends' house, I had little to distract me from what was going on in Ohio. Would it the package be in the regular delivery guy's pouch or with one of those special-assignment couriers driving around in the boxy jeeps with the steering on the right?

I'd been told the recipient wouldn't get the envelope without being at the house to sign the green slip. Had to produce an I.D., too, and the wife couldn't take it, nor the kids or a well-meaning, sitcom doofus neighbor who'd then misplace it so his sixth grader could find it and take it to school for Advanced Show & Tell with hilarious results.

It would arrive when he was in the middle of a second cup of something, sitting on a beige floral-print two-seat sofa watching a rerun of *Dual Survivor* or *Anti Drug Squad*, or right after coming home from the tire store. Or it would be further into the shade of the afternoon as a late winter's remnants of a snowstorm rolled up the valley from Tennessee on its way to Buffalo and Nashua, and if his mom Emily was visiting, wouldn't that make for a photogenic firestorm.

At some point the cop would decide how to handle this thing in his grasp. What does a retired big-city police investigator make of this, all four of his names hand-printed and up in the corner a nameless, sparse return address?

Was this some come-on for a vacation condo or a toxic white-powder revenge gift from a now-free criminal who, back in the day, yelled at the detective as they dragged him out of the courtroom, something about it not being over?

At a distant time, as a teenage boy I sat on my mother's bed and methodically unsealed a manila envelope that held I didn't know what. A half century later there was a chance this cop, a physical sort and a muscled onetime diver, was a ripper, the type to slash the package open with a scissor-bladed index finger and dig into its bowels.

Inside the big envelope, another one, a small one with just "Rodney" etched on it.

This is assuming, of course, that this Rod was You're Right You're Right, the correct cop in the correct town, not to mention Yes Yes Yes Yes.

The green postal receipt possessed a tracking number and the USPS website supplied immediate evidence of mail being signed for and when. There wasn't a damn thing I could do about whatever would result, so let the dinner company be a distraction. If there was no claim noted on the postal site, then relax, that's it for the Saturday mail, the tremors would wait until Monday.

Relax wasn't the right word. My mind was never calm, not in my sleep, not while listening intently to someone else talking, not while making tea or sitting in front of the TV with Mel, there was no relaxing possible, between my brain and this sciatica down my back and muscle inflammation along my neck from a newly discovered bone spur that was a tetherball twisting in one direction then hitting peak twirl, and slowly unwinding back the other way.

This whole thing, the secret brother, the father, Alice, no rest.

February 2019

I have a story to tell you. It's either new to you or it's somewhat familiar.

In late summer of 1951 Burton Hoster Mason came into Philadelphia following one leg of a voyage as a merchant seaman. Seeking diversion, possibly with some mates, he strolled into the Press Bar on North Broad Street, a place catering to the late-night shift of the Inquirer printing plant up the way from City Hall and the staff from Hahnemann Hospital across the avenue.

A few bio-lines about my mother and her marriage, followed by: Jean and her family discovered evidence that Burton was overdue on child support payments in Ohio, which was the first time Jean knew Burt had been previously married. Her car loan and other personal finances had been manipulated by Burt as well. Along with other accumulating information as to how Burt conducted himself, this led Jean to initiate a divorce. Burt had left the scene, back to Ohio.

In July of '52, the child came along. Burt had the opportunity to step up, be responsible, say, "OK, the thing with Jean didn't work out, but that's my kid." He chose not to.

For my entire life, as far as I've ever known, my father disavowed me.

And now you know who I am, and what that makes us.

I apologize for dropping you headlong into a story normally found on noisy and/or tearful cable TV shows, Jerry Springer territory. I chose to communicate by letter to give you whatever time you wanted to absorb this, in contrast to a phone call or a ringing of your doorbell. You can decide when and how to bring it, the sudden existence of me, to your wife and family.

I was certainly not going to surprise anyone at the door, nor command entry into a family, become a thing to explain to your kids and theirs at Christmas.

I have been in quite the two-year adventure since my accidental discovery of the YouTube with Burt on *To Tell the Truth* from 1961.

Beyond the extensive investigation I've already done and the distant unknown relatives and events that have come to light (discussion of which await another day), a multitude of questions percolate.

I want to know if you have known about me: "So the other kid Burton had finally showed up."

Or if all this is as sudden and stunning as a bag of flour to the face.

Questions about your experience as a son of Burt, if he was in your life at all and what it was like for you. To see if we are comically alike in some ways, or share nothing more than DNA and some facial resemblance. How you entered a new family - just as Bill Heyward took his stepfather's name Mason and later passed it along to Burt and Aunt Marilyn.

Maybe Burt did show up for you, did right by you - although I've doubted that, I know he had to be chased down back in the '50s after Waco, not handling his legal obligations to you and your mother. I know Aunt Marilyn sympathized with my mother Jean, sent her a note back in '51, and then went off into her own uneven New England life.

Also, I have no idea if you had a relationship with or even any knowledge of Margaret, who Burton sandwiched between your mother and mine.

I'm still working out if there's some family from yet another wife, where Burt had his picture taken in their swimming pool in the year before he died. Or about Margaret's children, cousins close to our age, spread out in Ohio and Florida and who knows where else?

218

(That might be a wrong tree... but I don't think so.) Then there's Clara and on and on, all the names from the Burt Galaxy. My virtual CSI blackboard has people and lines zipping in all directions.

And hovering above it all is my missing grandfather, Bill, and what happened to him in Texas.

Or I should say our grandfather.

You might have the answers to all of it, the complete story, the loose ends about where and to whom Burt spread himself, tidied up like a case closed by a veteran detective, in well-tended boxes of old pictures and mementoes in a closet. With all that I've found out, it seems we'd have many notes to compare.

I've spent many months delving into all of this Past. Now there's an entirely new voyage ahead of me that began last year when I went back to that game show Web page and, for the first time, another guy whose father was a diver.

That Future for me began when you opened this envelope.

To level the field, here's the brochure on me.

Several biographical paragraphs with a general upsell quality. Jean, Beatles, the bass, Eagle Scout, newspapers, stories and lives, marriage, kids, mess, second marriage, career.

Rod, I've spent my entire father- and sibling-free life barely thinking about who else might be out there carrying intimate connections to me. Then the YouTube and my subsequent investigations have opened so many possibilities, and my children and my partner are terribly excited for me.

From every indication, you and the family seem like nice people I'd like to know.

I'm leaving the choice about what comes next to you

(assuming your interest in this newfound WHAT!? that has landed in your lap).

I'm not on Facebook and don't tweet; Googling my name produces about two dozen of me from here to Australia (and very few of them are me).

So I think I'm most comfortable in asking you to write back in email, or postal if you wish. That will give you the opportunity to compose your thoughts as I have done here; I have tried to be most careful.

Now that I've kicked open this door to you, made my decision, I don't know if I'm to be met with cupcakes or caution, embrace or disdain. These revelations about the missing history of half my family line have disjointed my sense of self, my thinking, bouncing around in my head every day.

Imagine the uniqueness of it - of all the people in the world this could happen to, to find a missing father on an old TV game show, then an unknown grandfather violently fallen to human greed, followed by discovery of a half-brother and how many others, all in this raucous fashion. And it's happened to me, this regular guy from Jersey. That's just nuts.

Tag.

With hope, curiosity, trepidation and resolve,

signature

Bebe, that's Rod's wife, has one of her sisters visiting, and they saw the postman come down the sloping driveway late in the day. What the heck is that? The labels mystified them. They unsealed the diplomatic pouch, the inner envelope allowed to burst out its secrets. A quivering Bebe was the first to review it, then handed it to her sister for another reading, and soon they were both shaking.

Not long after, Bebe told Rod what had passed across the transom into their lives. She handled the conversation slowly, carefully. Had her reasons.

Sometime around seven, as I talked around a dinner table, an email vibe in my pocket advised me of my package's delivery. Now to wait and hope for no ringing demand that I pick up.

Bebe politely responded with an email the next day; meanwhile she spread tremors through the extended family. More letters followed with her assurances that I was being welcomed, that my appearance out of nowhere had been, for them, a delightful crash through their front door. Well, that was one relief, that my approach heralded good things. It was like attacking a wartime beachhead only to find no resistance, just flowers from the natives.

They had always known. Not much, but they felt it for years, that there was a Me. Bebe knew something from Rod's family, as did Margaret and her kids – after all, my mother's lawyer had been in an Ohio courtroom making noise in the early Fifties. For decades the buzz about an unknown son of Burt swirled around these families like dry-ice stage smoke. Now I'd galloped out of the foggy forest, not a myth but a real squire returned from the odyssey in the wilderness.

Through an email exchange we negotiated the first conversation. It had to be by appointment for a Sunday afternoon, my rules, not wanting my cell phone to ring while I was on the freeway. I wanted to be sitting in the right chair at the most conducive time of day, with notebook set up, the technicalities of journalism aligned, the right beverage. An uncluttered interview for me to meet my past and see what lay ahead, a light-overcast day that, for mood, was lacking only a pianist performing Liszt outside the window.

I didn't speak to Rod that first time. It was mid-day, usually one of his slots for napping because of his emerging medical state. Probably just as well. I wasn't sure I was ready for Rod in that first immense call, as though I needed some special preparation, a full-dress rehearsal before the big cue about fate.

Bebe and I discussed everything possible, and she represented, pursued and defended Rod's interests. This was the role she accepted and undertook with as much dedication and energy as any spouse could muster. Some days for Rod were better than others; most were manageable but his baseline stability could be interrupted at any time. There was no set pattern.

It was the plaques and tangles getting in the way, interfering with Rod's shaping a thought, his drawing it from the filing cabinets of the brain's vault and communicating it. They diluted his ability to take on life with the abandonment of the young cop who could ride standing atop a motorcycle, to apply the well-informed consideration of the older, mature father and resourceful detective.

Rod knew what he had but not its medical name, nor how the clock was set.

For two hours I downloaded the volumes, my explanations to her of where I came from and what my life had been composed of, mixed with Bebe's Tales of Rod and snapshots of other siblings in the mist. The stories went way back, who'd been treated well, or not so much, life's mixed bag, the missing pieces of the heart and psyche.

I heard about when Rod finally experienced some time to fill in the white space, get to know the man who co-produced him, when Burt came up from the South to visit his boy on a sort-of neutral ground.

On my end, the delight and amazement and holy-crap and a couple other swinging emotions challenged me like too many flavors on a swaying cone of soft ice cream. My identity was no longer strictly solo now that there was both Rod and the *et al*. There was an auto-connectivity to others beyond my control that I couldn't reactively buffer, even if I still wanted to. You can't dictate the Change.

After the we'll-do-this-again-soon parting, I was mentally pooped and my blood pressure was probably up. I collapsed on a couch, and Mellie was still upstairs; Burt and his first son caromed around my head like two squawky nephews.

I had to get my mind off all the noise from a few moments. On the big dark square coffee table that commands the living room there's a massive compendium of New Yorker cartoons across the decades. I pulled the weight toward me, this thing must be twenty pounds, and as my right hand was juggling a teacup I used my left to open the book, to just see something of a different time and place and lighter mindset than the racket of that call to Ohio. Some small chuckle.

The book squeaked open to the middle, the section of cartoons of the 1950s. At the top of a randomly-selected page, it was 225, the first thing I laid eyes on – I swear this is completely true – was a cartoon by Claude Smith. It's set in the visitors' room at a jail. To the left is a convict in the striped suit talking to his average-looking housewife. Another prisoner is self-satisfied and surrounded by four fur-lined, coifed and pearled women. The first guy is explaining to his wife,*"They all are. That's what he's in for."*

Clara Olmstead, Bill Mason's mother, kept an old genealogical record, the generations fore and aft. My father occupied a line alongside his sister Marilyn. In 1984 he scribbled some additional details into his family heirloom. Following Emily and her son William Rodney, Margaret and her half-dozen, then Nancy with Adam, he added Jerry Cooley to the spousal list. Jean from Jersey made no appearance.

He added to that document a miscellaneous, marginal notation: "I support zero population growth." Considering the man's authenticated penchant for bed-rollicking, one could make a supposition, simultaneously mean-spirited and reasonably warranted, on the likely favorable odds there would be undiscovered children of other past dalliances that he failed to record.

Burt also inherited his grandma's self-published collection of original little poems. In one of several notes he jotted on the cover to Clara's verses, he claimed being father to Adam "and others (seven or so)." That was the only evidence ever unearthed of Burt's recognizing there was, or might be, a Me.

Promoted at last. I'm an "or so."

It was on my second call a week later that Rod and I could speak in the few moments when he could convey his own story and express his pent-up emotions that had been drifting around in the back of his skull for years. The feeling, and then the confirmation, of another who'd been through the same life he'd experienced as a son of the diver.

He didn't stay on the phone long, but sharing the voices was enough. A start.

His utterances came out with determination but with a broken rhythm, similar to speaking after a hard run that exhausts the lungs.

"I was very excited for finding yet another brother. Gonna have some experiences when I finally get to see you. Shake your hand. Waiting 71 years."

I didn't feel like I was talking with a peer or an older brother. I became the older one, the guide, encouraging as he searched for a thought or even his ability to have one.

Rod would not cave to the Lewy body diagnosis, an abnormal protein buildup with increasing complications over time (ideally measured in years rather than months).

"I got this dementia nonsense. I just can't do much."

He reached for words that matched his feelings or the key to a response; Bebe said he could relate some of the old stories perfectly well. Rod recalled his amazement from decades before when he learned the full story of his father, the one I'd recently uncovered. "I don't know how that man and his wives survived trying to feed all them people every day."

Like me, Rod had vowed to be with, and for, his children in a fashion that was the opposite of Burt's.

I had to grip his decline in ways similar to when Melanie's mother went through it a few years before. There's a way you use small words, with few explanations, to not prod or fill in their blanks when the silence made the person appear stymied and confused, when what they're doing is crafting their own manner of reply-searching. I just "sat with him" and let him craft the pace of our talking.

He lasted about five minutes.

When Bebe took the phone from Rod and sat him down to rest, I went blank for a bit, I knew no template for reaction. The previous two-plus years had swamped me with strange supposition, and now there's this, in real time. It was overwhelming and somewhat clinical because of Rod's condition and the distance between us, and the call overcame little of my lifelong stoicism. Not that I expected to become all wishy-warm. A guard-rail was still up along this curve.

Meanwhile, Melanie sat next to me crying.

The further all this went along, the more I'd see him.

A guy came into the bookstore on a Tuesday around 9:30. On the raised platform of the café in the center of the shop, I was gazing around managerially, just a pretense to observe the young man. He's mid-twenties, a blocky Burt build, clear-rim glasses and a two-day beard that gives him the look of a third-generation Amish farmer selling countryside veggies and pie. Both at first glance and then as I study him, he shudders me, a chill wind to the face as from a door blown open.

The closer I saunter past him, the reflections shimmer differently, but stick him in a lineup of possible grandchildren, tell me "there's one of 'em in there," and I'd pick him out.

They start popping up every few days, other Burts at every stage of his life, like suspicious characters shadowing my visit to a shady foreign city, flashes in a mirror, in windows and closing elevator doors. (It was the same phenomena as when grandpop Edwin passed away and the world seemed full of balding, thin, old Lincolnesque guys.) There had been so many pixeled pictures of Burt in old newspapers, then the clearer shots of those relatives with shared genetic features on home-movie internet pages and Facebook properties who didn't know I was spying on their Christmas mornings and vacation dances for the camera. Now all these ingrained images took full 3-D form in some guy browsing lightbulbs at Home Depot.

A few months later, the midlife bearded Rodney walks through my store. Swept-back hair, the black glasses, gum in the left cheek rhythm, plaid working shirt. At the supermarket, a local fire chief permits me to photograph him with my phone after a fast, lame request to capture "a guy who looks just like my brother." Through the pizza parlor's front window, the Totally Lookalike delivery dude is walking around.

Every guy with a rubbery middle, round senior face and gray fuzz goatee seems to know what I'm seeing and feeling, and I imagine them to nod and salute, snapping two fingers against their brow as they pass, like the secret nose-rubbing signal of the shysters in *The Sting*. I'm surrounded, chased, infiltrated. It's a movie where the just-awakened hero with the bump on his head sees the maniacal/grinning/all-knowing antagonist in every face on the street. They're all Burt or Rod, depending on the distance, the profile, how the light strikes them and what mood I'm in. It's getting so common and undistinguished I dismiss it like flocks of birds on the tornado radar, "another ping, log it."

One day an older, small white couple, touch of southern European background, came up to the register with one of those books churned out by decidedly non-liberal political prevaricators and fabricators. Usually, the more questionable (morally or politically) the author or customer inquiry, the greater the effort it took to retain a retail banality.

At this moment, however, I was getting a bit of a charge from leading the couple down a path, so I refrained from hustling them along and kept up my insincere employee pleasantry. I leaned toward them and lowered my voice, playing to the appetite for conspiratorial fantasy held by a certain section of the electorate. I advised the customers to watch for a section in the book about Texas voter scams that the writer used as tinder in his blaze of blather that Lyndon Johnson was behind the Kennedy assassination. They'd see a line or two about a shady sheriff in Texas. I went for it: "That guy murdered my grandfather." Got the widening eyes on both folks, who paid and left the store impressed and chattering.

I realized a new-found fun in letting go of my closed-vest privacy, telling people the story of the ne'er-do-well ex-dad and the never-expected granddad who died in the street defending the First Amendment, and sometimes adding in the stuff about my brothers and sisters. One day at the tire shop, I showed the manager how he was just five separated degrees from one of the country's industrial kingpins: the mechanic > me > my father > the father's first wife > the wife's dad who was an intimate employee of > the CEO whose name was on the mechanic's shirt.

Strangers are mystified and excited. Good sport, this is becoming.

IV

THE MAN IN THE HELMET

Decades after his killing, my grandfather still unnerved southeast Texas.

When the academic Mary K. Sparks worked on her lengthy paper about Bill Mason's murder and its impact on American media practices, she spoke to a friend of Bill's in an Alice restaurant in the fall of 1991. She conducted a quiet, huddled conversation. But when a server or patron got too close, her guest changed the subject. Apparently, this dark asterisk on local history was not an appropriate topic to engage in publicly. She interviewed the then-publisher of the Alice newspaper and learned he was still being reminded by voices in town that the case was best left on ice.

(Neighboring Duval County still felt the heavy hand of law enforcement and the old-time Parr attitudes on social control. A twenty-year sheriff there was said to enlist all manner of pushing and shoving because he had a badge. Reporters who wrote about his grown son's bust for intoxication and fighting were threatened with arrest for "interfering with his business." Described by a county official as "a great politician and a terrible sheriff," the guy was finally tossed by the voters in 2008.)

Around 2004, Rod and Bebe were on the road. First it was Florida to see some old buddies and enjoy their deep-sea pursuits above and below the surface of the Gulf. Then a cross-country splurge would take them to some friends in Las Vegas. Rod had an idea.

"Let's go see Alice. I want to see where my grandfather lived."

Might as well, Bebe agreed. Rod was always a history buff and it was a logical, short detour.

From the Panhandle they rolled their gold Mercury Grand Marquis like a powerboat across Rt. 10, luggage piled high and her Shiatzu, Precious Baby, riding atop with the maps. At Houston they veered south toward Corpus Christi, coming to rest for a few nights at a motel on Mustang Island, one of those barriers against small Gulf storms, albeit ineffective for the big ones barreling into Galveston that folksingers serenade.

One day the couple bumped along fifty miles of Highway 44 past Aqua Dulce and other sneeze-and-miss-it burgs. Then came Alice, a big softball town and site of the winter meeting of the Pan American Golf Association, claiming the birthplace of Tejano music and two Nobel Prize winners: Professor Robert Curl, for Chemistry in 1996, and Dr. Jim Allison, a harmonica-toting cancer researcher awarded the Medicine laurels in 2018.

Alice holds a stop along the Texas Tropical Trail with the South Texas Museum, an Alamo-style structure stocked with saddles, animal heads and photographs of the bygone. It promotes the proud acquisition of the judge's bench from a George Parr tax evasion trial, along with "a range of artifacts including a lantern from the San Antonio and Aransas Pass Railroad and a rare horse collar woven from corn shucks." Available for a visitor's perusal is a typewritten notebook on Parr's regrettable place in local history, with a seven-page chapter on the intersecting lives and subsequent deaths of Bill Mason and Sam Smithwick.

(The museum normally does not exhibit anything on Lee Harvey Oswald. There were many sightings of the kid from Covington Elementary as he drifted in and out of Alice for weeks in October '63, tugging along his Russian wife Marina and a baby daughter. The Warren Commission on the Kennedy assassination, run by the one-time Berkeley D.A. who bumped heads with Bill Mason, didn't note the rumors Oswald had been there. Yet multiple Alice witnesses remembered the face on their tinny black-and-white TVs in late November. Local lore mentions a "second Oswald," an impersonator always hovering around town to thus "place" the soon-to-be shooter, yet who was unmasked by his assorted tells and mistakes. Who would want a spittin' image of an assassin hanging around Alice a month before the rifle shots in Dallas? *You* decide.)

As they drove around to locate the site of Bill's shooting, Bebe reconnoitered the book Emily saved (and finally relinquished to her son) of old newspaper clippings and handwritten memories about her young bride's life in Texas and her father-in-law's demise.

Any map could guide you to San Felipe Street, but it had all changed since the 1940s. The pipe company where Bill collapsed on the sidewalk, and the West Side Patio where Avellino Saenz cowered in a doorway as Sam Smithwick smacked his jammed pistol, were long gone. There was no evidence any commerce had ever been on San Felipe, now populated by small houses fenced by corrugated metal and playgrounds for chickens among old refrigerators in yards. Towering over the area in an open lot near the main road was a water tower announcing Alice as The Hub City. (Another white tank across town sports a cheer for the high school football squad, the Coyotes.)

Rod couldn't figure out spot X. After a half century, probably no one in town could. So they wouldn't want to be just hanging around on the street in what had become part of the expansive Rancho Alegre, the southern rump of town that, according to a current reporter, had been "overrun by drugs and crime for a long time."

About a mile away, just off the heart of Alice, they pulled up to the library, a small place on Third Street surrounded by trees. Inside, they greeted a woman at the counter. "I'm looking for slides of newspaper articles from back in the 1940s," Rod said.

"Is there something specific you were interested in?" came the helpful reply.

"We want to look at the stories about the murder of Bill Mason."

The librarian made a little face, then led them to the microfiche reader in the corner and briefly explained, in the manner of a North Korean tourist handler, how to view the spools of film.

Focusing on July '49, Rod twirled the slideshow across the lit screen and pages of the Alice Echo & Banner flew by. On the 30th, a front page exploded. Another report quickly followed, then a cascade. Bebe scribbled notes for the family history book.

They hunched and concentrated on the films a good half hour when Rod got the proverbial friendly tap on the shoulder. A sheriff of some rank in full regalia had a question. "What business do you have here?"

"I'm looking for Bill Mason. For the articles about his murder."

"What business would you have looking for that?" the cop pressed.

"He was my grandfather," Rod delivered back, and the deputy was startled.

"Well, get what you need," he muttered, and then in so many words, "get a move on."

Even to another police officer, Rod wasn't one to assert his secret identity to encourage someone's backing off. He'd accomplish what he had to on his own merits, without the badge-flashing.

The couple copied off some documents and then headed for the main road out of Alice back to the coast.

Rod the cop knew how to drive like one, quiet, keeping his head still, flicking his eyes up to the rear mirror and then left to the side, more or less continuously. They were five miles out on Rt. 44.

"We're being followed."

It took some minutes for Rod to shake the feeling, much less an actual tail.

Bill Mason's life and demise were reported, analyzed, reflected upon and at times drenched in nonsense. As was the man who gunned him down. Sam Smithwick has his own slice of dedicated space on the internet, in column inches on newspaper reproductions, bits from third-string history websites and vanity-published books about Lone Star politics.

Example: there's an odd YouTube video posted in 2018 by some Australian chap. This fellow wrote brief histories of subjects he deemed interesting, from the 1929 stock market crash to Bakelite plastic dinnerware to a "psychopathic prophet" from Scotland named Dowis (yes, all kinds of people came from Scotland). The Aussie deemed much of his work to be of such grand consequence, why, the world should find it fascinating to partake of it on video! So he created what were essentially slide shows, and apparently pleased with his own voice and ability to do cartoonish dialect, he added his own narration.

The tale of High Noon in Alice hit the Aussie's radar for some reason. His sketch of the facts of the event was slipshod, relying on limited sources. There are but two graphics filling the eleven minutes, a photo of Smithwick from an old paper and a clipping about his jailhouse suicide. Staring at Sam for eleven minutes is like listening to the on-hold music for CVS.

In this twisty telling, Smithwick's presence is far more chuck and gristle than sirloin. The Australian's writing has a lot of dime-store hoo-hah to inflate the drama. It portrayed Sam as the top-dog corruptor of Alice, not a low-rent part-time lawman who just went all stupid. No Sheriff Sain or Boss Parr, no other crooks or creeps mentioned. Details about the shooting are wrong and eyebrow-arching speculation abounds as to my grandfather's visiting Alice's "houses of ill fame." Aussie-isms pepper the tale (such as Sam's "weighing more than nineteen stone"). Supposedly verbatim scripting from Bill's last radio shows, quoted incorrectly, are overladen with noir.

Who knows where the Australian sourced his information? Probably lifted some of it from Inside Detective, one of those splashy magazines that hit their stride in mid-century. These fifteen-cent pulp mags usually had a damsel in distress on the cover, luring the reader with enticing stories like "If He Couldn't Have Her, His Shotgun Would," and "She Chopped Up Her Mother For Her Salad." The May, 1950, issue ran a spread on the Smithwick trial titled "Who's Bigger? Texas or Me?" that described Sam as a "huge scoundrel," a "king of vice," a "bloated deputy" with an "enormous appetite for food, liquor and fast women." Pictures confirmed the crappiness of Sam's neckties. (Although, in a weak effort at balance, the piece included a photo of Sam and his wife animatedly chatting at the trial as if discussing the menu at the upcoming church social.)

Of what little Sam deserved, at least the facts should count for something, and not in the overwrought style of Inside Detective and True Fact Crime and the Australian's nonsensical video.

There was no way I was going to Alice. Too expensive, more if my son went along, and all that time would chew up a busy summer. Airfares and schedules were convoluted, driving from Jersey never even contemplated.

All to stand at some spot on the few hundred yards of San Felipe Street, to bear distant witness to my grandfather's meeting some big lump with a badge, an automatic and a temper.

Beyond that, what else could I do in such a fraught town? Seek shade under storefront eaves where Wild Bill stood talking to a disgruntled shopkeeper undergoing a shakedown by one of Parr's *pistoleros*. The pole with the pants. The gravestone. See if my visit would end as it did for others who had come to town and were encouraged to be elsewhere by nightfall.

So without the actual trip to Texas, my attention instead turned to a name in Corpus Christi one of my sisters came across online. I unearthed an email address, and after a quick exchange of letters I arranged to call the man on a midsummer morning.

If I couldn't be in Alice personally, soak up that value, then maybe I could find some of what I was seeking in a long-distance, cellular Plan B. The target was unaware I'd designed an episode of theater for myself.

To be talking right at those moments, in that hour on the July day marking the seventieth anniversary of my grandfather's murder, with the great-grandson of the man who killed him.

"One's file, you know, is never quite complete, a case is never really closed, even after a century, when all the participants are dead," as per Graham Greene in "The Third Man."

Jim Smithwick's tale was about wide, flat spaces, and people who live in a place apart from my crunchy, concrete Mid-Atlantic. About how connected those people are in the Big Open West, all the space and time, how you can go into a store down in Ben Bolt or Rancho Banquete and bump into some stranger who you unravel as your mother's cousin's wife. It's easy around those parts to be pulled into the widening nebula of the family Smithwick, or any family in southeast Texas.

For those so connected in Jim Wells County, there's embrace, quiet, loyalty.

When he was young a great-grandmother told Jim about the George Parr business, what life was like back then around the Hub City at the crossroads of dust, poverty and violence. A place where then (as now) there could be twenty people to a house. Where a county clerk, a banker or a guy in a windbreaker with a shiny patch could decide some Tex-Mex farmhand's well-being.

That doesn't mean great-grandma would tolerate any discussion of Sam. Very few of the Smithwick elders would respond when the topic came up, the blot, the darkness, the unexplainable.

To ask a great-uncle in his eighties, who'd been an anxious teen back then, about what Sam had done, you'd get "ah, leave it alone." An aunt advised Jim, pretty much, "Don't believe everything you see in the papers." One old man offered a few factual fulminations but, "I didn't tell you this."

Any suggestion that what Sam committed was a deliberate, venal crime was quickly batted down. With a Great Silence, the family could split out Bad Sam from the Good Sam who deserved fond memory. Nobody from the old days wanted to dwell on "Sam ran a brothel," on how a man's character was trashed on the radio for an audience of scandalized house-wives and agreeably-nodding midtown barbershop customers and trac-tor-rolling farmers. Leave it alone, they advised Jim.

The young ones, or the ones way on the outside of the Smithwick *cojunto*, either didn't know at all about the events of 1949 or had barely heard a murmur about Sam. Detached from history, the kids learned to not question the oldsters; still, there were cousins who preferred curiosity over compliance and compiled scrapbooks.

The legend fascinated Jim, now in his mid-forties, and he knew many things by acquisition and admission. That his great-grandfather ran a shady bar, that a young female relative "worked there." How Sam supposedly didn't want to be part of the Ballot Box 13 cover-up engineered by Parr, that he had some shade of moral compass. Jim saw how the Australian's video was scattershot.

But the Smithwick family lore misrepresented who Bill Mason was and why he was in Alice. Their accepted backstory was a slander-slinging feud between Bill and Sam, and that George Parr deliberately hired my grandfather for his radio station, so as to direct him to bait Smithwick with his editorials on vice.

None of that was true, but it was what the Smithwick clan had long accepted. A way out of guilt and disappointment.

In Jim's telling, the Smithwick family was one of "gentle giants," stocky ranch guys of no extended education, with a physical, cow-wran-gling life. These were Christian believers who may have called on Sunday for compassion for all creatures while on weekdays still tamping down the Mexicans into an acquiescent social order, even as the Mexican bloodlines spun through the Smithwicks backwards and forwards.

In the proverbial box in a closet, an aunt hoarded mail from Sam the lifer up in Huntsville. While they weren't much for spelling and style, those letters expressed Sam in the way his family chose to know him: a get-along guy, not high-wattage, a man who took the deputy's badge to supplement both his ranching income and his civic pride. The aunt didn't give Jim access to Sam's letters, but her old back-porch conversations served up an image: an uneducated man, tripped up by emotion, pissed off by the grander men he'd served, conflicted, now feeling unsafe, seeing his end was nigh, that he wouldn't last in prison.

With loyalty to the family, the weight of disappointing his wife, his sons and so many people all over Jim Wells and Duval, shaming the name, Sam was one hefty mess. To offload his guilt, he dictated a missive to the ex-governor Coke Stevenson about Box 13, transcribed by a friendly guard. Suffering from what these days might be clinical depression, he'd take the ultimate responsibility.

The towel... Jim could see his great-grandfather doing it. He accepted Sam's death as suicide, an actual self-infliction, not a murder to quiet a witness. A giving up the ghost, a solo jump with no assist from a cell-crowding crew of bribed prison gangsters required to heft a huge, resistant man off the floor to dangle from a towel just so.

Thing is, about where this happened, the cell in Huntsville: under a spartan light bulb in a ceiling socket is a wood table, thirty inches wide and covered with a cotton spread. Jutting out in back of it is the lower level of the bunkbed barely a foot off the damp floor, and the upper deck is chest high to a tall man, neck-high to the short. It's a cheap metal frame with no springy brace, just a pallet of flat, thatched staves and a few inches of padding, the wafers of an old mattress. A tall man would also have to duck a bit to enter past the swinging gate of bars painted white a long time ago and now well-chipped.

A hanging made little sense, unless the victim was already dead or drunk and not struggling, in which case you could wrap him up on the pole and achieve whatever look you wanted. Otherwise, the bunkbed would have to be bolted to the concrete floor to resist the dragging, immense weight of the dangling man in whatever involuntary spasms he might engage before something cracked, a hyoid bone, the Adam's apple, to end the struggle. Not that the part-time doctor at Huntsville got too detailed about murderous strangulation versus the snapping force of rolling off a bed. Judge

Franklin's widow, the temporary justice of the peace, sure wouldn't have asked questions before she signed the record.

Anyway, they wouldn't have bolted the beds to the floor, not if they wanted to move the furniture around or confine a prisoner to a no-bed punishment. So Sam's jump would have disturbed the unsecured bed to the point of collapsing it and him. A voluntary hanging in this cell wasn't realistic.

Talking with Jim reminded me of those episodes in which a descendant of a violent wartime guard would humble himself in front of a POW's offspring. The younger man had nothing to do with the elder's terrible conduct, but still felt the outstretched arm of responsibility on his shoulder. The prisoner's family understood it was within the brutality of war, but still carried a terrible hurt, because even in the worst times individuals can decide to not inflict suffering. Neither party were sole representatives of their clans and countries, or of history itself. Just inheritors with a shared demonic memory.

There was perspective, I wouldn't call it defensiveness, to Jim's portrait of his ancestor, a hard-working, getting-by, pressured fella who lost his head. Alright, fine, so Sam was the product of poverty, open sky, a cultural upbringing where everybody was related to somebody across the county and an insult to one was an offense to all. A man who committed suicide under the grave weight of his failures. If Jim and his kin wanted it that way, I couldn't stop 'em.

For the members of another extended family, in Maine and Ohio, Florida, South Carolina and New Jersey, Sam Smithwick remained the thug who murdered a grandfather, the lawman who killed a reporter, who sent Bill's son Burton at age twenty-two off into a rootless life that did no favors for his own kids who were, in turn, fatherless in so many ways.

My contemporary relations preferred it had gone down differently back in '49. Sam could've slapped Bill's face with a dueling glove out "under the pants," he could've keyed Bill's car, left a dead fish in the mailbox or a horse's head on the pillow. But Sam made his temperamental choice on San Felipe Street. Three years later he supposedly chose again, to jump off the bunkbed and deny a lifetime of retribution to his victims.

Unless the final choice was made for him.

Maybe the hanging was Sam's idea, and maybe it wasn't. Seven decades later... whatever.

It was courteous of Jim, the musical great-grandson in Corpus Christi with a view of the world less provincial than his forbears, to meet in mid-field with the writer who was plumbing the tentacles of family and loyalty, violence and burial. And to do it (albeit unknowingly) on the anniversary moment of a murder that brought two American families into their *Rashomon*.

Nice of Jim to listen and receive the many truths and facts and corrections of the lore I imparted to him. Whether he went back to his clan to pass along any education, or if they accepted it, well, that's life in another county.

When the phone call was completed, both of us knew more than we did the day before, and we went back to our lives' pursuits with a more informed legend about a man bleeding in the street and another choking on a towel.

Daniel Bueno heard his own account as he grew up in the 1970s. The way he got it, Smithwick hadn't just tracked down Bill Mason on a side road. No, Sam got Bill on the phone and told him there was a body worth looking at, lying outside a bar on San Felipe. Bill showed up alone (no mention of a buddy in the passenger seat). At some point Bill is asking "where's this body?" and realized there wasn't one as Sam pulled out his gun.

When Bueno was young the corruptions of George Parr still infected the region, but things slowly changed once the Duke of Duval took his own life and the political landscape quieted down and began to grow some green grass of real law (although irritants like that more modern Duval sheriff popped up occasionally, and Bill's killing remained a dark shadow over Alice for quite some time).

Dan went into law enforcement himself and eventually was chief of police in Alice. After that came a spell as Sheriff of Jim Wells County. The tall, beefy guy directed the work of the constables (rather than "deputies") with a commitment to accountability.

Bueno had his memory of the Ballad of Sam Smithwick just as his contemporary Jim over in Corpus Christi had his, each with whatever tone and color their families imparted. Dan had no reason to doubt the veracity of what he'd heard as a boy. After all, his great-grandmother was Sam Smithwick's sister.

In a place like southeast Texas where everybody knew a lot of folk, there might be such stretching of kin lines a person might not realize all the people they were related to. Jim didn't know he had a cousin or an uncle of some sort in Alice, much less that the guy was a police chief and then county sheriff.

What is plain is that no one had the entire straight story about the killing of Bill Mason, not then, not now.

Two weeks short of their seventh anniversary, as Christmas approached in 1982, Burt dumped his sixth wife because she drank too much.

He'd married Jerry, in part, because Adam needed maternal care, but her example was more notorious than nurturing. She was known to crack the whip around the house. And she'd come down from the bedroom to the offices in her flimsy nightgown with no regard, or perhaps with deliberate show-off-iness, as to who might be there, the secretary or an antiques customer or a parent of one of Adam's friends. Burt had taken occasionally to sleeping in the car when her nighttime imbibing degraded her inhibitions in ways that didn't appeal.

Burt was accustomed to control, and while he engaged in salacious behavior with women throughout his life, it was to be when and how he wanted. Jerry wasn't responding to that and pressed her own chaos. For the first time, it was Burt who dissolved a marriage.

Three months later, a social request arrived at the house on Lee Road. The invitation, an 11x17 sheet of heavy, pale cream stock, came from Van Nuys, California, and carried the wedding portraits of Nancy Ross's parents: handsome, square-jawed, vested-suit Bill and light brunette Martha in an eight-foot flowing lace gown with even longer white toile.

The Rosses were celebrating their fiftieth anniversary in high style, with cocktails and dinner at the Ambassador Hotel in Los Angeles, and for entertainment, seats in the ballroom at the People's Choice Film Awards. Their son Peter was connected to the business and had a line on tickets to watch Jane Fonda, Katherine Hepburn and ET the Extra-Terrestrial accept their statuettes. The invitation read, "If your presence is not possible, you may be able to see us on television with some of your other favorite stars!"

Nancy's family certainly maintained their feelings for Adam after the fire that killed his mother, and stayed in contact with Burt. They might not have approved of how he handled his personal affairs as long as he took care of Adam, not that they knew about all the financial manipulations and the emotional and physical violence. They knew Burt married Jerry Cooley ten months after Nancy died, and also that he eventually divorced that dame and remarried another woman within weeks. They addressed the invitation to the California celebration to both Burt and his latest bride by name, the wife who'd phoned them out of the blue to discuss Adam's need for parental guidance and affection and her prospective role in it.

The Masons never went to the party.

In a tree-lined suburb there's an above-ground swimming pool and flopping around in it is Burton, in his sixties with a beard and ridiculous

Santa-suit suspenders on his trunks. And some older woman and a middle-aged guy.

The photos were on a mystery Web page with a pseudonymous host and no evident association with anybody I'd come across in two years of poking around.

And, strictly psycho-drama, why wasn't I invited for an afternoon cooling off in their water? Why do I only get to watch from across the fence again, like with those kids in my childhood who never asked me to go swimming? Whose car do I have to oil-change to get invited for a splash?

The couple in the pool is Eva and one of her sons. Eva was born in Chicago in the Depression just as my mother was. Eva's own mother gave her up at birth for the proverbial better life with another family. Twenty years later Eva and her adoptive mom moved down South, where she married young and raised six kids.

By the early 1980s that marriage was over and Eva was on her own, looking for work around Covington, Louisiana. She'd applied her office skills to temping with a big shampoo company, and then a newspaper ad for full-time secretarial and sales work caught her eye.

Burt wanted some women to drive around in attention-getting antique cars to sell a grease-cutting product invented by a friend that took the slippery crap off boat decks and gear. Eva, around five-eight, a short-blond round-faced middleweight with big glasses and a wide smile, was quickly called in for an interview. Burt's then-spouse, Jerry, sat in, and at mid-day they went out to lunch along with a second applicant.

Eva's first impression of Burt was the same as anyone's, the charismatic, funny and ambitious guy. Almost too good to be true, and a real character. Stepping carefully to avoid anything too wild or weird, after placing a few check-him-out calls, she moved into the next phase of her life with Burt as her boss.

Burt let Eva into his life in stages, but with a lot more candor than he'd allowed with other women. He freely discussed with her his extended families from previous marital adventures. (All except one.)

Eva witnessed the "outlandish things" Jerry did, her embarrassments. Then Jerry was deposed from Lee Road, ending up back in her hometown of De Ridder where she remarried, divorced again and died in 2003.

Not long after Jerry left town, Eva analyzed her prospects and said Yes to her boss's proposal.

On a state marriage document, Burt had to list any former wives. There were four; true to form, no Jean.

She signed up amid twenty years of his throwing business darts into the wall. He pounded doors looking for pay dirt at Getty Oil, Mobil, Esso Exploration, Raytheon Offshore, supply and pipe companies. A deal fell through with a submarine firm called Perry (designer of James Bond's underwater car in *The Spy Who Loved Me*). While working on-and-off for the barge and diesel company Kirby Industries, he put his mind to those seven patents for controls, mechanisms and parts, including a severing blade that would cut through tangled cables. He realized no profit.

He wasn't a wastrel, a total dreamer, all hat and no cow, as the saying goes. He just wasn't the one to bring the steer to market, and he never made it easy for anyone to help him or stick with him.

One of his visiting sons from Team Margaret ran around the Gulf states in a replica 1929 Mercedes, creating accounts to sell the deck cleaner originally branded as Cooley Wash, now relabeled Sea Wash. When he got back to Covington he was quickly sucked into Burt's next big thing: a deal with a Saudi investor for what might have been in the healthy six figures, to create an early engine analysis computer.

"I installed all the wiring for the prototype system," my brother remembered. "Spent six weeks sweating to death inside a hundred-twenty-five foot boat that was constructed in Lafitte. I put in the whole thing except the computer, and that was handled by a guy from Texas named Dennis, a very Southern guy in his fifties with a big hat. I was there the day they started the engines and turned on the analytics for the first time. It was basically a precursor of the handheld version today for car mechanics."

Might've been a viable concept, but Burt couldn't sell it. What capital remained, he split with the Texan. They never paid back the Saudi.

If the high-tech and mechanical ideas weren't productive, there were always corndogs to fall back on.

Eva and Burt picked up a four-wheeled trailer outfitted with upswinging doors and christened it Diver Dan's Depot. With a white van they pulled the stand to schools and churches, fairs and flea markets, parties and horse shows, then throw in a dunking machine that charged not only for the ball-throwing dunkers, but also dunkees who'd pay fifty cents for the fun of two splashes into the tank.

The "fine gourmet lunch" menu was printed (as was all their paperwork) with a deep-sea diver illustration, and the cuisine matched the rustic décor: mini-doughnuts, nachos and crawfish pies, chicken Kiev, chicken chops and "crunchy vegetables with cheesy spices."

A collection agency was on their tail for thirty-five bucks; they got into a tussle with a newspaper. Fanciful plans to expand to a second, permanent location outside Hot Springs, Arkansas, evaporated.

From his wartime yarn-spinning through the cub reporter days in Texas and playing the expert on diesel mechanics in industrial magazines, Burt fancied himself a storyteller. He got some histories of swamped boats and waterlogged treasures published in local newspapers in New England and Louisiana.

He had unsold stories in the drawer about setting off hundred-pound bundles of dynamite on a submarine (a tricky proposition if your timing was off). And he outlined a tale about a six-foot fish that followed his diving bell from job to job.

In "George the Grouper" the principal character, Sylvester Tripp, boasted accomplishments that reflected Burt's self-image, the man he wanted others to see and applaud, yet made grotesque for some operatic Phantom sympathy.

Sylvester was a fellow who wouldn't nominally qualify as a diver (out of shape, case-a-day beer belly, half-toothless head the size of a cantaloupe) yet still had status. The "diving fraternity held Sylvester in high esteem both for his performance underwater and his shore side reputation as a macho man… he almost never lost a barroom joust (his nickname was Mighty Mouse) and in spite of one crossed eye and permanent bad breath, he had bedded every waitress on Booze Alley Road (his other nickname was Long Dong)."

This Sylvester was a "giant of a man below the splash zone… who could set and secure a clamp in 300 feet of water faster and better than any diver in the Gulf of Mexico, probably in the whole world."

Burt figured he'd best humanize Sylvester. "We all have our hidden frailties. Sylvester had two. The irritating one was he stayed in permanent hock to everyone he knew and never paid back any loan, small or large. By the time he was 28 his casual friends could be counted on one finger."

The story describes his grand fear of fish; to Sylvester, as with Burt, they were all barracuda or great white. A ten-pound lobster grabbed the hero on the ass "with a claw a foot long that can grind a cement block into powder." Then a six-foot grouper named George shows up and falls in love with him.

Hard to say where that narrative was going. Burt made it only as far as the first few pages.

In Houston Burt tripped into a job with the transit company to deal with the city's old diesel bus inventory. With the profit from selling the Covington house and some attached land parcels, and whatever financial resources he'd pocketed from Adam's old insurance money, it was easy to pick up a new place in Humble, a suburb up north by the airport. The couple settled on a two-story number with lemon-mustardy siding and brown trim along steep Victorian gables with a white-post porch rail. Fifty-foot trees in the backyard swayed under the incoming traffic to a runway a mile off at the international airport, not yet named for the first President Bush.

Things were finally good for Burt. A British driving cap gave him a shade of class while a scruffy, graying beard was more in tune with an old hipster. The torso got heftier, pushing him back from dinner tables and offering little room for tiny doggies against a paunchy sweater.

A woman loved him, with whom he could be vulnerable after years of running from his own story, or at least the painful chapters of arrogance, narcissism and neglect.

Burt made up songs, spoke in rhymes, and they danced through aisles of the supermarket. There was the hilarity that comes of two people who are content with their oneness.

He may have filled her head with all sorts of fantasies about himself, dressed up with his victimhood and being misunderstood. She knew some of his raucous past, what with all the kids out there, and she saw the whole Jerry Cooley thing firsthand.

We can now only leave Eva alone in her backyard sunlight to feel what she feels, carry what she carries. As far as she knew, she fully had him.

What illuminates someone as they see the final credits approaching? You hear about people who get a feeling about what's coming (short of the doctor telling them) and how they're struck by conscience or regret in the face of the final bleedout. Cue the autumnal shadows and the Samuel Barber adagio from *Apocalypse Now*.

One of my half-sisters, the short one I'll just call Sis for the moment, had a relationship with her father that seemed a bit chipper than he had with her five siblings. She'd been through the same emotional and material deprivations as the others, and yet loved him immensely. She sometimes felt she'd been the favorite, if you could attribute Burt with favoring anybody over himself. He'd taken her out to sea as a kid when he went treasure-hunting with that teenage boy, and another time he'd also left her alone on a boat while he went diving, to imagine she'd been deserted, awaiting a whale or a gale.

It struck her odd when she and her dad were on the phone when she was in her early twenties, had two kids, and when the subject came up of how nice grandchildren were, Burt said, "Grandchildren? I don't have any grandchildren." It was intentional, not some super-early memory lapse, and she found it sad, sort of insulting, and she was disappointed both for him and her kids. Sis was convinced "he wanted to hurt my feelings."

If her father actually considered her with some level of special bond, perhaps that's why, when he concluded his runway was getting short, he confessed to Sis, albeit briefly, his regrets.

It was uncharacteristic of him to put effort into communicating with his children. So it confused her several times when she came home, long before cell phone ubiquity, to see his number beeping on her answering machine. She was home another night when he got through and they spoke for a lot longer than usual.

"It almost wasn't him, it wasn't how he conducted himself with me." She got a sense that this was one of Those Calls. "He knew he was going to die soon. So he was getting things off his chest, how he messed up, the things he did wrong. It was like he felt remorse. He confessed to having made many mistakes, that he didn't do right by his kids."

A letter came in a few weeks, not long after Burt's seventieth birthday. Most of it was his usual laughing chat, yet he also wrote to Sis how "our recent confab started me thinking about all the wrong roads I have been down and where I want my bones (read Ashes) to lie. Maybe we can hold a party and you can toss them out into Casco Bay!"

The last months of 1996 weren't good ones in Humble. Burt didn't hesitate to play doctor on himself, avoiding appointments with the certified ones. With his love of the sweets always lying around since his retirement from the transit company, his diabetes was particularly destabilizing. He wrote to his aunt Marian, Wild Bill's sister, as to family history with the problem, but she didn't know of any.

It didn't help that those valves and spare parts from a quadruple bypass surgery ten years before were wearing out.

Sadness ransacked the house in December. One of Eva's sons living in Los Angeles planted a neighbor's boy on the back of his motorcycle. Another neighbor's car collided with them, killing the boy on the spot and landing Eva's son in a weeklong coma from which he did not emerge.

Soon after the new year rolled in, the flu hit Burt. He was always napping. One night he was reading the paper in bed and asked Eva to bring some orange juice for his sugar level and raspy throat. She got up to provide it, feeling some cold symptoms herself. When she returned, he refused the glass, and within a moment of settling down under the blankets to ward off a Texas winter that had brought freezing rain and downed power lines, he fell asleep.

Sometime after two, Burt was coughing and Eva woke up. She cradled him in her arms and he slept again.

My father's myocardial infarction came around the same day his confessional letter slipped into Sis's mailbox. After that, what remained was the artificial, the boxes of photographs in somebody else's attic and copies of magazines and newspapers in which Burt played, first, a supporting role in his father's theater of blood, and then his own subsequent crash-bang across wharves and barges, U-boat hulls and sharky domains, courtrooms and jail cells, through the raucous, hungry, unattended lives of children who were more than willing to meet him halfway, if only Burt knew or could care where the fifty-yard line was.

Two weeks after Burt died, Eva organized a Life Celebration, informal and not particularly religious. Two hundred or so people showed up, from Houston Metro Transit and Gulf maritime circles, the semi-retired community from around Humble and Eva's church. They shared their stories of Mr. Charisma, and somebody threw together a remembrance DVD soundtracked by scratchy renditions of "Anchors Aweigh" and other nautical anthems.

I wasn't there; it would be another two decades before I found Burton, to see how he looked, spoke and ambled, and only because of some internetian good fortune courtesy of Goodson and Todman and Fremantle and those three guys who invented YouTube.

It felt palpably different, that Change brought about by the appearance of Number Two. I was an only child at sixty-four with barely a vague notion of possible others as reported in a magazine years ago. By the time I hit sixty-seven I was a lone golfer suddenly recruited onto a baseball team.

It brought to mind the oceanic stateroom in *A Night at the Opera*, when the stowaway Marx Brothers and the singer, the chambermaids and the floor cleaner, the plumber and his assistant, the four waiters with trays and the manicurist and Aunt Minnie's niece have crowded in only to have Mrs. Claypool open the door for them to all crash-tumble out.

My oldest sister, batting second after Rod in Burt's All-Star lineup, lived mostly in Connecticut and then Maine. She enjoyed a rural setting near the ocean. Her first husband had issues, but she got into a good relationship with a carpenter that endures to this day, a blended family with five children. Like her half-aunt Jean, she was a nurse for over thirty years, and also had specialized dementia training that allowed her to look after the aging Margaret's care. Sisters Two and Three, younger than me, amiable people, had careers and kids.

Their parents later produced three boys for the outfield. The middle one, a father to eight (five acquired through marriage), played the accordion as a boy, a second squeezebox specialist from the Mason School of the Arts, and became a singer and songwriter, a talented topiarist and budding novelist. It also turned out (*Strange Snick®*) he lived for some years in a suburb about an hour's drive from downtown Philadelphia, and thus from me. He might've stood next to me one day for pizza in the King of Prussia Mall, or maybe I gave him a cursing finger for being a jerk in the parking lot (or he to me, parking lots being a matter of perspective).

Marge's older and younger sons have their busy and complicated lives in different states. I don't know them well, but you can't be chummy with everybody.

A great teller of jokes, well-read and a pianist, Margaret was far tougher than most people credited her. After the six kids scruffed their way into adulthood, she had part-time work helping a private home-duty nurse, inspiring her at age fifty-two to care professionally for others. She entered the nursing program at Columbus State Community College, followed by more studies in Arizona, where a local newspaper captured her with a strawberry-blond coif under a crisp white hat, in the "nurse giving a kid a measles shot" pose.

After ten good years things began to happen, the challenges, the slip-ups, initiating a long decline. Her nurse-daughter who worked in a Maine facility helped attend to her.

Burt's second and fourth wife, mother to six of my half-siblings, passed at seventy-two, a few years after her own mom. Her death brought about a reconciliation between two of her estranged children, each holding her hand at the last. They took her from Bangor back to Ohio for burial.

Aunt Marilyn's place in the wider family was a tangled mish-mosh. When she visited Akron in the Fifties, she could enjoy her little nephew Rod's company as long as she didn't mention her brother Burt's name. Her two young children with Pete Krones enjoyed some summer lake swimming in New England with their friends, Margaret's brood, taking up a full row of seats to see Dick van Dyke in *Bye Bye Birdie*, yet without ever having been told they were actually cousins due to the, uh, family dynamics.

Aunt Marilyn didn't appear in my life at all until I was in my sixties and heard of a sympathetic letter to my mother bearing an opinion as to Burt's character.

My distant relation was significantly impacted by the pain in the neck that was life and struggle: her mother torn away in a car crash, the substitute Vera, the young marriage to Krones, followed by a father murdered in some corrupt town, the two kids, the struggles of domesticity and the illusory elation of alcohol, her leaving Pete, the bum choices at a cash register, and then another walk to the altar with a dentist named Lou.

That marriage collapsed after five years, and that's when Marilyn moved to California. She wed a machinist who worked in a defense plant, then got involved with a turkey farmer whose wife was dying of breast cancer in Sonora, out in gold rush country, followed by a hitch to some other guy in San Francisco...

Finally, something woke her up.

I don't know if it was a years-long itch or a newer curiosity, a "get serious and do some good," that attracted my aunt to nursing. Marilyn was in her forties when she started at the University of California at Berkeley, perhaps afforded by her settlement with the dentist.

Once a RN – part of quite the quartet, joining my mom, Margaret and her oldest daughter all in starched white – she became attracted to breast cancer research (an affinity, dare one speculate, possibly informed by the woman she met on the turkey farm, however sticky that situation might've been).

Then she found out about an East Coast opportunity in medical investigation. Like Jean two decades earlier, Marilyn ended up working in a Philadelphia hospital.

She settled in a nicely-appointed apartment across the bridge in

Jersey (four towns away from where my mom and I lived), and again a *Strange Snick®*: when I was on the zippy new Speedline train crossing the Delaware, growing my hair after high school and reviewing records for the underground newspaper where I got my start, my father's sister could've been on the same train headed for work from her place in Maple Shade, while her son, my slightly younger cousin, was checking out the bars along Route 73, including the Jug Handle Inn, still serving it up at an intersection I now pass through almost daily.

That same-train thing was a "maybe," of course, but close enough to qualify, as per published guidelines, as an authentic *Strange Snick®*.

Most nurses are serious about what they do, and Marilyn really dove in. Back at UC San Francisco alongside the noted Dr. Nick Petrakis, she took a role in developing a fluid extraction technique used in cancer diagnosis and treatment, and lectured on it at Johns Hopkins, the National Institutes of Health and several universities. It was also pretty committed of her to live in a grass hut in South Africa during field experiments with medically productive plants.

Jimmy Stanton, the guy she married in 1992, a career captain with a major airline, was mighty proud of her. Marilyn laid off the drinking and, as one of her kids said, "mellowed considerably."

Her grown children met Burt way back when, sharing everyone's experiences and conclusions, that he accomplished some stuff, very smart, amusing, shittiest possible dad, huge temper, turned Adam into a big mess. They knew nothing of The One Who Knocks until my digging brought me to their in-box.

I never caught up with my aunt or her handsome pilot with the pleasant house in Topeka. She died at ninety-one after a five-year cognizant decline, in November 2019, which I learned about two months later. Dammit, just missed her.

I wouldn't have passed judgement on Marilyn's up-and-down life or anything she did that was less than polished. But I would have liked to have told her it was nice that she wrote that letter to my mom.

Harriet Iris, born to Bill Mason and his high school sweetheart Hallie, an aunt to a fellow in Jersey she sure never heard of, the intelligent, witty, classy dame who sang on every Minneapolis stage, married a guy named Paul and had a daughter. In a second marriage to an engineer called Glenn, a lot happier than the first, she had two more girls and outlived her husband by thirty years.

It's not known whether Burt and his sister knew about Bill's first marriage and the two Harriets early in their adult lives, or not until they were a lot older. His relationship with his half-sister was estranged over unspecified, unfulfilled expectations that lasted until '91 when Burt and aunt Marilyn visited "H.I." in Minnesota. They trekked up to Lutsen, a Lake Superior fishing town, where they took some joyous photographs. Hi later settled in Virginia where she died in 2012 at ninety-one, attended to by two of her girls (one of whom owned that mystery Web page with the photos of Eva and Burt in his red-suspendered swim trunks in the pool).

For any kid whose mom brings them a new sibling, popping out of her funny belly, that's got to be an odd experience. It was a delight to watch my daughter beam at her baby brother. (That wears off, of course.)

Meeting a sib for the first time when you're all grown up is its own class of bizarro.

It's seven hours and change from Philadelphia to Akron. The route's Midway Island that held some promise for a civilized meeting ground is the town of State College. As Melanie and I headed west, the eastbound Bebe drove the entire trip for Rod, as he no longer operated a car.

Zeroing in on a workable week wasn't easy; we all had prepaid vacations blocked out that spring. The target was for when all those Penn State kids headed home at semester's end, their parents and SUVs no longer filling every available hotel room, with the summer school crowd not yet filtered in.

For this once-in-a-lifetime soiree we certainly couldn't lounge in a lobby or hotel bar for hours. I wanted a spacious suite with a desk and sitting space for everyone. There was one appropriate hotel away from the constant university thrall, the whipping street flags of rampant logos and the NFL-sized stadium carrying the Penn State perfume of the legendary Nittany Lions coach Joe Paterno and the squalid after-shave of his assistant who got deep time for getting touchy with students in the shower and the top administrators who refused to acknowledge it.

Mel and I planned to arrive in town a day before my brother, to give us time to prepare mentally for one of life's ultimate knocks on the door. Plenty to ponder: would Rod and I would cross our legs the same way, both prefer the shrimp over the shark steak, get thirsty at the same time, finish each other's sentences, exercise pointed sarcasm toward similar political targets, admire particular attributes in cinema, sports and women?

And lest anyone be flummoxed by two days yakking about BurtBurtBurt, we had to pipeline other topics. Let's see… Rod was a master scuba and rescue diver, while outside the pool I disliked water with anything but white sand under my feet. Maybe talk about his skydiving, as I always wanted to try that and never did (and not just because of Mel's homicidal threats should I dare it). However, I managed some lessons as a pilot, my life-dream, so for Rod and me, being up in the air was common ground.

I knew some stuff about him from his family Christmas home movie I stumbled across on the internet. When I first gazed at my brother, not certain at all this was the guy, he relaxed in his winter robe as grown children and loopy grandkids exchanged presents in front of a fireplace and made noise about breakfast and guffawed over gag gifts. On one hand, the episode was like watching an uninvolving film of strangers, as would a bored cat. Alternately, it was more scientific than emotional at that early stage, a secret glimpse at a laid-back man who could sort of be me, at one with his world. I was reminded again of the morning I'd spent observing that tribe of primates at the National Zoo, with its clambering youngsters and hairy grownups trying to maintain civility.

We'd just have to open the hotel room door and let it happen. Something was bound to.

At three o'clock the second day, in a farm-country town in the middle of Pennsylvania, the next Change.

Rod's affinity for poker came into play soon after they sat down. He admired my shirt, with a send-up of those gas station velvet glowlight tapestries of dogs playing cards, but with famous cartoon pooches, Scooby-Doo and Pluto, Snoopy and Stewie among others. I went into the bedroom and put on something else, came out and presented my brother with the best dog-poker shirt around. Made us both happy.

The perusing of volumes of pictures, clippings and memorabilia Bebe had lugged on the trip went through the afternoon.

No one at the hotel told us before booking that the well-reviewed dining room was being overhauled after a broken-pipe washout and there'd be no meals, thus forcing us downtown to some pipsqueak beef-n-beer that Melanie and I normally wouldn't have patronized even to escape the Horseman of Death coming down the street. A post-dinner sidewalk stroll followed, and the spouses warmed over the two brothers side by side, one carefully leading a conversation and another struggling, but managing, to hold up his end.

The following morning before we all gathered downstairs for the hotel's paltry breakfast, I visited Rod's room alone for a quick how-ya-doin'. I stayed for almost an hour. At one point his wife went into the bathroom to answer one of the several calls a day she was getting from her youngest son, who was really enthusiastic about the new uncle from Jersey.

I spoke to Rod methodically so that he could follow my lead. "You're so aware of what's challenging you now. When we first spoke on the phone for a few minutes last month, you told me you had this condition that slowed your thinking. You're aware that it's taking things away from you. Can you tell me… is there anything that's been given to you?" What I was trying for was some awareness, some philosophical peace or piss about life now that he was confronting a creeping deterioration.

Rod took a moment to situate the question in his head. Then he replied with slow deliberation, a story going back to when he was a freshly minted motorcycle cop. Another fellow in the station was a mentor in policing and pokering. His name was Keith and he taught Rod everything about cards. The two of them made the rounds of poker nights with other cops and friends of cops and they started taking all the money, gaining a fearsome reputation that made others wary of calling their hand with anything less than trip aces. At some point, the older policeman passed away. When Rod heard about a new brother appearing in his life, he said to his wife, and to himself, "Now I have a Keith again."

What a grand thing for me to be.

In late morning it's almost time to part company with the emissaries from Ohio, and I ushered them off the lobby to the hotel bar, a cushy, lamplit, dark-paneled library. There were model ships in bottles and books lying about on end tables, piles of Penn State alumni magazines and framed posters of the horsey, moneyed farm life. The day before during a recon stroll around the hotel, I'd spotted the same huge history of New Yorker cartoons as on my coffee table. Weeks before I'd emailed Bebe a copy of the art I came across, and now I wanted to show it to her in 3D.

So I lead the others over to this table, pull out the book from the bottom of the heavy stack, do a little show-off flaring of the hand, nothing up my sleeve, intending to search for the cartoon about the guy in jail. And with the fingers of my left hand I select a *completely random* page and pry open the weighty book with a thud… and again, it's 225, there's the fellow in stripes, smirking and surrounded by multiple wives. *"They all are. That's what he's in for."*

Maybe that was the thing about Burt. No matter where you were, regardless of the page you turned to, the husband you sought, the partner you required, he was so darn good at finding *you*, ready to be charmed out of your pants, your wallet, your childhood. He was on everybody's page 225.

Out in the parking lot, luggage in the cars, came the embraces. Hug, done. Hug, done. I wrapped my arm around Rod's shoulder, he's stockier than me, like a retired footballer at an autograph convention, and pulled him in.

I said quietly, "Love you."

"Love you, too."

Where the hell did that come from?

It just popped out of me, natural. Didn't prep it, no thoughtful inhalation to oxygenate it. I amazed myself for a second, felt the screaming "what?" inside me. Then just let it be.

Perhaps this resolved the longtime question, if I had an intrinsic human love in me to offer someone like that, in contrast to the kind which only time could develop. Then came a flash of doubt, if I'd done that for my older brother as a comforting gift because he's a bit diminished, a sympathy rather than a genuine piece of my heart.

No... I don't think so, I guess I'm okay with it being real and honest, I felt it, meant it, it had a life of its own.

And I don't believe he returned it to me just because his emotional enthusiasm was flowing in an easier, simpler form, some child in him returned because of those damn plaques and tangles. It came to him the same way it came to me. We didn't have to get to know each other across an entire summer, didn't need a lot of time to bring it to fruition like wine in the cask, spend a day fishin'. It was just there, of the moment, of the lifetime.

A love between Rod and me was just one more thing Burt left behind.

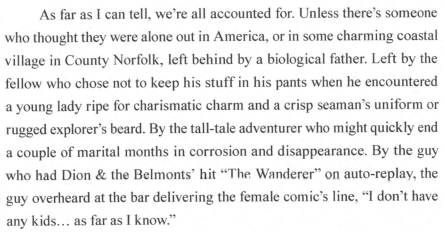

As far as I can tell, we're all accounted for. Unless there's someone who thought they were alone out in America, or in some charming coastal village in County Norfolk, left behind by a biological father. Left by the fellow who chose not to keep his stuff in his pants when he encountered a young lady ripe for charismatic charm and a crisp seaman's uniform or rugged explorer's beard. By the tall-tale adventurer who might quickly end a couple of marital months in corrosion and disappearance. By the guy who had Dion & the Belmonts' hit "The Wanderer" on auto-replay, the guy overheard at the bar delivering the female comic's line, "I don't have any kids... as far as I know."

Still, I have to be mentally prepared with some extra Club Burt T-shirts in the bin. It's conceivable someone will see the book in a Barnes & Noble or Amazon Reviews and recognize the circumstantial and possibly uncircumcised evidence of their own missing paternal link, followed at some point by relief or obscenity, or both.

Then one day, through the modernity of email, my doorbell chimes.

The chattering mob completed its tour of the lovely home Rod built by the pond and continued their requisite picture-taking. Then my son and the new family he'd just met in Akron went back upstairs to enjoy Bebe's dinner.

I took my boy to Ohio just after his thirtieth birthday for my second meeting with Rod. We shared a pair of seven-hour trips on the turnpike gaily wrapped with the political arguments between the experienced old liberal thinker and the young, progressive planet-saver, the perspectives on ridiculous relatives at home, and my induction into his current drillhammer taste in music that I tried to balance with Miles Davis and Bill Evans.

As the ensemble headed up to the table, I needed some time to myself, and when I melted back no one missed me amid the chattering and fawning over my kid.

I stood down there alone by the bar, me and a diving helmet.

Twenty-plus years before, Burt ordered T-shirts from a dive shop in Ventura, California. He sent along art for the front, a photo of a helmet made by George Swindell (the guy at the Connecticut diner with tales of U-853). Running the page through a copier twice, he planted his face into the window of the helmet, creating a spooky, disembodied emoji. He ordered three shirts to start and added in his letter, "If at a little extra cost you can include other stuff, please put front or back." The other stuff was a long list of Burt's claimed achievements, so that with these shirts he or his fans could wear his records, his identity, his secure place in posterity.

Among the braggadocios were a supposed world record of more than thirteen hours non-stop working on the ocean floor, diving in the Gulf of Mexico to five hundred and forty feet, and for another hundred and sixty-five dives in 1963.

How do you verify such achievements? Nobody goes down to the sea bottom with a Guinness checklist. You surface, look at your watch and exclaim, "Hey, how about that! Guys, look what I did!" Or if you hadn't noticed, the crew clocked what was happening and cheered when you came back up. Or instead, you're back on land with a little calculator and some sourcebook and you see you've set a record. And you brag loudly, or quietly, or not at all. Burt wanted to boast on his shirt.

He also wanted to brag on a ring, inscribing his feats in the tiniest font across the inside of a massive gold, or gold-looking, ring that Eva ordered through a Houston jeweler. On the face of it a 3D helmet burst out, capable of rending some damage in a bar fight. Rod had always wanted that ostentatious ring, a way for a son to carry a bit of his dad's legacy.

Both the ring and the helmet are featured accessories in a color portrait of Burt, overweight-stocky with a gray beard and big tortoiseshell glasses below a liver-spotted forehead, printed on the take-home card for his post-demise Celebration of Life in Humble.

Now the helmet, the one he photographed for the T-shirt order with the tiny Burt face looking out at you, was parked on his oldest child's bar.

Whatever archives and assets, mementoes, miscellany and money (his or Adam's) Burt left behind went to Eva and her kids. Rod and his six cousins would've appreciated seeing the memorabilia, like the ring Burt had promised to Rod, but after his passing Eva didn't contact Burt's children for a long time, and when they stopped by to see her in subsequent years, she didn't relinquish anything of Burt's.

Twenty years passed, and then a close friend persuaded Eva to clean out the attic. They piled a bunch of stuff in the car and headed north to see some people, and along the way stopped in Akron. That's when she offloaded a few boxes of Burt's old photos and other stuff.

Rod got his father's ring.

As for the helmet, it's a blue-painted, brass-looking outer-space hood for warding off underwater pressure and errant octopus suckers, with nozzles for air hoses and tightening knobs and a glass faceplate locked under sixteen big screws with a little microphone box. *B. Mason* is embossed on strips of metal and plastic glued on the top and sides, either to claim ownership or just let another diver know whose body was being retrieved after a mishap. It's the one he used on big ocean oil-platform repair jobs or simply borrowed from George Swindell one day and never returned, what he wore to set world diving records or maybe set no such thing.

That little spooky Burt face was no longer pasted onto the glass. But the diver still inhabited his helmet.

His ashes are in there.

In 1952, whiny, defensive Burt said I didn't exist. Well, here I am, standing in an All-American success story, the finished basement crafted by my brother, the exceptional policeman who in so many aspects was as unlike Burt as could be, a room with a big TV and table hockey and walls of posters and photographs, and on top of the brightly lit playroom bar with twinkling rows of glasses is this big blue diving helmet, and inside tucked into a box under a metal plate are the carbonized flakes of Number Two, and I exist and he doesn't, so screw him.

I stood there alone, below the low rumble of excited voices and chair-scraping above me, and tossed around the expectations one should have of such a theatrical moment, the remarkability of it all, the end of journey thing, the found it at last thing, the son meets disappointing wayward dad thing, the close to a hug from my father as I'll ever get thing.

"So… it's you."

It was close to three years since my father showed up in my cellar on *To Tell the Truth*, and now it was just me and him at the bar in his other son's cellar. The Trumbull Burt and the Akron Burt and the Waco Burt and the Kelly Station Burt and the Cherbourg Burt and the Covington Burt, just the two of us.

The moment reminded me of the ambient regard I experienced when I walked along Millbank in London, where Disraeli and Churchill had strolled by Parliament. The one in front of the rowhouse on Ashbury Street in San Francisco, talking with the current owner and his lovely golden retriever at the old Grateful Dead house where Garcia and Weir's band practiced their counterculture, an American shrine that mirrored the zigzag crossing at Abbey Road. It was the feeling a colonially dressed Olde Philadelphia guide hopes to instill in schoolkids when he explains they're padding the same cobblestones as Franklin and Jefferson. It's a sharing-history-space thing. Same square footage, same dirt or brick, inhabited by two people separated by time.

So now I occupied the same bar as Burt, resting on my elbow next to him, nobody telling stories, nobody singing an old song about his father.

One of the few volumes on self-realization I sometimes consult puts it one way: "If we don't forgive, we're never free. Unless we forgive, we are not forgiven; we remain chained to our wrongs, unable to free ourselves, leave the dark dungeon of our past, and walk free in the sunlight of love."

I've tried to earn forgiveness from those I've hurt and offended and disappointed; that long white list still sticks to my shoe like errant bathroom tissue. I forgave that dude who drove into me when I was sixteen on my bike, and for the kneecap scars I retain, because it was my fault in the first place to fly out of that driveway into the street. I forgave my mother her errors of parenting in that they were ridiculously far-outweighed by her miraculous success at raising me. On the flip side, there are a couple of people who shivved me in the heart years ago – all guys, actually – and I can't say today if I'll ever let those hurts go.

What do I do with Burt?

When I was fourteen, I knew I'd been stuck with those genetic qualities my father uploaded. The conscious space was something I could control, so I allotted this vaporous phantasm as little as I could manage. I was more dedicated to protecting my mother from memory, under the delusion I had influence over that.

Then he appeared on some pages from a pair of magazines and a small photograph under a paperclip, all of which I was willing to absorb but not invest much in, in that by his disappearance my father had squandered both my organic and voluntary interest.

When I was older, Burt took up slightly more space that came and went each time some woman asked across the second-date table, "Don't you want to know anything about your father?" and I replied, "Not particularly."

I wasn't going to dignify him with my curiosity.

Burt is a mark that stayed with me long after his initial appearance, like the pale shadowy suture streaks still apparent across my left patella from when I flooped onto the hood of that surprised guy's car and paid for the miscalculation with stitches in three places. The incident is long gone, barely a smudge retained, noticed only when I choose to see it.

The real contusion is what Burt inflicted on the other siblings he created and damaged, and the women who endured his disregard and violence. I'm grateful that Jean blocked him out legally, using his claim that I was not a product of their relationship to ward off any knocks at the door or demands for access to his boy, for money, for the opportunity to strike her or me for having unmasked and discarded him.

My paternal grandmother, Bill's second wife, died in October 1931 when Bill couldn't handle a car's tendency to wander off the asphalt when its trajectory exceeded his grasp. I had the wonderful Bess, the daughter of a Scottish mailman, who never got her name in anything but a Sunday church bulletin, for thirty-five years; I had Charlotte not at all.

Beyond a few old Bay Area news accounts, there's but one written family log of Charlotte, and it was Burt's, created years later. It would take an expert in memory retention to guess how much of Burt's recall of when he was four-ish came from facts and impressions he actually stored, what endured after his brain did what all brains do, reclaiming some of its real estate by wiping the old tapes and supplanting with new accumulating information. Could these recollections of his mother's death be so true, burned in, he could breathe life into them again when he was forty-six, reminiscing to a notebook aboard a rolling barge in the North Sea when he thought some audience would give a damn about his voyage through the space/time continuum?

How much can I depend on Burt to recreate his mother's death, or anything about his life, for me? What is salvaged reality and what is diary fill-in, dramatic license, emotional self-support, pompous playwriting?

My grandchildren (if and when) will know most everything in terms of the history. I began that process some months after the YouTube appeared. My two kids, plus my daughter's new husband, sat at a dinner table, and as I introduced my post-dessert "I have something to talk about" they sensed exactly what was about to hit them, the grand tale they'd never heard. I told them the story of my years inside the wall, the emerging older-guy curiosity and the sorta-casual casting about on the Web for Burton. Out came the laptop and the video of Number Two and the copies of old newspaper stories (barely a scratch of the stack of paper I ultimately compiled). I fielded their questions as best I could.

My daughter and her new spouse's wide-eyed fascination matched that of the celebrity panel when my father finally stood up in 1961. My son retreated to the bathroom for some quiet because the whole thing about his dad's dad, the male lineage inhabiting him, really slapped him.

So I packed him off some months later to Ohio for the astounding embrace of an uncle who, at some moments amid his decline, understood him and who he belonged to. Next were two of the sisters/aunts we both met for the first time as they passed through Akron with miraculous serendipity.

There came the big dinner, the fulfilling, story-sharing, raucous table of the long-suspected and recently met, after my private rec-room consultation with the man in the helmet. Then, a little gift.

In my grandfather Edwin's workshop amongst the drills and saws and a hardware store's worth of accumulated parts and constructive tidbits, a shelf held old magazines and flaking papers and a few bottles of alcoholic destiny. Some were just swill, fruity brandies from some North Philadelphia brewery whose chemical content and flavor probably rivaled the benzene on General Tire's factory floor. One bottle, however, was bequeathed to grandpop in the early Sixties by an aging comrade from the old wartime outfit of Camden soldiers. It was a somewhat rare and provocative three-sided dimpled bottle of a Haig & Haig Scotch called Pinch, wrapped in golden webbing and a sort-of royal seal waxed across the foil, already aged two decades, not that Scotch appreciated with the passing of time like a good wine, acquiring only character.

When Edwin died, it was one of the few things I conscripted from the workshop before other relatives came in to claim and clean. It sat in my own cabinets, in darkness and maturing calm, for another thirty-five years, awaiting the right setting and people, something with pageantry or a moment of funereal remembrance, worth a careful unwrapping and toasting. But an occasion never seemed to present itself, nor those qualified to share it, as the calendars came and went.

I packed the Pinch for Ohio while reserving a final decision about revealing it, but at this table clarification came quickly. I told my newly enlarged family the story of my grandfather's workshop, the wait for exceptional company and purpose to make the Pinch proud. With my usual cautious theatricality, I opened it and poured for Burt's children and his grandson, my travel partner. Both Rod and I considered it to be one of the most noble tastes of our lives. He and his own son, a young policeman, shared seconds with me and my boy.

Then I gave the rest of the bottle to my descendant to celebrate his birthday, along with an admonition, well, let's call it a serious encouragement, to keep it for posterity, for as many years as necessary to await the next distinguished celebration and companions to enjoy it.

With luck, I'd be at that table.

A few months after our visit to the Buckeye State, the dreadful weeks started piling up for Rod. The hallucinations called "sundowning," his recognition of people only with his wife's prompting, "you remember Bob from the office," trouble with personal care, then with walking.

When the pandemic attacked in the spring, there were no more trips to the hospital for the drug trials and the therapy that gave him a few hours of lucidity before an inevitable slip-back once he got home.

The nautical reference was "fading into the red sky," the mind relinquishing its command over body.

In August, cradled by his wife and with a grandson hugging tight, Rod left us all, the daughters and sons and sailing friends and grateful colleagues and a brother from far off. As with his grandfather in a town down South, people waved off the summer heat to stand with tribute and hymns.

I had so little of him, but eighteen months was better than nothing. The best part was knowing, if only for a year and a half, that my brother knew he had me.

His wife bequeathed to me the thought Rod shared after I drove off from Ohio.

"Keith is the most like me."

Those who remain today from Burton's careening across the landscape are stuck, far more than I, with the upsetting Rolodex of memory. Each carries what they wish, as best they can edit their remembrance and truth, of the man who made them, or charmed them, the fond and the rough and the wistful.

Burt's physical presence may last only until the day, should it come about, someone scatters the residue from the diving helmet unceremoniously off a fishing pier.

But my father's name will rattle about, apparently forever, in those old newspapers digitally salvaged from history's internment. And on YouTube. And as a sub-reference in Wikipedia, unless someone edits him out of a page on U-boats.

I think I did a little better, posterity-wise. When NASA asked people to get on board a little project to inform the galaxy about us Earthlings, I said "count me in" and they etched my name with a bunch of others alongside a micro-portrait of Leonardo da Vinci on a dime-size chip mounted to the 2001 Mars Curiosity Rover, now resting *ad infinitum* on the Red Planet.

Look me up sometime.

ACKNOWLEDGEMENTS

There's not enough space on the page to thank enough the brothers and sisters who popped into my life and welcomed me into their universe. There are also cousins and partners from far afield who passed along their stories and literal and figurative images of people I couldn't know and would never meet.

I'm grateful to all those folks, be they family of one degree or another, or non-relatives going about their jobs and lives, who opened the door to me. I can't think of anyone in the entire process, the family or research contacts, who turned me away (although I may have worn out my welcome with a couple of people).

I offer my appreciation to Melanie, for generously giving me time, patience and encouragement as I undertook a life's journey, and for seeing what I had to do and letting me do it, lonely though it may have been for her at times, with love beyond any measure.

My gratitude goes to Jean, who gave me everything a parent should, to the best of her ability and heart to do; Catherine and Alec, for adding such light to my life and giving me the remarkable, singular opportunity to be a parent in so many dimensions I've lost count; Elizabeth and Edwin, who gave me a home in which to be a child, and filled in the blank spaces when they could.

Thanks to Rod, who in the short hours we had to experience each other was as fine a big brother as anyone could ask for; to his wife for representing him and his experiences with detail; to newly-acquired siblings and cousins for history, perspective and emotion; to the divers and others out on the horizon who chipped in to my knowledge and far-flung sense of connection.

Thanks as well to Gregg Feistman, professor at Temple University, for an early flashlight in the dark; Susan Jolley, Michael McDevitt and other early readers for pointing things out; Ben Yagoda and others with experienced voices who reflected on the manuscript; Dave Margolis of Damarcom for artistic drafting and Jayne Bierman at Classy Websites for the many pixels; Steve Allen for inspiring agility and Salman Rushdie for inspiring possibility.

For additional photographs, other information
and contacting the author, visit:
www.pleasestandupmason.com

SOURCES

Reporting

The Associated Press (particularly reporter William Barnard)
in the 1940s and 1950s providing accounts of events to
news outlets far and wide, large and small; United Press
International, for a bit of the same

Hartford, CT, Courant (particularly reporter/photographer
Stan Simon)
Naugatuck, CT, Daily News
Bridgeport, CT, Telegram
Bridgeport, CT, Post
Bangor, ME, Daily News
Newport, RI, Daily News
Wakefield, RI, Independent (Lynne M. Heinzmann)
Providence, RI, Journal-Bulletin (Robert Frederikson)
Boston, MA, Globe
Pittsfield, MA, Berkshire Eagle
Rochester, NY, Democrat & Chronicle
New York, NY, Daily News (Tom Allen)
New York, NY, Times

Alice, TX, Daily Echo & Banner (particularly, but not limited to,
reporter Martha Cole)
Waco, TX, News-Tribune
Galveston, TX, Daily News
Pampa, TX, Daily News
Denton, TX, Record-Chronicle
Brownsville, TX, Herald
Sweetwater, TX, Reporter

Breckinridge, TX, American

Waxahachie, TX, Daily Light

Victoria, TX, Advocate

Corsicana, TX, Daily Sun

Del Rio, TX, News Herald

Abilene, TX, Reporter-News

Marshall, TX, News Messenger

Harlingen, TX, Morning Star

McAllen, TX, Monitor

Lubbock, TX, Morning Avalanche

Coleman, TX, Daily Democrat-Voice

Goose Creek, TX, Sun

Albuquerque, NM, Journal

Akron, OH, Beacon Journal (particularly, but not limited to,
    Matt Hall, Kenneth Nichols, Robert Hoiles)

Fremont, OH, News-Messenger

Cincinnati, OH, Enquirer

Mansfield, OH, News-Journal

Columbus, OH, Dispatch

Pittsburgh, PA, Press

Chicago, IL, Tribune

Minneapolis, MN, Star Tribune

Munster, IN, Times

Valparaiso, IN, Vidette-Messenger

San Francisco, CA, Examiner

Oakland, CA, Tribune

San Mateo, CA, Times

Napa, CA, Register

Petaluma, CA, Argus-Courier

Grass Valley, CA, Morning Union

St. Tammany, LA, Farmer
Bogalusa, LA, Daily News
Hammond, LA, Daily Star
Alexandria, LA, Town Talk

Reference

Newsweek Magazine, 1948 - 1961
Naval History, Adam Lynch, U.S. Naval Institute
Yankee Magazine, Lawrence Williard (assistance from Joe Bills)
Saturday Evening Post, Harold Martin (assistance from
    Jeff Nilsson)

Inside Detective, May 1950 (Dell)
True (Roy Bongartz), January 1969 (Fawcett)
Broadcasting Magazine

Mary Sparks, Texas Women's University and American
    Journalism Historians Association
Anthony R. Carrozza, "Dukes of Duval County: The Parr Family
    and Texas Politics" (Univ. of Oklahoma Press)
Joan Mellon, "Faustian Bargains" (Bloomsbury)
Earl Warren Oral History Project (University of California)

Eve Ensler, "The Apology" (Bloomsbury)
Abby Ellin, "Duped" (Hatchette)
M.E. Thomas, "Confessions of a Sociopath" (Crown)
Robert Kurson, "Shadow Divers" (Random House)
Robert A. Caro, "Means of Ascent" (Vintage)
Gregg Allman, "My Cross to Bear" (William Morrow)
Rick Atkinson, "The Guns at Last Light" (Picador)
Anna Chopek, The Ukrainian Weekly
Claude Smith, The New Yorker

Consultations

David Trisko, James Bunch, William Palmer and
William Campbell, with gratitude for time, knowledge and
perspective

Louis R. Koerner, Jr., Esq., New Orleans, LA
William Mysing, Esq., Covington, LA
Stephen J. Zaloga, historian, "Cherbourg, 1944" (Osprey)
Pat McTaggart, historian
Robin Perkins, St. Tammany Parish, LA records office
Nahketah Bagby and JoAnn Rucker, Covington, LA planning &
zoning offices
Aimee Faucheux, Covington, LA cultural arts director
Jack Terry, Covington, LA historian

Lauren Blankenship, Beauregard, LA
Elona Weston, Beauregard Museum, DeRidder, LA
Office of LA State Fire Marshall
Akron, OH Police Department
Cleveland, OH Public Library
Shammas Malik, Assistant Director of Law, City of Akron, OH
Lt. Dawn Westerfield, Gary, IN Police Dept.

Cecilia Martinez, South Texas Museum, Alice, TX
Texas State Library & Archives Commission
Texas Dept. of Health, Bureau of Vital Statistics
Waco, TX, records office
Sheriff Daniel Bueno, Jim Wells County, TX
Rhonda Hebert, Connecticut Dept. of Justice, Hartford, CT
California Highway Patrol, Vallejo, CA
Sean Demers, Samuel French, Inc.

James Moore, *texastotheworld.com*

axishistory.com

justia.com

uboat.net

historictexas.net

Collection of Coke Stevenson family

James Smithwick